The Myth of Christian Uniqueness

The Myth of
Christian Uniqueness

Edited by
John Hick and Paul F. Knitter

SCM PRESS LTD

290

British Library Cataloguing in Publication Data

The Myth of Christian uniqueness.
1. Religion. Pluralism
I. Hick, John, *1922–* II. Knitter, Paul F.
291

ISBN 0–334–01066–7

2002316⁷

First published 1987 by
Orbis Books, Maryknoll, NY 10545

First published in Britain 1988
by SCM Press Ltd
26–30 Tottenham Road, London N1 4BZ

Printed by Billings & Sons Ltd, Worcester

Contents

III
THE ETHICO-PRACTICAL BRIDGE:
JUSTICE

POSTSCRIPT

Preface

Insofar as it might be misleading, the title of this book makes its point. We are calling "Christian uniqueness" a "myth" not because we think that talk of the uniqueness of Christianity is purely and simply false, and so to be discarded. Rather, we feel that such talk, like all mythic language, must be understood carefully; it must be interpreted; its "truth" lies not on its literal surface but within its ever-changing historical and personal meaning. This book, then, rather than intending to deny Christian uniqueness, wants to interpret it anew. In fact, we shall suggest, from various perspectives, that the myth of Christian uniqueness requires a genuinely new interpretation—one so different that, perhaps, some will say that the word "uniqueness" is no longer appropriate.

Christianity, of course, is unique in the precise and literal sense in which every religious tradition is unique—namely that there is only one of it and that there is therefore nothing else exactly like it. But in much Christian discourse, "the uniqueness of Christianity" has taken on a larger mythological meaning. It has come to signify the unique definitiveness, absoluteness, normativeness, superiority of Christianity in comparison with other religions of the world. It is this mythological sense of the phrase, with all that goes with it, that we are criticizing in this book.

The general context that provides the meaning and motivation of this volume is the same that has inspired a spate of recent publications dealing with "Christianity and World Religions" or "Christ in a Pluralistic World." More and more Christians, along with peoples of other faiths and ideologies, are experiencing *religious pluralism* in a new way—that is, they are feeling not only the *reality* of so many other religious paths, but also their vitality, their influence in our modern world, their depths, beauty, and attractiveness. And because of this new experience of pluralism, Christians are feeling the need for a more productive dialogue and cooperation with other religions, a new attitude toward them.

What makes this present volume different from most recent proposals for a Christian theology of religions is contained in the vision of what its subtitle calls a *pluralistic* theology of religions. A pluralistic model represents a new turn—what might be called a "paradigm shift"—in the efforts of Christian theologians, both past and present, to understand the world of other religions and Christianity's place in that world. A paradigm shift represents a turn that is both genuinely different from, yet dependent upon, what went before.

Through this collection of essays we hope to show that such a pluralist turn is taking shape, that it is being proposed by a variety of reputable Christian thinkers, and that therefore it represents a viable, though still inchoate and controversial, option for Christian believers. Our intent as editors, then, was to assemble a representative mix of Christian theologians—Protestant and Catholic, female and male, East and West, First and Third World—who felt both the urgency and complexity of exploring genuinely new Christian understandings of other religions and of Christianity in light of other faiths. We tried to spell out the conditions and objectives of our project as tightly as possible so that only those who felt they could clearly endorse them came aboard.

"New understandings" were described as any effort to move beyond the two general models that have dominated Christian attitudes toward other religions up to the present: the "conservative" *exclusivist* approach, which finds salvation only in Christ and little, if any, value elsewhere; and the "liberal" *inclusivist* attitude, which recognizes the salvific richness of other faiths but then views this richness as the result of Christ's redemptive work and as having to be fulfilled in Christ. We wanted to gather theologians who were exploring the possibilities of a *pluralist* position—a move away from insistence on the superiority or finality of Christ and Christianity toward a recognition of the independent validity of other ways. Such a move came to be described by participants in our project as the crossing of a theological Rubicon. In the words of Langdon Gilkey, it represents "a monstrous shift indeed . . . a position quite new to the churches, even to the liberal churches."

Recognizing the complexity and the perils of this so-called pluralist paradigm, we wanted to proceed as cautiously as possible. Part of the purpose of this book is to "expose" this new approach, to bring it out into the open so that other theologians, together with the Christian community at large, might better evaluate its content and coherence, and judge how adequate it is to human experience, how appropriate and faithful to Christian tradition. So we thought that a fitting first step would be to gather the authors for a meeting at which the first drafts of these chapters could be subjected not only to mutual criticism (there turned out to be plenty of that!) but also and especially to the criticism of others.

We met at the Claremont Graduate School, Claremont, California, March 7–8, 1986. The critics included theologians who—like John B. Cobb, Jr., Schubert Ogden, David Tracy—are ardent advocates of interreligious dialogue but who feel that the pluralist move is either unwarranted, unnecessary, or ill-timed. All the manuscripts were read in advance so that each of our six daily sessions could open with a critic's comments, followed by the author's response, and then a fast-moving, always animated discussion. In light of these discussions, each author went home to revise their chapter. Though we could not include the comments and suggestions of the critics in this volume, they are at least implicitly present, to some degree, in the revised, final products that make up each chapter. Tom Driver's is the only essay written after this meeting; his task was to observe the dynamic, the new issues, and critical concerns, and then to draw some bottom lines as to what are the major problems and most promising directions in a pluralistic theology of religions.

The order of these essays as here presented is also ex post facto to the Claremont meeting. The authors had been asked to formulate their views on why they felt the contemporary context was pressing Christians toward a new pluralist approach toward other religions, how such an approach might best be elaborated, whether it was in line with past tradition and present Christian experience, and what might be its implications for other areas of Christian doctrine and practice. Both in the essays themselves and in our discussions of them, the viewpoints of the authors turned out to be much more richly varied than we had expected, and often in tension with one another. In going about our editorial toils, however, it seemed to us that the varied perspectives sifted down to three principal ways in which our authors were making the pluralist move—or, if we retain the somewhat labored image of the Rubicon, three "bridges" by which they were crossing over from the shores of exclusivism or inclusivism to pluralism. Although most of the contributors make "multiple crossings," these three bridges can, we think, help make clear the diversity and productive tension, as well as the underlying unity, within this collection of essays.

THE HISTORICO-CULTURAL BRIDGE: RELATIVITY

The starting point and guiding light for the essays in part I is *historical consciousness*—the ever more impelling awareness of the historico-cultural limitation of all knowledge and religious beliefs, and the difficulty, if not impossibility, of judging the truth claims of another culture or religion on the basis of one's own. Gordon Kaufman and John Hick are the clearest voices in this camp. Arguing that the threat of the mushroom cloud impels all religions to dialogue and cooperation, Kaufman proposes as a necessary condition for such dialogue that believers recognize the historical relativity of all religious forms and so abandon past claims of being the "only" or the "highest" form of religion.

John Hick gives a further twist to this awareness of historical relativity. Nowadays, he suggests, if any religion is going to make claims of superiority, it will have to do so on the basis of an "examination of the facts"—i.e., some form of empirical or experiential data available to all. Such data would have to be found in the ability of a religion to promote the welfare of humanity better than other religions. Hick's conclusion:

It seems impossible to make the global judgment that any one religious tradition has contributed more good or less evil, or a more favorable balance of good over evil, than the others. As vast complex totalities, the world traditions seem to be more or less on a par with each other. None can be singled out as manifestly superior.

Langdon Gilkey offers a more cautious, dialectical endorsement of historical consciousness. On the one hand he confesses that he can no longer make the
claims of finality for Christianity or Christ that he had made for most of his
life, because today "no one revelation is or can be the universal criterion for all
the others." On the other hand, Gilkey is also painfully aware of how such a
recognition of historical relativity easily leads to the quicksand of historical
relativism in which no one is allowed to make "absolute" judgments on anyone
else. But especially today, confronted by the intolerable evils that humans
inflict on other humans (many such evils imposed or sanctioned by religion),
we must be able to be so grounded in truth that we can speak and defend
absolute nonacceptance of such intolerables. But how, if every religious claim
is relative? In his wrestling with the dilemma of how to put together the
relativity of religious pluralism with the commitment of prophetic praxis,
Gilkey suggests how we might make use of the paradox of "relative absoluteness."

THE THEOLOGICO-MYSTICAL BRIDGE: MYSTERY

The theologians in part 2 make their proposal for a pluralist theology of
religions impelled by the recognition not only that our means of religious
perception are historically relative but also, and more importantly, that the
object or content of authentic religious experience is infinite—Mystery beyond
all forms, exceeding our every grasp of it. The infinity and ineffability of God-
Mystery demands religious pluralism and forbids any one religion from having
the "only" or "final" word.

W. C. Smith uses the time-honored notion of idolatry to state the reason why
a new attitude toward other faiths is needed. For him, however, idolatry
describes not other religions but our own. "Christianity has been our idol."
Christians have given in to the temptation to equate their religion with God by
making it absolute or final. To repent of this idolatry is to cease all exclusive or
inclusive claims and to be open to the possible equality of other ways.

Raimundo Panikkar and Stanley Samartha draw on their Hindu experience
to lay a mystical foundation for Smith's warnings against idolatry. For them,
the Ultimate Mystery is as ineffable *(neti-neti)* as it is real; all religions can
participate in and reflect this Mystery; none can own it. Samartha proposes an
Indian theocentric christology, and so shows that Christians can even make an
idol out of Jesus Christ. With their Eastern insistence on the limitations of
reason, both Samartha and Panikkar warn their Western colleagues against
making a pluralist theology of religions "too reasonable."

Panikkar is particularly insistent on the limitations of reason and so stands
in a certain tension with some of the other proposals. For him, the Ultimate is
not only ineluctably ineffable, it is also radically pluralistic. So, too, is all
reality. Panikkar suggests that many of his colleagues who endorse a new
pluralism and plunge across the Rubicon do not really know what this means.
Pluralism tells us that there is no "one" that can be imposed on the "many."

There will always be many; there will always be difference and disagreement. Panikkar warns:

> Pluralism does not allow for a universal system. A pluralistic system would be a contradiction in terms. The incommensurability of ultimate systems is unbridgeable. This incompatibility is not a lesser evil . . . but a revelation itself of the nature of reality.

Confronting Mystery within the context of his Buddhist experience of Emptiness *(Sunyata)* or Formlessness, Seiichi Yagi offers an essay that is in a sense unique among the contributions to this book. He uses a concrete example of Christian-Buddhist dialogue in order to lay the groundwork for a pluralist theology of religions. From a Buddhist perspective, but drawing as well on New Testament scholarship, he presents a reinterpretation of the "I" of Jesus that will enable Christians to move beyond both an exclusivistic and inclusivistic understanding of the uniqueness of Christ. Such a christology preserves the uniqueness of both Jesus and Buddha.

THE ETHICO-PRACTICAL BRIDGE: JUSTICE

For the authors in part 3, the main motivation to cross over to a pluralist approach to other faiths is not a consciousness of historical relativity or of absolute Mystery, but the confrontation with the sufferings of humanity and the need to put an end to such outrages. The need to promote justice becomes, for this perspective, the need for a new Christian attitude toward other faiths. What we have here are the beginnings of a "liberation theology of religions."

From their feminist experience, Rosemary Ruether and Marjorie Suchocki make clear how traditional understandings of Christianity as the bearer of the only or highest revelation have led to "an outrageous and absurd religious chauvinism. It is astonishing that even Christian liberals and radicals fail to seriously question this assumption" (Ruether). To hold up Christianity or Christ as the "norm" for all other religions is just as exploitive as is the attempt of sexism to render male experience the universal norm for humanity. In agreement with such charges, Aloysius Pieris and Paul Knitter add some positive reasons for a new attitude toward other faiths—not only to prevent injustice but to promote justice. "Economic, political, and especially nuclear liberation is too big a job for any one nation, or culture, or religion. . . . A worldwide liberation movement needs a worldwide interreligious dialogue" (Knitter).

Pieris explores the implications of such a liberation approach for christology. After tracing the similarities and resulting conflicts between the "absolute" claims that have been made in both christology and buddhology, he suggests that if Buddhists and Christians meet on "the one Path of liberation," Buddha and Christ can complement, rather than compete with, each other.

Suchocki and Knitter expand on Pieris's suggestions. Agreeing with Gilkey on the limits of tolerance and on the need to resist the intolerable evils that infest our modern world, they recommend that the religions of the world accept a shared concern for justice as the starting point and guiding norm for their efforts at dialogue. Well aware of the variety of ways for understanding "justice" or "salvation" or "human welfare," these authors still suggest that something like a "preferential option" for those most in need might well serve as the context for a new meeting of religions. Persons of different religious traditions could enter into a *shared* liberative praxis for the poor and suffering, as well as a *shared* reflection on how that praxis relates to their religious beliefs; this would provide them, it is suggested, with a workable means of better understanding and judging each other. Praxis and commitment would lead to doctrinal clarification and revision.

In his Postscript, Tom Driver sounds some final warnings and provides some needed guidelines for further explorations of a pluralist theology of religions. There is a danger of understanding the case for pluralism too naively. Given the disjunctions and discontinuities existing between religious traditions, it is impossible and imperialistic to subsume the religions under universal categories. Resonating with the last set of essays, Driver concludes that the case for pluralism is at bottom a moral or ethical one, not the result of any salvific, revelational, or rational harmony.

The discussion of all these essays at Claremont, which led to the gathering of their final fruits in this book, was made possible by financial support from the James A. Blaisdell Programs in World Religions and Cultures, together with the encouragement and facilities of the Department of Religion at the Claremont Graduate School. For such assistance, and also for the enthusiastic and industrious cooperation of all the participants in our Claremont meeting, we are deeply grateful. We hope that the broader community of believers, thinkers, and dreamers will share this gratitude.

—Paul F. Knitter

PART I

The Historico-Cultural Bridge: Relativity

1

Religious Diversity, Historical Consciousness, and Christian Theology

GORDON D. KAUFMAN

I

How can persons and communities with radically differing conceptions of the world and of human life, and quite diverse views of the most urgent problems facing human beings and the most effective ways to address those problems, come to understanding and appreciation of each others' ways of being human? How, in all our diversity, can we humans learn to live together fruitfully, productively and in peace in today's complexly interconnected world, instead of regularly moving into the sort of conflict and struggle that may erupt into a nuclear holocaust that will destroy us all? These are questions that raise special issues for Christians because of the absolutistic claims about divine revelation and ultimate truth that have often been regarded as central to faith; these claims require careful theological scrutiny. Serious attention to these issues, in my opinion, suggests that we must today become self-conscious about Christian faith in new ways—ways that will enable us to move toward some fundamental revisions of the tasks and methods of Christian theology. I shall try to explain these contentions in this chapter.

Among ordinary Christian believers as well as most theologians, it is usually taken for granted that the fundamental truths and values needed for the proper ordering of human life are available and known in and to the Christian tradition: they have been provided by divine revelation (however that may be understood). The task of theologians and other teachers in the church, thus, is understood to be one of interpreting and passing on these truths and values of the tradition, not fundamentally questioning, criticizing, or reconstructing them. Hence, when other religious (or secular) positions are encountered that make divergent or even contradictory claims, they are either to be refuted as mistaken or to be interpreted in light of the basic principles that Christians accept.[1]

To many Christians, however, this sort of practice, which has stood the churches in good stead for two millennia, seems more and more faulty and dangerous. In the first place, it is apparent that there are a number of other religious (and secular) communities and traditions—Buddhism, Judaism, certain forms of secular humanism, and so forth—that have quite impressive resources for interpreting and orienting human existence and for giving significant formation to human individual and social life. It seems a narrow sort of self-impoverishment to refuse to learn from these differing ways of being human, however alien some of them may at first appear. Secondly, and much more importantly, it has become obvious today that if we humans do not learn to appreciate each others' commitments well enough to enable us all to live together in our diversity, if we continue to attempt—as most communities and traditions have throughout the past—to live largely from and to ourselves, moving willingly even to destroy those whom we regard as our enemies, we may well succeed only in bringing all of human life on earth to its final end. We live now in a single interconnected and interdependent world, whether we like it or not, and it is no longer possible either to ignore the other ways of being human or to move toward eliminating them. We must learn instead to encounter these others on equal terms, seeking, as sympathetically as we can, to understand and appreciate both their insights into the human condition and the forms of belief and practice they recommend and inculcate.

The following remarks take as their fundamental premise that it is a necessity today for religious and secular communities that differ and disagree to come to sufficient understanding and appreciation of each other to enable them to enter into positive dialogue and other interaction, instead of persisting in the sort of separation, distrust, and even warfare that may destroy us all. With this general problem in mind, I wish to propose certain theological moves for Christians that will, I think, help to open up our self-understanding in such a way as to facilitate significant interchange with others on matters of fundamental conviction and faith. If Christians are to take other faiths, other life-orientations, with full seriousness, it is necessary for them to reexamine certain theological claims they often make. I shall suggest that modern historical consciousness makes possible just the sort of reassessment that is called for here, and thus can provide a basis for the theological reconstruction that is needed.

II

It should be clear that if our objective is to proceed along a road toward greater mutual understanding with those with whom we now disagree on fundamental issues, we cannot continue to follow our usual practice of simply taking it for granted that our received religious traditions provide us with everything we need. It is just this sort of parochial approach to thinking and living that gives rise to the problem we are trying to address.

Some suggest we should attempt to overcome our traditional parochialism by moving to what they claim is a "universally human" position, one that penetrates beneath all the "accidental" and "historical" differences among humans and their religions to some supposed "essential oneness" we all share. Then, on the basis of this deep unity underlying everything human, we can understand and negotiate the differences with which the several great religious traditions confront us.[2] But there really is no such universally human position available to us; every religious (or secular) understanding and way of life we might uncover is a *particular* one, that has grown up in a particular history, makes particular claims, is accompanied by particular practices and injunctions, and hence is to be distinguished from all other particular religious and secular orientations. Doubtless there are similarities, parallels, and overlappings of many different sorts within this enormous human diversity—and it is just as important to grasp these connections as to apprehend the differences—but it seems undeniable that every position to which we might turn is itself historically specific. A universal frame of orientation for human understanding and life is no more available to us than is a universal language.

Instead of searching for a single "universal position" that sets forth, supposedly, the "essence" of the human or of human religiousness, I want to acknowledge immediately that in my view it is impossible simply to move out of and leave behind the particular symbolic, linguistic, and conceptual frames of reference within which one does all one's thinking and living. Nevertheless, if we are to approach sympathetically, and enter into dialogue with, others of quite different commitments and convictions, we must find ways of relativizing and opening up our basic symbol system. The tendencies toward absoluteness and exclusivity in traditional Christian faith easily lead to a kind of idolatry that makes it difficult to take other faiths seriously in their own terms,[3] searching out their insights into human existence and the deepest human problems, attending carefully to their proposals regarding how those problems should be approached.

To address this problem inherent in traditional Christian faith and theology, I want to make a relatively modest and simple proposal: that we follow out certain implications of our modern historical consciousness, and the kind of reflection it engenders, as we work out our theological understanding of Christian faith. Many Christians already accept modern historical methods as appropriate for understanding the origins of Christianity as well as the institutions, practices, and beliefs of other religious traditions. I want to suggest now that the complex of attitudes and consciousness that underlies modern attempts to engage in historical and comparative studies of human religiousness can provide a way to break through the tendencies toward absoluteness and self-idolatry that often obstruct interaction between Christians and others.

Modern historical and comparative studies direct attention to precisely the particularity and concreteness of communities and traditions, attempting thus to understand their full human significance and import. As we begin to appreciate the richness and meaning of life in a community or tradition, we move into a position from which we are able to take seriously its integrity and its unique claims. As we gradually come to see how it has gained its unique structure, emphasis, and character in and through the history in which it was created, we grasp its special historicity.

Let us take note of what it means to understand a religious position in this historical way. It means grasping the patterns of life before us, the ritual practices, the customs, the values, the ideas, the ways of thinking and meditating, the worldviews, all in connection with their specific historical context, in order to see how and why they came into being with just the special qualities and characteristics they have come to have. It is clear that widely diverse patterns of life, structures of roles and institutions, religious practices and experiences, have developed in the various societies around the world and in different historical periods. Thus, the women and men who grew up in those societies and historical periods were formed in different ways, came to have different skills, different interests, different needs, different patterns of relationship to other humans. They became quite different persons than they would have been had they grown up in some other society or some other period. Each of us would be a very different person had we grown to maturity in, say, an Indian village (as a low-caste Hindu), in a commune in central China, or in a Roman emperor's family. (These observations are, of course, commonplace in modern historical understanding.)

With this awareness of human historicity in mind, let us turn for a moment to the rise and development of human religiousness itself. Human life, as we today believe, gradually evolved from animal origins to forms shaped by cultural activity, and only over the course of many generations did it become historical in the sense we have just been considering. The development of language and culture enabled men and women to become conscious of themselves and of the world around them to a much greater degree than was possible for other forms of animal life, and they thus increasingly oriented themselves and their lives in terms of this growing linguistic and cultural consciousness. In time, unifying ideas or pictures of the world began to appear to the more imaginative and poetic, ideas that enabled persons to see and understand their world better, making it possible to adapt to it more effectively and live within it. And notions of what humans themselves are, what their deepest needs are and how these needs are to be met, also began to be formulated.

The earliest versions of these conceptions of the human and of the world were apparently in the form of stories, poems, and songs told and sung generation after generation. These presented imaginative pictures of human life, showing the problems that must be faced and the tasks to be performed. They enabled men and women to gain some idea of what the world in which they lived was like, what were the powers or beings that must be dealt with in human existence. Human life could be seen, for example, as a journey through hazardous territory where one might encounter wild beasts and evil monsters as one sought to get to the safety of home; or it might be depicted as participation in a great warfare between the forces of light and the forces of darkness. It might be set forth essentially as responsible citizenship in a quasi-political order, the kingdom of God; or as but one stage in a never-ending transmigration of the soul from one form of life to another. The human individual or self might be seen as a soul fallen out of its proper home in heaven above and become trapped in a physical body from which it must find some way to escape. Or, in sharp contrast, the very sense of self or soul might be regarded as an illusion, as the product of ignorance, the veil of *maya*, which right insight can dispel, thus dissolving the deep human problems that arise out of this false consciousness. Or human existence might be understood to be a product of the accidental collocation of material atoms, or of blind evolutionary processes that could just as well have gone in other directions and formed other patterns.

In the course of history, women and men have developed many diverse worldviews, many different conceptions of what life in the world is all about, of what the central human problems are and what could be solutions to those problems. Every great civilization, indeed every isolated tribe, has worked out one or more such conceptual or imagistic frames for understanding, interpreting, and orienting human life; and humans have shaped and reshaped their lives, institutions, values, and practices in accord with these various visions of reality and the human. It is out of primordial visions of this sort that the different religious traditions have grown. In their religious practices, institutions, and rituals humans have found orientation in life, have found an interpretation of what human existence is all about and how it is to be lived. Or rather, we should say it was in their search for orientation in life, in their attempt to come to an understanding of what human existence is all about and how it is to be lived, that humans created and developed the various religious traditions, thus giving life the variant meanings it has come to have.

Of course the great religious poets, prophets, and storytellers have rarely understood themselves to be directly creating traditions of value and meaning to serve in this way as interpretations of the ultimate Mystery of things, as bulwarks against the void. They have taken themselves, rather, to be directly expressing *how things really are*, simply depicting what human life is all about. Inasmuch as humans have always come to consciousness and self-consciousness within a community and a tradition already there, which has been handed on by the elders, the mothers and fathers, as the wisdom about life, no one has ever experienced himself or herself as building up a conception of the world and of the human simply from scratch. Living and working within the framework of understanding handed down to it, each new generation makes only such changes and additions—and subtractions—as its experience demands. No one, thus, has understood herself or himself to be simply creating or constructing a picture of the world and of the human within the world;

rather, each was, at most, making small corrections in received pictures believed to be substantially true. From our modern historical vantage point, however, looking back at the many great and diverse cultural and religious traditions that have appeared in human history, all of these diverse conceptions and pictures seem best understood as the product of human imaginative creativity in the face of the great mystery that life is to us all. Out of and on the basis of such traditions of meaning, value, and truth, all men and women live.

III

Such a historical approach to the understanding of human religiousness, its origins and functions, has long been accepted in the scholarly study of religion (including the study of Christianity), but it has not often been made a point of departure for Christian theological construction. I want to suggest, now, that a theological self-understanding informed by modern historical consciousness can provide an interpretation of Christian faith that will—without destroying or undercutting the fundamental significance of the central symbols of God and Christ for the orientation of life—enable Christians to give other religious traditions their full integrity and meaning, neither patronizing nor otherwise demeaning them.

If our self-understanding is informed by a historical conception of human existence of the sort I have outlined, we must think of ourselves as historical beings like everyone else, and we will see the traditions of value, meaning, and truth by which we are living and which orient our lives as themselves historical in character—that is, as creations of the human imagination in and through history, like those of any other people or community. This sort of historicist self-interpretation, of course, gives rise to some theological questions that must be faced clearly; indeed, some may believe it undermines the very meaning of Christian faith. If we agree that everything religious—including our own commitments and convictions—is historical in character, is not the normative significance of faith undercut? If the Christian meanings and values, insights and understandings, by which we live are taken to be basically products of historical development, instead of held to be grounded simply and directly in divine revelation, do they not lose their point?

I do not think these consequences need follow from the proposal I am making, though it must certainly be granted that the sense of the *absoluteness* of our religious convictions will be weakened. This does not mean, however, that they are thereby rendered inoperative or ineffective. In fact, an understanding of human existence as historical in the way I am proposing—precisely because it emphasizes the function and importance of worldviews and conceptual frameworks for ongoing human life—shows clearly how humanly significant, indeed indispensable, are religious language and reflection. There is no reason to suppose that imaginative construction of holistic frames of orientation, of world-pictures, either can or should be discontinued today. It is as necessary for contemporary women and men to have a worldview or conceptual frame for ordering and understanding their lives as it has been for any other generation. Religious frames of orientation, then, and religious reflection, are as important today as ever—but (in the light of modern historical understanding) they should be conceived now much more explicitly in terms of human imaginative creativity. Our religious activities are still to be carried on, but now in a critical and self-conscious way that was not possible earlier.

What does this mean for Christian theology? If we understand human historicity in the sense I am urging here, Christian faith (like every other faith) will be seen as one perspective, one worldview, which has developed in and through a long history alongside other traditions, many of which are vying for the attention and loyalty of us all today. When one applies the concept "worldview" to one's own tradition in this way, one simultaneously distinguishes it from and relates it to other worldviews. This involves a certain distancing of oneself from one's tradition, taking a step back from simple, unmediated commitment to it. We now see the great theologians of Christian history, for example, not simply as setting out the truth that is ultimately salvific for all humanity (as they have often been understood in the past), but rather as essentially engaged in discerning and articulating one particular perspective on life among many others.

Reflective interpretation of Christian faith today involves a similar activity of discernment and articulation; however, it must now be taken up in a much more self-conscious way. This change in degree of self-consciousness transforms the critical questions for Christian theology. In the past we could ask, What are the principal doctrines or ideas prescribed by tradition for Christians to believe, and how should we interpret them today? It now becomes necessary to direct attention to questions like, How does one articulate a worldview—specifically, the Christian worldview—and how does one assess its significance for human life today? Refocusing religious reflection in this way leads one to attend to a rather different agenda from that followed by most theologians in the past. Instead of concentrating on familiar doctrines and dogmas, one is led to inquire into the fundamental categories—the basic conceptual and symbolic framework—that has given Christian perspectives their unique structure, order, and experiential flavor. If these can be ascertained, one can begin to explore how well these categories can order and provide orientation for contemporary human life.

A human frame of orientation, of course, is given its full character and meaning by a historically complex pattern of institutions and customs, words and symbols, liturgical practices and moral claims, stories and myths handed down from generation to generation, shaping and interpreting the experience of those living within it. However, not all these expressions, patterns, and practices are of equal weight: the basic structure and character of every worldview is defined largely by a few fundamental categories that give it shape and order. These are connected and interrelated in various ways by the wider vocabulary of terms and symbols used in ritual and meditation, ideology and story, thus providing concreteness and filling in details of an overall picture, or developing a complex of pictures, that accommodates and interprets the infinite variations and nuances of the experience of many generations. This configuration of defining terms and symbols—worked out in many different ways, with different nuances of meaning and diverse behavioral and institutional implications—I call the *categorial* structure of the worldview. The task of Christian theologians today (from the perspective I am presenting here) is to penetrate through the multiplicity of Christian institutions, practices, and liturgies, of Christian philosophies, theologies, and myths, to the basic categorial pattern that informs them. With this categorial pattern in mind, the theologian is in a position, on the one hand, to engage in the most fundamental sort of analysis and criticism of Christian worldviews, taking into account insights and understandings provided by other religious and secular positions, both ancient and modern. And, on the other hand, the theologian is in a position to proceed to the construction of a contemporary Christian understanding of human life, the world, and God.

I cannot here provide a detailed analysis, criticism, and reconstruction of the basic Christian categorial scheme.[4] Instead I will briefly sketch what I take to be the four principal symbols or categories that give Christian worldviews their basic structure and character: God, world, humanity, Christ. (The first three of these categories, it may be noted, are not uniquely Christian; they have also figured importantly in Jewish and Muslim perspectives.) These four categories provide principal benchmarks or reference points in terms of which Christian maps of reality are drawn. Or, to change the metaphor, they are principal hooks or fasteners to which Christian webs of experience, life, interpretation are attached, determining their basic patterns and character. Let me say just a few words about each of these categories.

"God" is, of course, the ultimate point of reference in Christian perspectives. Christian traditions have expressed this by speaking of God as the source of all that is, as the ultimate ground of all reality, as the creator of the world and the lord of history. In the biblical documents God is portrayed as a quasi-personal or agential reality—that is, the model in terms of which the notion of God is constructed is the human self or agent. In classic Christian theology, however, this was greatly complicated by the development of trinitarian conceptions. Just how this "ultimate point of reference" for all human life and thought can properly be conceived today is a major issue for contemporary constructive theology.

The second term of the categorial scheme, "world," refers to the overall context within which human life takes place. In the earlier mythopoeic versions of the Christian perspective, this context was characterized simply as "the heavens and the earth." But today we are obliged to think of it as an unimaginably immense universe, hundreds of millions of light years across and billions of years old. Within this universe are millions of galaxies, and within one of these galaxies is the solar system that provides the immediate context for planet Earth. Earth in turn is a complex ecosystem without which human life would not be possible. All of this, in Christian worldviews, is understood as in some sense God's "creation."

The third principal category, "humanity," refers to those creatures living here on earth who are sufficiently self-conscious and capable of taking responsibility for their own actions and lives (for they were "created in God's image") as to require that they have a symbolical framework for orienting and ordering all their activities. Orientation is gained, as we have noted, as humans imaginatively created world-pictures and interpretations of human existence that set out various possibilities, problems, and parameters of life in ways relevant to their historical experience and their accumulated knowledge. It is a principal part of the task of contemporary Christian theology to show how and why an adequate modern world-picture and understanding of the human requires—or at least can usefully employ—the symbols "God" and "Christ" to help orient life today.

The fourth category is "Christ," that figure from human history who is believed by Christians to reveal or define, on the one hand, who or what God really is, and, on the other hand, what true humanity consists in. The historical figure of Jesus Christ thus gives concreteness and specificity to the understanding of both God and humanity, in this way significantly shaping these central symbols that define what is normative for orienting human existence in Christian terms.

This fourfold categorial scheme—God/world/humanity/Christ—has significantly defined and given shape to Christian understandings of life and the world. Other terms in the Christian vocabulary—for example, sin, salvation, church, sacrament, trinity, faith, hope, love, creation, revelation, holy spirit, and the like—all help to elaborate and fill out this categorial structure so that it can give a full interpretation or picture of what human life is all about, how it is to be carried on in the world, and toward what human devotion, worship, love, and service should be directed.

Careful and thoughtful reflection on the four terms of this categorial pattern is essential in developing a Christian theology informed (as I am proposing here) by modern historical consciousness. It is necessary for theologians to learn as much as possible about the different ways of thinking about God and the world, humanity and Christ, that have appeared in Christian history, and theologians must seek to understand the principal arguments for these various views. They will then be in a position to raise some important questions that others in the past have often failed to ask: Which of these Christian views have been destructive, damaging, or oppressive to humans, and thus evil? Which ones have promoted the love, creativity, peace, and justice—human fulfillment—for which Christian faith hopes? Which ones, however powerful and significant historically, must now be regarded as archaic and misleading, as the "mythology" of another age? Which promise to provide adequate, full, and insightful understanding of our contemporary existence, its problems and possibilities? A theologian working with the sort of historical self-consciousness I am advocating is able to examine and to assess traditional theological positions both sympathetically and critically.

Ordinarily one would expect this attempt at comprehensive and critical historical assessment to prepare the way for a constructive interpretation of the

Christian perspective on life and the world, an interpretation that can effectively orient the existence of women and men today. In some instances,
however, it may bring a theologian to the conclusion that the traditional
categorial scheme orders and interprets human life in a way no longer viable or
helpful. Perhaps one or more of the principal categories requires drastic
revision, drawing on ideas suggested by other religious or secular traditions.
The theologian may even feel forced to conclude (as some have in recent years)
that such central Christian symbols as "God" or "Christ" must be given up
entirely, other images or concepts being given categorial status in their stead.
There is, of course, an almost unlimited range of theological possibilities and
permutations. For a theology that wishes to remain "Christian," however, the
fundamental task is quite straightforward: to work carefully and critically
through the proposals for understanding human life and the world presented
by the Christian tradition (and by theological reflection on that tradition); to
try to grasp our contemporary experience and life in terms of these categories,
images, and concepts; and to reconstruct them in whatever respects are required to enable them to serve as the framework for a worldview that can
provide adequate orientation for life today.

A contemporary theology, informed in this way by a thoroughgoing historical consciousness, would not be in a position to claim—as Christian theology
has so often in the past—that its assertions were directly and uniquely authorized or warranted by divine revelation. (This does not mean, of course, that
they are not in some significant sense grounded in God, as "ultimate point of
reference"; nor does it mean that there are no ways at all in which the concept
of revelation might be used to articulate that grounding.) Christian theology
would understand itself in essentially the same terms that it understands other
religious activity and reflection—namely, as human imaginative response to
the necessity to find orientation for life in a particular historical situation. It
would, thus, keep itself open to insights, criticism, and correction from other
points of view, including other religious and secular perspectives and worldviews.

Surely this is an enormous gain over more traditional approaches. As our
modern historical knowledge vividly shows us, every theological position has
always been taken, and every claim has been made, by some particular, limited,
finite, human being, whether named Paul of Tarsus or Thomas Aquinas or
John Calvin or Karl Barth. Beliefs about divine inspiration and revelation have
all too often enabled theologians in the past to obscure this fact by claiming
that this or that affirmation or position is grounded directly in the very truth of
God. And heretics were burned at the stake for not properly acknowledging
what God had so distinctly revealed, and what this or that theologian or
authoritative church official knew with such certainty. To acknowledge
forthrightly and regularly that our theological statements and claims are
simply *ours*—that they are the product of our own human study and reflection,
and of the spontaneity and creativity of our own human powers imaginatively
to envision a world and our human place within that world—is to set us free

from these all too easy but false moves toward authoritarianism, which has characterized so much Christian theology in the past. And simultaneously we are opened to the broad ranges of experience, life, and insight lying outside our own tradition, and provided with a powerful incentive to engage in dialogue and other interchange—on equal terms—with representatives of other religious and secular points of view.

IV

Let me now attempt to draw together the points I have been making. None of us—Christian or non-Christian—possesses absolute or final truth, truth adequate to orient humankind in face of the enormous problems we confront in today's world. At best we Christians, like all others, have available to ourselves the insights and understanding of our forebears. But these were, in all cases, their own imaginative constructions, formed under the influence of their own experience and of the problems they faced in their time, and thus finite, limited, and relative. They have been corrected, amplified, and transformed in the past by other imaginative and creative women and men. And they can surely benefit today from exposure to images and concepts, perspectives and worldviews, developed in other quite different traditions.

Interreligious dialogue has become important for us. The problems with which modernity confronts us—extending even to the possibility that we may obliterate humankind completely in a nuclear holocaust—demand that we bring together all the wisdom, devotion, and insight that humanity has accumulated in its long history, as we attempt to find orientation in today's world. We simply cannot afford not to enter into conversation with representatives of other traditions, making available to each other whatever resources each of our traditions has to offer, and learning from each other whatever we can.

Such dialogue today should not have as its objective just talking together to get information about points of view different from our own. We must enter into serious exchange with each other in order to help humanity—including, of course, ourselves—find adequate orientation in today's world; in order, that is, to enable us to construct religious frameworks that can provide genuine guidance with respect to the unprecedented problems we today confront. We moderns must seek to learn, thus, how to discern the basic patterns and frameworks of the several great religious and secular traditions of orientation that have been created by humankind in its long history—to discern what I have called their fundamental categorial structures—so that we will be able to compare them with each other directly, evaluating the strong points and the weak points of each as frames of orientation for life today. Thus we will come into a better position to construct frames of orientation that can provide significant guidance for contemporary human existence.

Religious claims have always had to make their way, finally, in the open marketplace of human experience and ideas. Though dogmatic appeal to revelatory authority, or to special insight, enlightenment, or truth, might for a time have given a position special attention and credence, in the long run of human history only the power to explain, interpret, and orient actual human life has enabled some positions and claims to survive and to grow in intellectual and cultural power, whereas others, gradually or quickly, have died out. Acknowledgment that our religious activity is *our own* imaginative and intellectual individual and communal activity—not an unmediated expression of or reflection on divine revelation—can only be salutary in forcing us to do our work as well as we can, even while we are as open as possible to insights and understanding from other quite different religious and secular perspectives.

In the twentieth century particularly, humankind, which for most of its history developed in quite diverse ways in various geographical settings around the globe, has been growing together into one humanity. Now the threat of nuclear war has irrevocably bound us all together in one common fate, whether we like it or not. It is no longer possible, therefore, or desirable, for us to continue living simply and uncritically out of the parochial religious and cultural traditions we have inherited. Entering into dialogue with others and trying to understand each other, exposing the weaknesses and problems of our own perspectives to each other as well as their respective strengths and values, learning to appreciate the insights and understanding of positions quite different from our own—these sorts of moves are now demanded of us all.[5]

I have tried to sketch here a way to understand the task of Christian theology today that will help Christians move more easily and wholeheartedly into genuine interreligious understanding and fruitful dialogue. This perspective, as we have seen, grows out of modern Western historical thinking, and it is in that respect, of course—like all other perspectives—particular, relative, and limited; we do not know what sorts of theological self-understandings may succeed it at some later time. But it is an approach that enables us to break the grip of the absolutistic commitments that have characterized much traditional Christian faith and theology, thus enabling us to encounter other significant religious and secular traditions *in their own terms* instead of as defined by our categories. Moves of this sort can help provide us with the understanding and sympathy for others that is so much needed to help bring peace in our time. Only as we find ways of stepping back from, and thus not remaining confined within, those features of our traditions (both religious and secular) that wall us off from others, can we hope to come into genuine understanding of and community with them. Building such community with others, it seems to me, is the most profound religious necessity of our time. Promoting it, therefore, is the most important task to which Christian theology today can attend.

NOTES

1. It is worth noting that living and thinking out of a received tradition in this way is characteristic not only of Christians. It is in fact the common practice of most individuals and groups, including those who regard their commitments as fundamentally "secular"—e.g., Marxists, Freudians, nationalistic patriots, humanists. Men

and women ordinarily orient themselves in life more or less unquestioningly in terms of the values and truths they have inherited from the community or communities with which they are most closely associated. Christian beliefs about God's revelation, however, deepen and harden this allegiance to living tradition by giving it a seemingly divine authorization and making it a matter of religious faithfulness and obedience.

2. In the present volume such a position seems represented especially clearly by John Hick and Wilfred C. Smith, and in a somewhat qualified way by Paul Knitter and Marjorie Suchocki.

3. I am, of course, not arguing here that there are no dimensions of Christian faith that motivate and sustain interaction with and sympathy for non-Christian persons and communities. The central Christian moral imperative that we love both our neighbors and our enemies as impartially as does God, who "makes [the] sun rise on the evil and on the good, and sends rain on the just and on the unjust" (Matt. 5:45), requires Christians to concern themselves directly and wholeheartedly with human suffering and need, wherever it is found. This imperative has in the past initiated not only worldwide missionary activity; it has also motivated efforts to alleviate physical suffering through the establishment of medical centers, through engaging in relief and rehabilitation work around the world, through providing agricultural assistance of many sorts, etc. But, however helpful these activities have been in breaking down barriers between Christians and others, they have not, for the most part, affected the Christian sense of *religious superiority*—they may even have enhanced it!—a sense grounded in the conviction that Christians have a unique and universally valid gospel needed by all peoples. It is a gospel whose ultimate truth is believed to be grounded in God's own special revelation in and through Jesus Christ; this in a special way is taken to set Christian faith apart from all other religious orientations. The barriers to genuine interreligious dialogue and community raised by these special truth-claims are what I am trying to address in this chapter.

4. For further elaboration of my conception of "the Christian categorial scheme" and its reconstruction—but one expressed in static-structural language, and insufficiently attentive to the historicity of the structure of categories—see my *The Theological Imagination* (Philadelphia: Westminster Press, 1981), chap. 4; and also *Theology for a Nuclear Age* (Manchester: University of Manchester Press, and Philadelphia: Westminster Press, 1985), esp. chap. 3 and 4. For a fuller discussion of theology as imaginative construction of the sort I am here recommending, see my *Essay on Theological Method* (Missoula, Montana: Scholars Press, rev. ed. 1979), and *The Theological Imagination*, esp. chap. 1 and 10.

5. I have argued in some detail the claim that "nuclear eschatology" puts new and quite unexpected demands on Christian theology, in *Theology for a Nuclear Age*.

2

The Non-Absoluteness of Christianity

JOHN HICK

I

Ernst Troeltsch's famous book, *The Absoluteness of Christianity* (1901), focused on what has always been from the point of view of the Christian church the central issue in its relationship to other streams of religious life. Until fairly recently it was a virtually universal Christian assumption, an implicit dogma with almost credal status, that Christ/the Christian gospel/ Christianity is "absolute," "unique," "final," "normative," "ultimate"— decisively superior to all other saviors, gospels, religions. Troeltsch's own intellectual journey illustrates how this implicit dogma has now come under serious question. In the lecture that he wrote for delivery at Oxford in 1923 (he died before delivering it), he criticized his own earlier position and opted for the very different view that Christianity is "absolute" for Christians, and the other world faiths are likewise "absolute" for their own adherents.[1] Clearly the "relative absoluteness" of his 1923 paper is very different in its implications from the unqualified absoluteness of his 1901 book.

The Christian mind has always been composed of many segments and layers, exhibiting very different degrees of self-consciousness and self-critical reflection. But in its more intellectual hemisphere there has been, during the period since the first world war, a marked development in ways of conceiving Christianity's place within the total religious life of the world. We are now at a critical point at which that development may be halted or may proceed to its logical conclusion. Hence the symbol of the river Rubicon, to cross which is to take a step that closes one range of options while opening another. In order to see where this theological Rubicon runs, we must go back for a moment to the medieval assumption—medieval, but continuing effectively until about the end of the nineteenth century—of a Christian monopoly of salvific truth and life, expressed in the doctrine *extra ecclesiam nulla salus*. This exclusivist

Roman doctrine had its equally emphatic Protestant equivalent in the conviction that outside Christianity there is no salvation, so that missionaries were sent out to save souls who must otherwise have forfeited eternal life. It was a virtually unchallenged assumption that Christianity was to spread throughout the world, replacing the non-Christian traditions. Thus as late as 1913 Julius Richter defined his subject of missiology as "that branch of theology which in opposition to the non-Christian religions, shows the Christian religion to be the Way, the Truth, and the Life; which seeks to dispossess the non-Christian religions and to plant in their stead in the soil of heathen national life the evangelic faith and the Christian life."[2]

What has led many, perhaps most, thinking Christians during the last seventy or so years gradually to abandon this absolutist position? The full answer would be many-sided. Perhaps the most important factor has been the modern explosion of knowledge among Christians in the West concerning the other great religious traditions of the world. Between the two world wars, and even more so since the second, ill-informed and hostile Western stereotypes of the other faith communities have increasingly been replaced by more accurate knowledge and more sympathetic understanding. The immense spiritual riches of Judaism and Islam, of Hinduism, Buddhism, and Sikhism, of Confucianism and Taoism and African primal religion, have become better known in the West and have tended to erode the plausibility of the old Christian exclusivism. More about this presently. Another factor has been the realization that Christian absolutism, in collaboration with acquisitive and violent human nature, has done much to poison the relationships between the Christian minority and the non-Christian majority of the world's population by sanctifying exploitation and oppression on a gigantic scale. I want to look here at some of the large-scale ways in which Christian absolutism has lent itself—human nature being what it is—to the validation and encouragement of political and economic evil.

That phrase "human nature being what it is" is important. For we can imagine a very different world in which Christians have always believed their gospel to be uniquely superior to others but in which they have had no desire to dominate and exploit others. In that imagined world Christianity would have liberated its adherents from acquisitive desires, so that none of the evils that we are about to look at would have occurred. Thus the connection between Christian absolutism and these historical evils is not one of a priori logical necessity but is a factual link via a "fallen" human nature that Christianity has been largely powerless to redeem. But of course this very powerlessness is itself a major factor in the accounting. The picture would be very different if Christianity, commensurate with its claim to absolute truth and unique validity, had shown a unique capacity to transform human nature for the better.

It should be added at this point that the claims of other religions to absolute validity and to a consequent superiority have likewise, given the same human nature, sanctified violent aggression, exploitation, and intolerance. A worldwide and history-long study of the harmful effects of religious absolutism would draw material from almost every tradition—Christianity and Islam probably providing the greatest number of examples, and Buddhism perhaps the least. However, I am writing here as a Christian specifically about our Christian attitude to other religions, and accordingly I shall be concerned with Christian rather than with other forms of religious absolutism.

II

The main destructive effects of the assumption of Christain superiority have occurred in the relationships between European and North American Christians on the one hand, and both the black and brown peoples of the world and, for an even longer period, the Jews, on the other.

As regards the Jews, there is a clear connection between fifteen or so centuries of the "absoluteness" of Christianity, with its corollary of the radical inferiority and perverseness of the Judaism it "superseded," and the consequent endemic anti-Semitism of Christian civilization, which has continued with undiminished virulence into and through our twentieth century. This connection has only become a matter of Christian consciousness—within very limited circles—since the mid-1950s. One of those responsible for bringing it to Christian awareness, Rosemary Ruether, has written about it in another chapter of this book, and so I shall not enlarge upon the theme here. She has also written about the long-standing destructive effects upon Christian women of the absoluteness claimed by the church's traditional patriarchal system of ideas; and I shall likewise not attempt to repeat that here. Instead I will supplement what she has written by adding a note about the way in which the Christian superiority complex supported and sanctified the Western imperialistic exploitation of what today we call the Third World.

European colonization, reaching out forcefully into Africa, India, southeast Asia, China, South America, and the Pacific islands, and establishing white hegemony over vast brown and black populations, constitutes a complex historical tapestry woven with many and varied threads. The patterns of damage caused by organized exploitation and, within it, the elements that also occurred of incidental benefit, are well depicted as regards one major part of the story in James Morris's recent three-volume history of the flourishing and fall of the British Empire.[3] Carved out by the aggressive might of Western military technology, this empire at its height covered a quarter of the surface of the globe and included a quarter of its human population. It placed Britain at the center of a vast trading network, drawing cheap raw materials to feed its nineteenth-century industrial expansion, and then exporting manufactured goods to huge captive markets. In some cases trade followed the flag, whereas in others the flag was planted to protect an established flow of trade. The basic motives were acquisitiveness and aggrandizement—though within the structures created by these forces there was also room for shining threads of personal idealism and courage, and sometimes for a genuine, if paternalistic, spirit of service to the subject peoples.[4]

The racist attitudes that continue to poison the human community after the colonial structures have collapsed formed a powerful ingredient in the mentality that created and maintained them. For during the period when it was accepted as right that Britons, Frenchmen, Germans, Dutchmen, Spaniards, Italians, and Portuguese should rule over whole black and brown populations, it was psychologically almost inevitable that they should see those whom they dominated as inferior and as in need of a higher guardianship. This categorizing of black and brown humanity as inferior included their cultures and religions. Although there were individual colonial administrators—some of them remarkable and admirable men—who came genuinely to respect the peoples over whom they ruled, more usually their cultures were seen as barbarous and their religions as idolatrous superstitions. For the moral validation of the imperial enterprise rested upon the conviction that it was a great civilizing and uplifting mission, one of whose tasks was to draw the unfortunate heathen up into the higher, indeed highest, religion of Christianity. Accordingly the gospel played a vital role in the self-justification of Western imperialism. Writing of early nineteenth-century India, Morris says,

> The Indian territories were allotted by providence to Great Britain, wrote Charles Grant, the evangelical chairman of the [East India] Company's Court of Directors, "not merely that we might draw an annual profit from them, but that we might diffuse among their inhabitants, once sunk in darkness, vice, and misery, the light and benign influence of the truth, the blessings of a well-regulated society, the improvements and comforts of active industry. . . . " James Stephen wrote of the "barbarous and obscene rites of Hindoo superstition" and Wilberforce declared the Christian mission in India to be the greatest of all causes. "Let us endeavor to strike our roots into their soil," he wrote, "by the gradual introduction and establishment of our own principles and opinions; of our laws, institutions, and manners; above all, as the source of every other improvement of our religion, and consequently of our morals."[5]

David Livingstone, the great explorer and missionary, told a British audience in 1857, "I go back to Africa to try to make an open path for commerce and Christianity."[6] Indeed, says Morris, "The mission stations which, throughout the second half of the century, sprang up throughout the tropical possessions, were manned by and large by militants with no doubts—this was a Christian Empire, and it was the imperial duty to spread the Christian word among its heathen subjects."[7] He summarizes:

> The administrators of Empire, too, and very often its conquerors, were generally speaking practicing Christians: the new public schools at which so many of them were educated were invariably Church of England foundations, with parson-headmasters. . . . Explorers like Speke or Grant saw themselves as God's scouts—even Stanley turned evangelist in 1875, and converted the King of Uganda and all his court to Christianity. Generals like Havelock and Nicholson slaughtered their enemies in the absolute certainty of a biblical mandate . . . and most of the imperial

heroes were identified in the public mind with the Christianness of Empire—not simply humanitarianism, not Burke's sense of trusteeship, but a Christian militancy, a ruling faith, whose Defender on earth was the Queen herself, and whose supreme commander needed no identification. Every aspect of Empire was an aspect of Christ.[8]

Much more could be said. But without going into further detail it is, I think, clear that in the eighteenth and nineteenth centuries the conviction of the decisive superiority of Christianity infused the imperial expansion of the West with a powerful moral impetus and an effective religious validation without which the enterprise might well not have been psychologically viable.

A brief word should be said at this point about the missionaries themselves. Most of them were not concerned with the effects of their work on empire-building and the development of trade. They had genuinely dedicated their lives to the saving of heathen souls, and in this cause many of them willingly endured immense hardships and dangers, including the ever-present threat of fatal tropical diseases. They also usually had to accept separation from their children when they were sent back home to school. Again, although many seem to have regarded the indigenous primal or Hindu or Buddhist or Muslim religious life as valueless or even as demonic, and their adult converts as children to be commanded and instructed, there were others who developed a deep respect and affection for the people to whom they had gone; and they were able to recognize elements of profound wisdom and of inspiring ideals within these alien traditions. To note the ways in which the Christian mission-ary imperative was used within national consciousness to motivate and validate imperialism does not require us to impugn the motives of the missionaries themselves.[9]

III

To refer to our twentieth-century awareness of the values of the other great world traditions, and to our concomitant new awareness of the pernicious side of Christian absolutism in history, is not to tell the full story of the modern erosion of theological exclusivism. But these two factors have probably been the most important. At any rate such an erosion has undoubtedly occurred. The Second Vatican Council (1963–1965) highlighted and consolidated the new thinking that had been taking place for a number of years among some of the more adventurous Roman Catholic theologians. Vatican II in effect—though not of course in so many words—repealed the *extra ecclesiam nulla salus* doctrine by declaring that there *is* salvation outside the visible church; the redemption bought by the blood of Christ is offered to all human beings even without their formal entry into the church. Thus, speaking of Christ's redeem-ing sacrifice, Vatican II taught:

All this holds true not only for Christians, but for all men of good will in whose hearts grace works in an unseen way. For, since Christ died for all men, and since the ultimate vocation of man is in fact one, and divine, we ought to believe that the Holy Spirit in a manner known only to God offers to every man the possibility of being associated with this paschal mystery.[10]

The possibility of salvation was thus officially extended in principle to the whole world. This extension was reiterated even more strongly in the first encyclical, *Redemptor Hominis* (1979), of Pope John Paul II, in which it is declared that "man—every man without exception whatever—has been redeemed by Christ, . . . because with man—with each man without any exception whatever—Christ is in a way united, even when man is unaware of it."[11]

All this does not mean, however, that the old sense of Christian superiority has died out or that the traditional claim to the unique finality of the Christian gospel has been rescinded. In the past that claim took very explicit forms: Christianity alone possesses the full knowledge of God because it alone is based on and is the continuing vehicle of God's direct self-revelation; Christianity arose from and alone proclaims God's saving act in the atoning death of Christ; Christianity, despite all its historical defects, is the only religious movement to have been founded on earth by God in person. The claim has now come to be expressed in less blatant and less offensive ways.

In the modern reaction against the triumphalism of the past the church's still cherished assumption of Christian superiority has moved discreetly into the background. In, for example, the Vatican II Declaration on the Relationship of the Church to Non-Christian Religions (*Nostra Aetate*), which was in effect addressed to the members of those other traditions, the decisive superiority of Christ/the gospel/the church was not openly stated, although it was delicately and indirectly implied. In this document the headline-catching theme was that "The Catholic Church rejects nothing which is true and holy in these religions."[12] However, in the Dogmatic Constitution on the Church (significantly beginning with the words *Lumen Gentium*), in which the church was clarifying its beliefs for the benefit of its own members, it was stated openly that "Whatever goodness or truth is found among them [i.e., among "those who through no fault of their own do not know the gospel of Christ" and "those who, without blame on their part, have not yet arrived at an explicit knowledge of God"] is looked upon by the Church as a *preparation* for the gospel."[13] And another of the Vatican II pronouncements, the Decree on the Missionary Activity of the Church (*Ad Gentes*), emphatically declares:

All must be converted to [Christ] as He is made known by the Church's preaching. All must be incorporated into Him by baptism, and into the Church which is His body. . . . Therefore, though God in ways known to Himself can lead those inculpably ignorant of the gospel to that faith without which it is impossible to please Him, yet a necessity lies on the Church, and at the same time a sacred duty, to preach the gospel. Hence missionary activity today as always retains its power and necessity.[14]

Protestant thinking, insofar as it has been expressed through the World Council of Churches, has moved to a significant extent in the same direction. The work of the Council's Subunit on Dialogue with People of Living Faiths and Ideologies is hardly compatible with the old exclusivist theology. At the same time, however, another powerful element within the World Council, heard at its Uppsala (1968), Nairobi (1975), and Vancouver (1983) Assemblies, has continued to talk in ways reminiscent of the old exclusivism. Indeed the Catholic scholar Arnulf Camps is probably right in his opinion, concerning the continuing tension within Protestant thinking between a basically Barthian absolutism and a more liberal acceptance of interfaith dialogue, that "neither the International Missionary Council nor the World Council of Churches has managed to get beyond this dilemma."[15] This being acknowledged, however, it can, I think still be said that there has been, since the early 1960s, a general, even if not wholehearted and consistent, movement within the Protestant as well as the Catholic understanding of other religions.

The new consensus, or near consensus, that has emerged out of this trend away from the old exclusivism is today generally called inclusivism. The Christian mind has now for the most part made the move from an intolerant exclusivism to a benevolent inclusivism. But the latter, no less than the former, rests upon the claim to Christianity's unique finality as the locus of the only full divine revelation and the only adequate saving event. Non-Christians can be saved because, unknown to them, Christ is secretly "in a way united" with them. But the saving truth unknown to them is known to the church, which is God's instrument in making redemption known. To abandon this claim to an ultimate religious superiority is therefore to pass a critical point, entering new territory from which the whole terrain of Christian truth is bound to look different. For on the other side of this divide Christianity is seen in a pluralistic context as *one* of the great world faiths, *one* of the streams of religious life through which human beings can be savingly related to that ultimate Reality Christians know as the heavenly Father.

From one point of view, to cross this theological Rubicon seems an almost inevitable next step, following to its natural conclusion the trajectory whose path we have traced from an exclusivist to an inclusivist view of other religions. For once it is granted that salvation is in fact taking place not only within the Christian but also within the other great traditions, it seems arbitrary and unrealistic to go on insisting that the Christ-event is the sole and exclusive source of human salvation. When it is acknowledged that Jews are being saved within and through the Jewish stream of religious life, Muslims within and through the Islamic stream, Hindus within and through the Hindu streams, and so on, can it be more than a hangover from the old religious imperialism of the past to insist upon attaching a Christian label to salvation within these other households of faith? This would be like the anomaly of accepting the Copernican revolution in astronomy, in which the earth ceased to be regarded as the center of the universe and was seen instead as one of the planets circling the sun, but still insisting that the sun's life-giving rays can reach the other planets only by first being reflected from the earth!

But the move from Christian inclusivism to pluralism, although in one way seemingly so natural and inevitable, sets Christianity in a new and to some an alarming light in which there can no longer be any a priori assumption of overall superiority. For the Christian tradition is now seen as one of a plurality of contexts of salvation—contexts, that is to say, within which the transformation of human existence from self-centeredness to God—or Reality-centeredness is occurring. Accordingly, if it is now claimed that Christianity constitutes a more favorable setting for this transformation than the other traditions, this must be shown by historical evidence. It can no longer be established simply by defining salvation as inclusion within the scope of the divine pardon bought by Christ's atoning death. From that definition it does follow that Christianity, as Christ's continuing agency on earth, is superior to all other religions. But this kind of arbitrary superiority-by-definition no longer seems defensible, even to many Christians. Today we cannot help feeling that the question of superiority has to be posed as an empirical issue, to be settled (if indeed it *can* be settled) by examination of the facts.

IV

The observable facts—constituting the fruits of religious faith in human life—are bewildering in their variety and scope. However, two threads are available to guide us: we can look for both individual and social transformation. We find the former in its most evident form in those who are recognized as the saints of the different traditions—granting that there are different patterns of sainthood, some pursuing the inner paths of prayer, contemplation, and meditation, and others the outer paths of social service and political action. But if we mean by a saint a person who is much further advanced than most of us in the transformation from self-centeredness to Reality-centeredness, then I venture the proposition that each of the great religious traditions seems, so far as we can tell, to promote this transformation in one form or another to about the same extent. Relating this to the traditional assumption of superiority, I am thus suggesting that we have no good grounds for maintaining that Christianity has produced or is producing more saints, in proportion to population, or a higher quality of saintliness, than any other of the great streams of religious life.

A challenging recent example is set by Gandhi, recognized by hundreds of millions in India as a Mahatma or great soul. Most of us have come to see in him a human being who, in response to the claim of God on his life, realized the human moral and spiritual potential to a rare degree, inspiring many others to rise to a new level of effective self-giving love for others. Gandhi was a Hindu, and the name of God that was on his lips as he was struck down by an assassin's bullets in 1948 was not that of the Christian Heavenly Father or Holy Trinity but that of the Hindu Rama. But if human salvation, or liberation, has any concrete meaning for men and women in this world, it must include the kind of transformation of human existence seen in Gandhi and, in varying ways and degrees, in the saints of all the great traditions. But this transformation, with its further influence upon other individuals and through them, more remotely, upon societies, is manifestly not confined to the Christian areas of the world. There are persons who have in varying degrees given themselves to God, or to the ultimate Reality, within each of the great traditions.

I recognize that this cannot be proved. The reason why it cannot be proved— or disproved—is that we do not at present command the conceptual precision or the exhaustive information necessary for objective comparative judgments. All that we have is a variety of overlapping concepts of saintliness and a very partial and unsystematic body of historical knowledge. Accordingly, we each have to rely upon our own working conception of a saint, our own limited range of contemporary observation, and our own reading within the vast literature of the history of religions—a literature that was not created and is not organized to answer our present question. What I am proposing on this basis, as a Christian attempting both to survey the contemporary world and to look back down the long vistas of history, is that we are not in a position to assert a greater power in Christianity than in any of the other great world faiths to bring about the kind of transformation in human beings that we all desire.

V

The thread of saintliness, then, I suggest, does not lead us to the conclusion that Christianity is manifestly superior. The other thread to be followed is that of the social outworkings of the different faiths. Here much Christian thought starts from a firm assumption of manifest superiority and, when challenged, presents a picture of the relatively affluent, just, peaceful, enlightened, democratic, Northern hemisphere, owing its virtues to Christianity, in contrast to the relatively poor, unjust, violent, backward, and undemocratic Southern hemisphere, held back by its non-Christan faiths. However, this picture has to be deconstructed on several levels. To begin on the surface, Buddhist-Shinto Japan is not poor or technologically backward, and several other non-Christian nations of the Pacific rim are also rapidly becoming major industrial powers. Muslim Saudi Arabia and the other Gulf states are far from poverty-stricken; and Hindu India, which has recently produced a number of front-rank physicists, is also the largest democracy in the world. Social injustice is indeed endemic in varying degrees in all these countries; but it is, alas, endemic in virtually every country in the world, affluent as well as poverty-stricken, Western as well as Eastern, Christian as well as non-Christian.

And on the other side of the same coin, there are very large Christian populations that are desperately poor—particularly in the southern half of the Americas and in the southern half of Africa; there are Christian countries, in Latin America and South Africa, whose social structures are profoundly unjust and where the insignia of democracy are a mockery; there are Christian populations, in Ireland and in Lebanon, currently engaged in political violence; and others, in the United States and in most European countries, turning the earth's precious resources into weapons of destruction on an appalling scale. Again, the Amnesty International report *Torture in the Eighties*[16] impartially cites as guilty of torture a number of Muslim countries (including Turkey, Iran, Irak, Libya, Pakistan, and Bangladesh), a number of Christian countries (including South Africa, Spain, Argentina, Brazil, Chile, El Salvador, Guatemala, Paraguay, and Peru), Hindu India, Buddhist Sri Lanka, and Jewish Israel.

However, it remains true that the Christian, post-Christian, and Marxist West constitutes the relatively affluent First and Second Worlds, whereas the non-Christian East and partly Christian South constitutes the generally poverty-stricken Third World; and also that our modern liberal ideals of political freedom and human equality have initially developed primarily in the West. And so we have to ask to what extent this affluence and these ideals are gifts of the Christian religion and evidence of its moral and intellectual superiority.

Western economic prosperity is the product of modern science and technology. It has been suggested by several authors that the birth of modern science required the intellectual environment of Christianity, with its belief in a rational creator producing an orderly and law-governed universe. And it seems clear that science needed for its birth and early growth the hospitality of a worldview that sees the cosmos as a system subject to universal laws. But all the great religious traditions in their different ways—those of Semitic and those of Indian origin—see the universe in this way. The Hindu and Buddhist cosmologies have indeed greater affinities than the traditional Christian cosmology with some major modern scientific theories. The ancient Hindu conception of the vast successive Kalpas, each leading to the conflagration of the universe and then its renewal, to go again through the same development, is close to one of the current scientific models of an endlessly expanding and contracting universe. The Buddhist emphasis upon incessant process in an interdependent flux of beginningless and endless change agrees well with the physicists' picture of the universe as a field of energy undergoing perpetual transformations.

But neither Hinduism, nor Buddhism, nor Christianity during the first fifteen centuries of its history, in fact gave birth to modern science. And so we have to ask what other factor entered to enable the human mind to awaken from its long prescientific slumber. The answer seems to be the rebirth, in the European Renaissance and then in the Enlightenment, of the Greek spirit of free inquiry, gradually liberating minds from the thrall of unquestioned dogmas and enabling them to turn to observation, experimentation, and reason to understand the universe in which we find ourselves. Once modern science had thus been launched, it quickly became an autonomous enterprise, of ever increasing power, obeying its own methodological rules and emphatically asserting its independence from the religious ethos within which it had been born. This independence created painful tensions and conflicts with the religious establishment as, first, astronomy moved our world from the center of the universe to the position of one of the sun's satellites; and then as geology established the age of the earth as enormously greater than the biblical chronology had imagined; and then finally as biology traced the place of homo sapiens within the whole evolution of life, thereby erasing the biblical picture of the special creation of humanity and, as a further by-product of the scientific outlook and method, as the objective study of ancient scriptures soon began to undermine their customary literal authority.

In fact the birth of modern science within the Christian culture of Europe reminds us of a cuckoo hatching in a thrush's nest and rapidly growing up to attack its hosts! In the science versus religion debates of the nineteenth century, as in the church's earlier treatment of Galileo and its attempts to suppress the new cosmology, Christianity, far from seeing science as its own distinctive gift to the world, fought a long but unsuccessful battle against it! This led—despite a resurgence today of fundamentalist resistance—to a belated acceptance of the new scientific knowledge and a consequent massive rethinking of Christian doctrine. Thus Christianity can claim no proprietary interest in the modern scientific enterprise. Its special relationship consists simply in the fact that it was the first of the world faiths to be hit by the impact of the new empirical knowledge and outlook. But the same impact is now inevitably affecting the rest of the world. We may speculate that Islam will find this encounter as traumatic as has Christianity, whereas Hinduism and Buddhism may be able to adjust to it without great difficulty. But in each case the deeper effect must be, as in the Christian West, a progressive secularization both of thought and of society. And the deeper challenge will be to develop forms of faith through which the human spirit can be transformingly related to the Transcendent within the context of our modern knowledge of ourselves and of our environment.

Similar considerations apply to the modern explosion of technology, with its fruits of hitherto undreamed of material affluence. The firstness of the First World consists in its being the first part of the globe to have become industrialized and so to have benefited from the mass production of consumer goods. But it does not follow from this that the poor of the largely non-Christian Third World would not also like to have plentiful food and a large array of consumer goods! It is true that there is a strong strand of Hindu and Buddhist teaching that is world- and wealth-renouncing, treating the ever-changing material world as ultimately unreal. Hence the famous Hindu prayer, "lead me from the unreal to the Real." But it is also true that there is an equally strong strand of world-renouncing Christian teaching, virtually conflating "the world, the flesh, and the devil." This began in the New Testament, where Jesus tells his disciples "If ye were of the world, the world would love his own: but because ye are not of the world, but I have chosen you out of the world, therefore the world hateth you" (John 15:19), and "If any man come to me, and hate not his father, and mother, and wife, and children, and brethren and sisters, yea, and his own life also, he cannot be my disciple" (Luke 14:26). We read elsewhere in the New Testament that "the whole world lieth in wickedness" (1 John 5:19); and it was a widespread early Christian conviction that the earth is to be under the devil's rule until the last day. Such teaching has not, however, prevented the development of Western capitalism and the general desire that it feeds for more and more possessions, including ever more sophisticated luxuries.

Hindu teaching is no more likely to inhibit the scramble for consumer goods in a rapidly industrializing India. For the basis of India's relative poverty in the modern period—ancient India having been fully as prosperous as Europe[17]—is the fact that its medieval phase has only now, in the second half of the twentieth century, given way to industrial revolution. And if we ask why Britain's eighteenth- and nineteenth-century industrial transformation did not spread to India, as it did to the United States and to the white British dominions, the answer is that it was in Britain's interest to keep the Indian subcontinent a source of raw materials and a captive market rather than encourage it to become an independent industrial competitor. To quote from Dutt's *Economic History of India*:

It is, unfortunately, true that the East Indian Company and the British Parliament, following the selfish commercial policy of a hundred years ago, discouraged Indian manufacturers in the early years of British rule in order to encourage the rising manufactures of England. Their fixed policy, pursued during the last decades of the eighteenth century and the first decades of the nineteenth, was to make India subservient to the industries of Great Britain, and to make the Indian people grow raw produce only, in order to supply material for the looms and manufactories of Great Britain.[18]

As late as the 1920s, Gandhi was campaigning against Indians being compelled to export their raw cotton to Lancashire and then buy it back in the form of finished cloth, to the profit of the Lancashire mills and to the detriment of the Indian masses. It is only since independence in 1947 that India has begun to become industrialized on a large scale.

The general situation, then, seems to be this. The wealth-creating industrial revolution, transforming human society from its feudal to its modern phase, occurred first in Europe, and was greatly helped by the concurrent European imperial expansion, which gave privileged access to raw materials and to vast new markets. The industrial process had to begin somewhere; and if it had not started when and where it did, it would have started at some other time or place. But it does not seem possible to establish any exclusive causal connection between industrialization and Christianity, such that without Christianity industrialization would not have occurred within human societies.

VI

The other main area in which contemporary Christianity is inclined to see itself as superior is in its adoption of the modern liberal ideals of human equality and freedom, expressed politically in democratic forms of government. These liberal ideals emerged out of the deconstruction of the medieval dogmatic-hierarchical world of thought. That they are not purely Christian ideals, but the product of a creative interaction of cultural influences, is shown by the fact that for the previous thousand years the Christian West had been strongly hierarchical, sanctifying serfdom and the subjugation of women, believing not in the rights of humanity but in the divine right of kings, burning heretics and witches, and brutally suppressing both social unrest and deviant intelletual speculation. The dawning concepts of human rights and of individual freedom and equality were initially as powerfully opposed by the church as was modern science in its early days. For example, what became in the nineteenth century the Christian campaign against slavery began as a small minority movement within the churches, opposed by many churchmen acting on behalf of slave-owning interests. And the other endeavors by such groups as the Quakers, and then by the social gospel and Christian socialist movements, to achieve greater social justice within Western societies, have always been an uphill struggle, generally opposed by the ecclesiastical establishments. The belated and still often wavering conversion of the churches to the ideals of human equality and freedom is a very recent development, which is now also occurring within the other world traditions.

Once again, then, Christianity does not have a proprietary interest in these powerful secular ideals of the modern world. They have a secure theoretical basis in the teachings of each of the great faiths, but in each case their emergence as a real force is largely due to the hierarchy-dissolving influences of modernity. Christianity has, however, the distinction—and herein lies its genuine historical uniqueness—of being the first of the world religions to have been to a great extent transformed by modernity.

The results in the Christian West have been partly beneficial and creative, and partly harmful and destructive. On the credit side, science has made possible ever more advanced technologies, which have in turn spawned an immense proliferation of wealth, so that the Western world now enjoys the highest material standard of living in history. This has at the same time stimulated an enormous growth and extension of education and an unprecedented explosion of cultural activity. On the debit side, the same expansion of scientific knowledge has produced ever more powerful weapons of mass destruction, so that the whole human enterprise now trembles under the threat of a massive nuclear exchange that could abruptly terminate civilization in the West and might produce a "nuclear winter," reducing the human race to scattered pockets of survivors facing a new stone age. Further, our modern affluence has been achieved at the expense of a galloping consumption of the earth's nonrenewable resources, and of a polarization between the overrich Northern and the desperately poor Southern hemispheres, while setting up in the affluent regions social and psychological stresses and strains with frightening levels of drug addiction, suicide, divorce, crime, urban violence, and a tragic sense of meaninglessness and general frustration.

VII

When we try, then, to look at the religious traditions as long-lived historical entities we find in each case a complex mixture of valuable and harmful elements. Each has provided an effective framework of meaning for millions of adherents, carrying them through the different stages of life, affording consolation in sickness, need, and calamity, and enabling them to celebrate communally their times of health, well-being, and creativity. Within the ordered psychic space created by a living faith, as expressed in the institutions and customs of a society, millions of men and women in generation after generation have coped with life's pains and challenges and rejoiced in its blessings; and some have gone beyond ego-domination into a transforming relationship with the Eternal. Many have responded—again, in their varying degrees—to the moral claim of love/compassion mediated by the great traditions and widely formulated as the Golden Rule: "Let not any man do unto another any act that he wisheth not done to himself by others, knowing it to be painful to himself" (the Hindu *Mahabharata,* Shanti parva, cclx.21); "Do not do to others what you would not want them to do to you" (Confucius, *Analects,* Book XII, #2); "Hurt not others with that which pains yourself" (The Buddhist *Udanavarga,* v. 18); "As ye would that men should do to you, do ye also to them likewise" (Jesus, *Luke* 6:31); "No man is a true believer unless he desires for his brother that which he desires for himself" (The Muslim *Hadtih, Muslim, imam* 71-2).

This is the good side of the great traditions. But each has at the same time sanctified vicious human evils. Hinduism, though constituting an immensely rich and powerful universe of meaning, and pointing the way to inner liberation, also validates the hierarchical caste system of India, including the relegation of millions to the position of outcasts—an injustice which still lingers despite its official abolition in the 1947 Constitution. Hindu society tolerated the former practice of suttee and still tolerates the continuing cruel persecution and sometimes murder of brides whose dowry is deemed insufficient. Buddhism, although basically peaceful and tolerant, and suffusing millions with the ideal of unself-centered existence, has been indifferent until very recently to questions of social justice, so that many Buddhist lands have long remained in a state of feudal inequality. Islam, though calling the faithful to submission to and peace with God, and promoting a Muslim brotherhood that is notably free from color prejudice, has sanctioned "holy wars," fanatical intolerance, and the barbaric punishments of mutilation and flogging, and still generally consigns women to a protected but narrowly confined life. Christianity, though providing in recent centuries a birthplace for modern science and a home for the modern liberal ideals of equality and freedom, has generated savage wars of religion and supported unnumerable "just wars"; has tortured and burned multitudes of heretics and witches in the name of God;[19] has motivated and authorized the persecution of the Jews;[20] has validated systematic racism; and has tolerated the Western capitalist "rape of the earth," the misuse of nuclear energy, and the basic injustice of the North-South division into rich and poor nations.

The conclusion to be drawn seems to be that each tradition has constituted its own unique mixture of good and evil. Each is a long-lived social reality that has gone through times of flourishing and times of decline; and each is internally highly diverse, some of its aspects promoting human good and others damaging the human family. In face of these complexities it seems impossible to make the global judgment that any one religious tradition has contributed more good or less evil, or a more favorable balance of good and evil, than the others. It is of course possible that, to the eye of omniscience, one tradition is in fact, on balance, superior to the rest. But to our partial and fallible human view they constitute different ways of being human in relation to the Eternal, each with both its cultural glories and its episodes of violent destructiveness, each raising vast populations to a higher moral and spiritual level and yet each at times functioning as a vehicle of human chauvinism, cupidity, and sadism. We may well judge that in some respects, or in some periods or regions, the fruits of one tradition are better than, whereas in other respects or periods or regions inferior to, those of another. But as vast complex totalities, the world traditions seem to be more or less on a par with each other. None can be singled out as manifestly superior.

If this is so, we may begin to consider how this truth is likely to affect the ongoing work of Christian theology.

VIII

The three central doctrines of trinity, incarnation, and atonement cohere together. Given a juridical conception of atonement, Jesus had to be God, as St. Anselm demonstrated in his *Cur Deus Homo*? For only a sacrifice of divine, and therefore infinite, value could give adequate satisfaction for the wrong done by human sin to the creator and lord of the universe; or could meet the inexorable requirements of divine justice, thereby enabling God to regard sinful men and women as just and as fit to be received into the kingdom. And given that Jesus was God, the Godhead had to be a trinity (or at least a binity); for God was incarnate on earth as Jesus of Nazareth, and God was also in heaven, sustaining the universe, and hearing and answering prayer. It was therefore necessary to think of God as at least two in one, Father and Son, who were respectively (for a brief period) in heaven and on earth. But Christian thinking in fact went on to include the divine presence in human life outside the thirty or so years of the incarnation as a third person, the Holy Spirit. It would in theory have been possible to account for this presence with a more economic binitarian doctrine by attributing what came to be regarded as the work of the Holy Spirit to the eternal Christ-spirit or Logos; and there was indeed a period before the Holy Spirit and the Spirit of Christ had been distinguished as two distinct realities. However, eventually the trinitarian pattern became established and now pervades Christian theological and liturgical language.

Approaching this cluster of doctrines through the idea of incarnation, it is widely agreed today by New Testament scholars, including even relatively conservative ones, that the historical Jesus did not himself teach that he was God the Son, the second person of a divine trinity, living a human life. He was intensely conscious of God as the heavenly Father, his life (certainly during the two or three years of his ministry) being dedicated to proclaiming the imminent coming of God's kingdom, to manifesting its power in acts of healing, and to teaching others how to live so as to become part of the kingdom that was presently to be established. He probably thought of himself as the final prophet, the one whose mission was to herald the end of the age. He may have applied to himself either of the two main titles that Jewish tradition offered for the fulfiller of this role—that of the son of man who was to come in glory on the clouds of heaven, and that of the messiah who was to rule the world from its new center, Jerusalem. Neither of these roles, it should be noted, amounted to being God; both figures were exalted human servants of God. But it is equally possible that Jesus refused all identifications, and that it was his followers who bestowed these and other titles upon him. Or he may have used the term "son of man" simply as a Hebraicism, a term that could be claimed by anyone.

The "son of God" title, which was to become standard in the church's theology, probably began in the Old Testament and wider ancient Near Eastern usage in which it signified a special servant of God. In this sense kings, emperors, pharaohs, great philosophers, miracle workers, and other holy men were commonly called son of God. But as the gospel went out beyond its Hebraic setting into the gentile world of the Roman Empire, this poetry was transformed into prose and the living metaphor congealed into a rigid and literal dogma. It was to accommodate this resulting metaphysical sonship that the church, after some three centuries of clashing debates, settled upon the theory that Jesus had two natures, one divine and the other human, being in one nature of one substance with God the Father and in the other of one substance with humanity—a philosophical construction as far removed from the thought world and teaching of Jesus himself as is the in some ways parallel Mayahana Buddhist doctrine of the Trikaya from that of the historical Gautama.

But there have always been other strands of christological thinking, even though the variations were officially suppressed during the long and relatively monolithic period of medieval Christendom. The earliest strand of language in the New Testament documents probably expressed an inspiration christology, seeing Jesus as a great prophet filled with the divine Spirit. This type of christology has become a live option again today, some recent English-language versions being D. M. Baillie's *God Was in Christ* (1958), several of the contributions to *The Myth of God Incarnate* (1977), and Geoffrey Lampe's *God As Spirit* (1977).[21] The basic thought is that to speak of God's love becoming incarnate is to speak of men and women in whose lives God's inspiration, or grace, is effectively at work so that they have become instruments of the divine purpose on earth. To "be to the Eternal Goodness what his own hand is to a man"[22] is to be a locus of divine incarnation. Incarnation in this sense has occurred and is occurring in many different ways and degrees in many different persons. Whether it happened more fully in the case of Jesus than in that of any other human being, or even perhaps absolutely in Jesus, cannot properly be settled a priori (though that seems to be how Baillie and Lampe settled it) but only on the basis of historical information. This means in practice that it cannot be definitively settled, for we lack the kind of evidence, touching every moment and aspect of Jesus' inner and outer life, that could entitle one to make such a judgment.

This type of inspiration or paradox-of-grace christology falls within the range of options open to those who are not credal fundamentalists insisting upon the verbal inspiration of the Nicene and Chalcedonian formulations. Such a christology is at the same time compatible with the religious pluralism being advocated in this book. It would seem to point out the direction— although it is not the only possible direction—in which christology is likely to develop within those theological circles that have moved beyond inclusivism to a pluralist understanding of the place of Christianity in the total life of the world.

An inspiration christology coheres better with some ways of understanding trinitarian language than with others. It does not require or support the notion of three divine persons in the modern sense in which a person is a distinct center of consciousness, will, and emotion—so that one could speak of the Father, the Son, and the Holy Spirit as loving one another within the eternal family of the trinity, and of the Son coming down to earth to make atonement on behalf of human beings to his Father. An inspiration christology is, however, fully compatible with the conception of the trinity as affirming three distinguishable ways in which the one God is experienced as acting in relation to, and is accordingly known by, us—namely, as creator, redeemer, and inspirer. On this interpretation, the three persons are not three different centers of consciousness but three major aspects of the one divine nature. They no more resolve God into three personal beings than do the various names of God in Jewish tradition or the ninety-nine Beautiful Names of God in the Qur'ān. Such an "economic" understanding of the trinity is as orthodox as a "social" one and would seem to represent the direction that trinitarian thought is likely to follow in theologies that accept a pluralistic understanding of the human religious situation.

Atonement theory has also taken a number of forms, some cohering better than others with an inspiration christology and an economic or modal trinitarianism. As in the case of christology, the kind of atonement thinking most hospitable to religious pluralism is nearest to what appears to have been the teaching of Jesus himself. Here we find, in the familiar words of the Lord's Prayer and in such parables as that of the prodigal son, the assumption of a direct relationship to God in which if we are truly penitent we can ask for and receive forgiveness and new life. The father in the parable did not require a blood sacrifice to appease his sense of justice: as soon as he saw his son returning he "had compassion, and ran, and fell on his neck, and kissed him . . . [and said] 'For this my son was dead and is alive again; he was lost and is found' " (Luke 15:20, 24). And the only condition for God's forgiveness in the Lord's Prayer is that we also forgive one another.

This is far removed from the idea that God can forgive sinners only because Jesus has borne our just punishment by his death on the cross, or has somehow by that death satisfied the divine justice. A forgiveness that has to be bought by full payment of the moral debt is not in fact forgiveness at all. But Jesus did speak of the authentic miracle of forgiveness, a miracle not captured in the standard atonement theories. Their merit would seem to be that they offer one way of focusing attention upon Jesus' death as an expression of the self-giving love that was incarnate in his life. And in accordance with the contemporary Jewish belief that the death of a righteous martyr somehow worked for the good of Israel, Jesus himself may well have thought of his own approaching death as a source of blessing to many (cf. Mark 10:45)[23]—as indeed it has proved to be through many different appropriations of it down the centuries.

In the case of each of these doctrines, then, the existing theological spectrum of the Christian tradition, as it has become diversified in the modern period, offers ample resources for theologies that can incorporate religious pluralism. What the pluralistic vision accordingly requires is not a radical departure from the diverse and ever-growing Christian tradition, but its further development in ways suggested by the discovery of God's presence and saving activity within other streams of human life. The resulting perception is that Christianity is not the one and only way of salvation, but one among several.

At the same time two other major insights—which I have not had time even to attempt to treat here—are also calling for parallel developments. One is the realization, expressed in liberation theology, that God is at work wherever there is a costly commitment to the struggle for human justice, and is accordingly present in secular and Marxist liberation movements as much as, and sometimes more than, in the church. Indeed too often dominant sections of the church have been and are today on the wrong side of the liberation struggles. Whereas Christian absolutism can easily blind one to that fact, the pluralist outlook enables us to recognize it and to participate in a worldwide movement for human liberation not restricted within the borders of any one tradition. The other new insight is that expressed in contemporary feminist theology: that God is the source of life and meaning for women as truly as for men, and that our religious understanding must accordingly be brought into a new balance. Openness to the wider religious life of humankind with its rich plurality of ways—female as well as male—of symbolizing the divine, can help to free us from the grip of an absolutized Christian patriarchalism.

These three concerns are today creating a new network of options for Christian thought. As in the case of the last great transformation of Christian self-awareness—in the nineteenth-century response to modern science—new options will be taken up and developed in a variety of ways by some but will equally certainly be rejected and opposed by others. Our task is to try to expound and explain the new vision that is gradually coming into focus so that as many as possible can recognize in it a contemporary illumination of the Spirit, and can respond through it to God's challenging presence.

Finally, in this chapter I have been treating the question of the place of Christianity within the wider religious life of humanity as a topic in Christian theology. I have accordingly used our Christian term, God, to refer to the ultimate Reality to which, as I conceive, the great religious traditions constitute different human responses. But when one stands back from one's own tradition to attempt a philosophical interpretation of the fact of religious plurality one has to take full account of nonpersonal as well as of personal awarenesses of the Ultimate. I have tried to do this elsewhere;[24] but it was not necessary to complicate this study, as an intra-Christian discussion, in that way.

NOTES

1. "The Place of Christianity among the World Religions," reprinted in John Hick and Brian Hebblethwaite, eds., *Christianity and Other Religions* (London: Collins, and Philadelphia: Fortress, 1980).

2. Julius Richter, "Missionary Apologetics: Its Problems and Its Methods," *International Review of Missions,* 2 (1913) 540.

3. James Morris, *Heaven's Command: An Imperial Progress* (London: Faber & Faber, 1968); *Pax Britannica: The Climax of Empire* (London: Faber & Faber, 1968); *Farewell the Trumpets: An Imperial Retreat* (London: Faber & Faber, 1978).

4. Perhaps as good an account as any of the dedicated service given by the best colonial administrators, and of their gradual realization that paternalism must give way to independence, is that of Leonard Woolf in the second volume of his *Autobiography*, covering his years in Ceylon before the first world war, *Growing* (New York and London: Harcourt Brace, 1961).

5. *Heaven's Command*, p. 74.

6. Ibid., p. 393.

7. Ibid., p. 318

8. Ibid., p. 319

9. James Michener's portrait of the early nineteenth-century American missionaries in Hawaii, in part 2 of his novel *Hawaii* (1959), probably gives a fair impression of the motives and sacrifices, as well as the narrow paternalism and prejudices, of much of the missionary movement of that time.

10. Pastoral Constitution on the Church, par. 22.

11. *Redemptor Hominis* (London: Catholic Truth Society, 1979), par. 14.

12. Par. 2.

13. Chap. 2, par. 16, emphasis added.

14. Par. 7.

15. Arnulf Camps, *Partners in Dialogue*, trans. John Drury (Maryknoll, N.Y.: Orbis Books, 1983), p. 12.

16. London: Amnesty International Publications, 1984.

17. Trevor Ling, after describing the prosperous condition of northern India in the sixth century B.C.E. adds: "This picture of India in the Buddha's time as a land of abundant food is one which some readers may find surprising, since it is commonly believed in the West that India has an 'age-old problem of poverty and hunger,' to quote one recent example of this sort of ignorance. The widespread hunger of the Indian peasants, who invaded the city of Calcutta in the Bengal famine of 1943, is a relatively modern phenomenon. In 1943 the reason lay partly in distribution problems but the long-term reason was the low productivity of Indian agriculture by the end of the British period. Under British rule a landlord system developed which led to insecurity of tenure by tenant-cultivators, in the division and redivision of plots of land, to the point where farming became uneconomical. Cultivators fell into the hands of excessively usurious money lenders. In these circumstances they had little opportunity of increasing the productivity of the land. Moreover, the rate of population increase might have been less serious in its effects had India been able to develop industrially as the Western countries themselves had done and as Japan, free from foreign rule, was able to do. India's industrial development was limited to a few enterprises which were compatible with British economic interests—railways, coal mining to supply the fuel, a small iron industry mainly for the same purpose, jute and cotton milling, the development of which was limited by the interests of Dundee and Lancashire rivals, some sugar refining, glassware and matches. The Industrial Revolution which was needed to relieve India's growing population of its equally fast-growing poverty was not allowed to begin until independent India embarked on the first of her five-years plans in 1951" (*The Buddha* [London: Penguin Books, 1976], pp. 304–5).

18. Romesh Dutt, *The Economic History of India*, vol. I (London: Routledge & Kegan Paul, 1906, 2nd ed.), p. x.

19. Matilda Joslyn Gage, *Women, Church and State* (New York: Arno Press, 1972 [2nd ed. 1983]), says "It is computed from historical records that nine millions of persons were put to death for witchcraft after 1484, or during a period of three hundred years, and this estimate does not include the vast number who were sacrificed in the preceding centuries upon the same accusation" (p. 274; cited by Mary Daly, *Gyn/Ecology* [Boston: Beacon Press, 1978], p. 183).

20. In his history of the offense of blasphemy, Leonard Levy recalls that "A crusader considered himself unworthy of redeeming the Holy Land from the Moslems until he first killed a Jew, for the crusader believed that avenging Christ by killing Jews earned a crusader remission of his sins. . . . During the Shepherd's Crusade in 1251, almost every Jew in southern France was slaughtered" (*Treason Against God* [New York: Schocken Books, 1981], p. 115). See also Rosemary Radford Ruether, *Faith and Fratricide* (New York: Seabury Press, 1979).

21. It is also to be found, though in guardedly obscure forms, in such pioneering Catholic writers as Karl Rahner, Edward Schillebeeckx, and Hans Küng. On Rahner's christology, see my *Problems of Religious Pluralism* (London: Macmillan, and New York: St. Martin's Press, 1985), chap. 4.

22. *Theologica Germanica*, chap. 10.

23. Cf. John Downing, "Jesus and Martyrdom," *Journal of Theological Studies*, 14 (1963).

24. Particularly in *Problems of Religious Pluralism* (London: Macmillan, and New York: St. Martin's Press, 1985).

3

Plurality and Its Theological Implications

LANGDON GILKEY

I

My subject is the impingement of the plurality of religions on theology; or, more accurately stated, the effect of the present sense or understanding of plurality on theology. For the Christian churches have always known that religions were plural, that there were other religions than our own. This consciousness of plurality raised few theological problems, because the church was convinced on a number of grounds that Christianity was the only truly valid religion, the only effective "way." That we now speak of theological implications of plurality, and clearly intend *serious* implications, thus bespeaks a new sense or understanding of plurality, a new assessment of its meaning. This new understanding of plurality, therefore, includes and adds the concept of "parity," or of "rough parity," to that of plurality: we recognize, often against our will, that in some sense the sole efficacy or even superiority of Christianity are claims we can no longer make, or can make only with great discomfort. I assume we are all agreed on this, otherwise a serious discussion of diversity and its theological meaning would not be undertaken, nor would serious and authentic dialogue between religions be possible.

When we ask what the causes are of this new understanding of plurality as rough parity, we find, it seems to me, both theological and cultural causes—and the latter, I think, are definitive. Let us begin with the theological. What is there in recent developments of Christian theology that has helped to encourage this recognition of the co-validity and the co-efficacy of other religions? These same developments have, I think, fostered the new views of each other by the various churches (resulting from the ecumenical movement); new ways of relating to Jews; new conceptions of relationships between diverse

37

races and between the sexes—and new interpretations of Christian obligations toward the world. In short, the attitude of Christian groups toward strong diversity on many fronts has, over the past century and a half or so, gradually changed. Now that relationships to other religions have moved center stage, these theological developments have been effective there also.

The most important development, I think, is the shift in the balance between what were called the requirements of faith and those of love; or, better put, a new assessment of how God views these requirements. Previously, "defending the faith" and its purity against other religious viewpoints was regarded as an unquestionable Christian demand, one that clearly outranked the obligation to love the other (cf. Calvin in relation to Servetus). In the modern period— largely, I think, with the help of the Enlightenment—this dominance of faith over love shifted: love became the major obligation, and the one who killed in defense of the purity of faith was regarded not as heroic but as morally dubious, as a misguided fanatic. Correspondingly, and through many of the same cultural forces, the doctrines of faith—creeds, confessions and even the words of scripture itself—began to be seen as human, as therefore historical and hence relative expressions of a truth that transcended any single expression. Their defense is no longer the defense of God—and becomes morally dubious.

These two shifts were largely accomplished by Protestant liberalism. It is, therefore, no surprise that the first ecumenical rapprochement began under the aegis of that theological period, as did the first large-scale recognition of the truth and validity of other religions. It is also no surprise that the churches that have not at all participated in the Enlightenment and in the liberal theology that grew out of it have no interest in, in fact distrust, the ecumenical movement in all its phases, and they defend with every means available the absolute truth of their own doctrines and the sole efficacy of their modes of salvation.

One other theological factor is relevant, inasmuch as participants in the neoorthodox movement continued, with only a few qualifications, the ecumenical spirit established by liberalism. Why? First, despite their emphasis on the finality and uniqueness of Christian revelation, nevertheless they accepted the relativity of doctrines, confessions, and laws—the realm of "religion" in Barth's sense—and also they seconded the priority of love over the demands of doctrinal and legal exactness, with a vast emphasis on the inwardness of religion and on justification by faith. It was central to their interpretation of Christianity that salvation came through neither perfection of life nor perfection of faith—for they recognized their own fallibility in both. All that we have or can give, then, is relative; whatever the partiality or the waywardness of our religious life, all must be and has been justified by an alien grace—neither our works nor our faith will here suffice.

To those who said this—that the agape of God covers all the relativity, especially the religious relativity, of their existence, and that the inward commitment and love in their life were all that was significant—it was inconceivable that suddenly all this should stop, and stop, so to speak, at the boundary of the Christian church. Could the divine agape choose us because of the external "religion" in which we live, and not reach out to others because of the external religions in which they grew up and which they now affirm? Is not this same all-encompassing love that justifies *my* paltry and relative faith capable of justifying another (different) but also relative faith, provided, as Kierkegaard said, that they are inwardly serious? Can the divine love base itself on religious any more than on social or moral externals? In this case, am I not justified by my work of Christian belief, poor as it is?

Thus agape so interpreted suddenly overflowed the bounds of one tradition and expanded to include others beyond the now relative bounds of the church—Jews, authentic secular saints, and committed members of other traditions. The relativity of religion and its doctrines, plus the reemphasis on the width of the divine love, plus the inwardness of faith and love, have been the theological sources of this new assessment of plurality.

Important as these theological developments were, it has been, I think, the cultural changes that our century has witnessed that have represented the major causes of the development of parity. The theological changes just referred to were enough to force the *inclusion* of other religions into the area of truth and of grace, if I may so put it. Liberals and most neoorthodox alike admitted this: divine self-revelation has taken place elsewhere and God's grace is present there (as is well known, Barth's position is strangely ambiguous on this). However, liberals and most neoorthodox alike—from Schleiermacher and Ritschl through the dialectical theologians Bultmann, Brunner, the Niebuhrs, and Tillich—retained a sense of what Schleiermacher called "the absoluteness of Christianity," or what they would rather term the superiority, finality, and absolute uniqueness of the revelation in Christ. Few recognized the kind of parity with which we began, except of course vis-à-vis (for example, for Tillich and the Niebuhrs) the Jews. My suggestion is, therefore, that cultural changes since their period (the 1920s, 30s, and 40s) have effected the further move toward parity—that is, from Christianity as the definitive revelation among other revelations to some sort of plurality of revelations—a monstrous shift indeed.

My point is that, historically, Western culture has recently undergone precisely this same shift: from a position of clear superiority to one of rough parity, and that this shift in cultural consciousness has in turn had vast effect on our theological consciousness—namely, the parallel shift toward parity. The West had been dominant in almost every sphere, at almost every level, for four centuries: militarily, scientifically, industrially, politically, sociologically, morally, and religiously—or at least the West had no doubt of that dominance. Altogether—as *Passage to India* shows—this total domination up and down the line, a domination over each of these spheres, created an unbelievable assumption of superiority—not the first such sense in world history but surely one as apodictically certain as any preceding one! This lasted through the neoorthodox period—that is, through the second world war. Such a grandiose superiority carried all along with it: morals, democracy, religion, customs—all.

And again as *Passage to India* shows, its devastating character is shown by the fact that it was *assented to* by those who were demeaned by it—by Indians, Japanese, and Chinese alike. To them there was hardly any point at which they could claim even parity, much less superiority. Hence their vast repressed anger, evident in the depth of their successive reactions against the West.

After 1945, this began to collapse, and to collapse on all levels—military, political, moral, and religious. Colonies vanished, Europe disappeared as a major power, other non-Western power centers appeared representing other ways of life and other religions. The West no longer ruled the world; Western ways were no longer unassailable; Western religion became one among the other world religions; and (not insignificantly) the Christian faith became the one now most morally culpable, the chief imperialistic, nonspiritual, and in fact barely moral faith! Correspondingly, Western culture became radically open to non-Western religions; missionary influence flowed in the opposite direction; and the spiritual power of other faiths began to assert itself on Christian turf. Here were vast changes from even the mid-1940s. Christianity now stood not as the accuser but as the morally accused by other religions. At home it found itself passive, almost dried up and lifeless in relation to vibrant and effective other religions around it. Christian families had to deal with the conversion of their members into other traditions.

This dramatic new situation has forced—and this is the right word I think—a new understanding of the interrelationships of religions, a new balance of spiritual power, so to speak, on all: a sense of ascending equality, if not superiority, on other religions; a sense of descending status, lucky if it achieves equality, on many Christians. It is this that has pushed us all into parity, a position quite new to the churches, even to the liberal churches. Thus, as always, religious changes and cultural changes appear and recede together; and, I believe, neither one can be understood out of relation to the other. All this is of no little significance also to the secular academy, which regards our discovery of religious parity among the world religions as a kind of childlike awakening from naivety and self-centeredness. And yet the same academy has not yet conceived the shock that is to come to it when the cultural parity of the West, among the world's other cultures, comes to the forefront of consciousness. The plurality of cultures viewed as parity, rather than as an ascending series up to our scientific and liberal culture, is just around the corner; it has already arrived and is already effective in theological reflection in the area of religion.

II

Plurality as parity has devastating theological effects—or at least, I believe, it should have. To be sure, this new situation is fascinating, in Otto's sense at once alluring and threatening. To recognize, as one does or must in dialogues, the presence of truth and of grace, validity of symbol and efficacy of practice, in another faith is radically to relativize not only one's own religious faith but the *referent* of that faith, the revelation on which it is dependent. Thus to be in dialogue is also to be driven on a new theological quest—namely, the effort so to interpret one's symbols as neither to exclude nor offend this other. That is to say, some mode of new theological self-understanding is necessary, an understanding that includes and supplements what the other offers instead of rejecting it as false or incorporating it as merely one vista in the panorama shaped by one's own viewpoint. The liberal effort to include and so to incorporate—for the two go together—thus begins to seem to be the imperial effort to take over, absorb, and dominate (not unlike a colonial domination in order to "raise" the other).

Note that this quest—at present the central one of theology, I think—is more radical than just that of "modernizing," "demythologizing," or even "representing" or "revising." The latter relativized only past expressions of traditional symbols in favor of modern expressions. Far more radical—painful and yet exciting—is to relativize the symbols themselves—and that is our situation, the newness of our situation.

Let us, then, begin to think about these theological effects—for that is about all we can as yet do. The first important point to make is that the problematic involves *all* theological doctrines, not just some of them. That is, it is not that only the symbols of revelation and christology are at issue so that a more liberal understanding of revelation and of Christ, perhaps their elimination all together, will resolve it. Several such efforts have appeared, for example that of John Hick. For then one is left with God the creator, moral ruler, and, presumably, redeemer as well; and unfortunately such a classic theism is as particular as is any orthodox theology; it is Semitic and Western in form, strikingly different from Hindu, Buddhist, or Confucian conceptions. Each system of religious symbols forms a coherent, interrelated whole; and each *Gestalt* of symbols is particular, at variance with, other *Gestalten*. Thus each doctrine or symbol within any given system differs significantly from analogous symbols in other systems. As a result, no one doctrine in any such system of symbols (again, for example, God or human being) can be abstracted out and be established as universal in all religions, a point of unity with other religious traditions. God is as similar—*and* as different—from the ultimate principals of Hinduism and Buddhism as are the Christ and Krishna or the Christ and a Bodhisattva.

Nor, so I believe, is there a philosophical way to transcend these particularities and achieve a universal standpoint, a standpoint above and so neutral to the fundamental differences between religions. It is possible to translate the religious symbols of a given tradition into fundamental metaphysical terms—though, as the efforts of Hegel and Whitehead show, much thereby is lost as well as gained. Such philosophical systems, however, reveal themselves in the end to be as particular as were the theologies they absorbed and transcended. The particularity in this case is, of course, that of a *culture,* in this case Western culture, rather than that of a certain religious tradition. Thus to the philosopher, and to the academy where he or she works, there appears the illusion of a new universality, the universality of the culture as a whole as opposed to the partiality of the church within the culture. But looked at on the scale we are here considering, modern Western philosophy is as particular, as located in space and time, as are the Christian or the Buddhist traditions—and that philosophy is as alien from the corresponding philosophies of India and China as the relevant sets of religious symbols are from one another. Recent decades have shown us clearly that no religious tradition is universal, and as a consequence that its claims to be universal distort rather than express its message. The coming decades, I am sure, will reveal that Western culture, which certainly thought it was universal, is also not so—and that its claims, and the claims of its modes of philosophy, to universality and finality will soon seem as ludicrous as were the same claims of religion.

If dispensing with or toning down certain doctrines (revelation and christology) does not work, and if translation into metaphysical categories does not work, what does? The other familiar move—and to me more fruitful—is to try to find a religious or theological mode of universality—that is, an interpretation of religious symbols that is inclusive of other traditions. I shall mention two. The first effort, pioneered by Schleiermacher and continued by Tillich and most of the liberal neoorthodox, is to propose on the one hand a wide understanding of general revelation through which the truth and the grace evident in other religions (and cultures) can be theologically explicated, and on the other hand some form of universal salvation through which the efficacy of these other religious ways can be affirmed. Thus other religions are included as valid and effective within a Christian theology of revelation and incarnation. In all of these, however, Christian revelation remains "final and definitive," to use Tillich's words. That is, it is the Christian God of justice and love who is revealed and at work elsewhere, and it is that same God who saves all who are saved. Although Christian revelation is thus no longer exclusivist, it does claim to represent the final and so the universal criterion for all faiths, and thus it provides the principle through which they are more validly interpreted than when they are interpreted on their own terms.

This is, I believe, precisely the method used by Hinduism and Buddhism. Recognizing other religions as valid ways to the truth, nevertheless they use their own version of mystical pantheism to define how far each of the others progresses on the true way, how far they each climb up, so to speak, the real mountain. And they regard the higher consciousness through which their understanding appears, and the symbols appropriate to that consciousness, as the only way finally that reality can be known and understood.

In both the Christian and the mystical versions, however, these efforts—and I must admit to using them myself—now seem to remain parochial, inadequate to the new situation. For each incorporates others into its own world, interprets and defines them from an alien perspective—as when Christianity or Judaism are seen by mystical religions as "really" mystical. Thus in effect such an interpretation deconstructs them, transforms them into something they are not. One can hardly carry on a dialogue on this basis—for each, in seeing the other through its own eyes, can never hear what the other has to say.

The second form of this effort is to me the more interesting, although I find its theological implications very alien indeed. I refer to the attempt to interpret all religions as particular expressions of a perennial religious/philosophical center, or, as Schuon terms them, exoteric manifestations of an esoteric heart. There is, he says, a mystical core in each religion, a core that can be grasped by intellect and articulated in a philosophy of absolutism. This universal core is participated in and borne by the elite in each religion. The exoteric or outer clothing of the religion, its particular *Gestalt* of symbols, its moral laws, sacraments, and liturgical customs, are *revealed*, for the divine understands that not all men and women are elite, and that different cultures need different religious homes, so to speak. Thus each particular religion is *true* and yet *relative*, a true revelation for that community, relative to other true revelations to other communities, and relative to the Absolute that each only partially and so somewhat distortedly manifests.

Clearly the ultimacy and finality is here drained from Christian revelation, the Jewish law, the Qur'ān, the Four Noble Truths, and so on; and a fortiori theology is reduced to an in-house exercise. Only the mystical core within each tradition and its philosophical expression in absolutism remain as of universal relevance. Just as the first alternative, centered on general as distinct from special revelation, raised a particular tradition above all the others, so now this second resolution raises an *aspect* of religion (mysticism) and its philosophical equivalent to supreme status over other aspects of the religious. Thus other religions, centered on those other aspects—for example, commitment and obedience to the divine will, creative political action for justice, sacramental and liturgical participation in a sacramental community, and so on—are reduced to the relativity of the merely exoteric. As in the first, the Christian incorporates the Buddhist and the Hindu into his or her perspective, so here the mystical incorporates the nonmystical into an alien framework. In neither case is universality achieved, and in neither case is dialogue possible.

Interestingly, in each of these recent efforts at genuine ecumenicity some element of absolutism clearly remains. In the first, Christian revelation, now inclusive of all others, retains its "final" status; in the second, the mystical alone is unrelative. If, then, both of these resolutions are found wanting and discarded, as I feel they must be, then clearly in so doing the last hold against relativity appears to be relinquished. If no revelation is held to be finally valid, how is any truth to be known—unless one retreats to science, philosophy, or common sense and so embraces the alternative absolutism of Western culture? If no one aspect of religion is absolute but all aspects are relative, what now are the bases for confidence in religion itself?

There seems here no firm ground to stand on, either in a given tradition and its symbols, or in religious experience and its various aspects. And note, this is *real* relativism: if they are relativized, God, Christ, grace and salvation, higher consciousness, *dharma*, nirvana, and *mukti* alike begin to recede in authority, to take on the aspect of mere projections relative to the cultural and individual subjectivity of the projectors, and so in the end they vanish like bloodless ghosts. We have no grounds for speaking of salvation at all, a situation of relativity far beyond asking about the salvation of *all*. A drift toward radical relativity has come to light, and any theological basis we might suggest for stopping that drift also begins itself to drift. The rough parity of religions, by removing the absolute starting point of each, seems to drain each of whatever it has to say and give to us, and so to leave us empty—and incapable of moving to some other more solid ground. Ecumenical tolerance represents an impressive moral and religious gain, a step toward love and understanding. But it has its own deep risks, and one of them is this specter of relativity, this loss of any place to stand, this elimination of the very heart of the religious as ultimate concern.

III

Plurality, as we have seen, drives in the direction of ecumenical tolerance. Plurality, however, has another face than this, a face fully as terrifying as is the relativity just described. For within the plurality of religions that surround us are forms of the religious that are intolerable, and intolerable because they are demonic. Toleration is here checked by the intolerable; and plurality means *both*.

This aspect of diversity we have always seen out of the corner of the eye. We know there were religious cannibals, religious sacrifices of human victims, religious wars of aggression, religious murders, religious caste—and so on. Most of these have been pushed aside in our consciousness through the need, and it is a real need, to be tolerant and to free religion from its baleful faults of intolerance, fanaticism, and unbridled cruelty. But this too was dialectical—and twentieth-century experience has also illustrated this point extravagantly. For in our century intolerable forms of religion and the religious have appeared: in a virulently nationalistic Shinto, in Nazism, in aspects of Stalinism and Maoism, in Khomenei—and in each of these situations an absolute religion sanctions an oppressive class, race, or national power. These represent the "shadow side" of religion, and they are radically destructive. When faced with one of them, we *must* resist, and we must liberate ourselves and others from them.

This danger implicit in plurality—namely, that demonic possibilities lie within even the religions of our land—has appeared before us in the recent rise to considerable political power of the Religious Right. To be sure, like the poor it scorns, the Religious Right has always been with us. But recently it has moved from the fringes of our culture close to the centers of political power, and—as usually happens—its political demands have, in consequence, vastly increased. Mind you, I do not think them to be an immediate danger; the countering forces of pluralism in religion and in lifestyle are too great, the mainline churches and the academies too strong, and the Constitution is for the nonce unchanged. Still, if the level of anxiety within our common life rises, surprising things can happen—as they happened to other cultures repeatedly in this century: Japanese, German, Italian, Russian, Chinese, Islamic—to name a few. Despite our confidence in ourselves, we are by no means immune to this disease; and when the fever of anxiety gets high enough, even constitutional safeguards, not to mention diversity of custom and of ecclesiastical centers, may not be sufficient.

I bring up the Religious Right, however, to illustrate the complexity and ambiguity of plurality, and to point to the dialectical opposition, even the paradoxes and contradictions, that are latent within diversity. For like the cases of Hitler and Khomenei, the Religious Right represents something we cannot tolerate. I do not mean that we cannot tolerate its fundamentalist theology; we can and have to. I refer rather to its stated goal of theocracy, of establishing a "Christian America": a national community in which Christianity is the preferred religion, "Christians" are placed in crucial political roles, a certain sort of religious observance permeates the public sphere (that is, in schools and in public places), fundamentalist doctrine dominates the teaching of science, social science, and history—and in which the supremacy of the nation is identified totally with the will and aims of God. As Jerry Falwell has said: "It is high time that Christians take back the power to run their own country. . . . The constitution in the hands of Christians is a holy document; in the hands of non-Christians it can be used by the devil to defeat us." Here religion takes over and uses the public sphere; here religion—and the absolutist politics it spawns—manifests an intolerable face, as the secular religion of Nazism did. Against such religion—traditional or secular—resistance is imperative.

Now the point is that in order to resist—and we must, paradoxically on ecumenical grounds, if for no other reasons—we must ourselves stand somewhere. That is, we must assert some sort of ultimate values—in the face of heaven knows what social, intellectual, moral, and religious pressures—in this case the values of persons and of their rights, and correspondingly, the value of the free, just, and equal community so deeply threatened by this theocratic tyranny. And to assert our ultimate value or values is to assert a "world," a view of all of reality. For each affirmed political, moral, or religious value presupposes a certain understanding of humankind, society, and history, and so a certain understanding of the whole in which they exist. Our view of existence as a whole gives locus in reality to the values we defend. Consequently any practical political action, in resistance to tyranny or in liberation from it, presupposes ultimate values and an ultimate vision of things, an ethic and so a theology. And it presupposes an absolute commitment to this understanding of things. This union of resistance, commitment, and "world" was made crystal clear by the Barman confession: to confess our adherence to one Lord is at once to resist the Nazi claim on our allegiance; conversely to resist Nazi ideology, allegiance alone to one Lord and to one Word was required. The necessity of action, liberating action, calls first for the relinquishment of all relativity and secondly for the assertion of some alternative absolute standpoint. Paradoxically, plurality, precisely by its own ambiguity, implies both relativity and absoluteness, a juxtaposition or synthesis of the relative and the absolute that is frustrating intellectually and yet necessary practically.

IV

We have seen the theoretical dilemma that plurality has forced upon us. On the one hand, the inescapable drive toward ecumenical community, toward respect for and recognition of the other as other, and of the religious validity and power he or she embodies, has pushed us toward a relativity that seems to defy intellectual resolution. There seems no consistent theological way to relativize and yet to assert our own symbols—and yet we must do both in dialogue. On the other hand, the shadow side of religious plurality frequently forces us to resist, to stand somewhere, and also to hold some alternative religious position with absolute fidelity, courage, and perseverance. How are we to understand and resolve this contradiction or puzzle dealt us by plurality?

Faced with this reflective impasse, I suggest we refer to the venerable, practical American tradition. The puzzle that to *reflection* may represent a hopeless contradiction, said John Dewey, can through *intelligent practice* be fruitfully entered into and successfully resolved. As James reminds us, moreover, praxis brings with it a *forced* option, one that cannot be avoided. When praxis is called for, puzzled immobility before a contradiction or indifferent acceptance of a plurality of options must both cease—for to exist humanly we must wager, and must enact our wager. So is it with the dilemma forced on us by an oppressive ideology: faced with that menace, we *must* act—that is, we *will* act whether we wish to or not. More specifically, we will *either* conform *or* we will resist; and both are actions, choices that transform much about ourselves that went before, not least our relationship to our social environment. Praxis and its demands do not leave us alone. Thus does praxis push as well as lure us into the heart of our puzzle.

That puzzle has revealed itself as the apparent contradiction between the requirement within political action for some fixed or absolute center and an equally unavoidable relativism. Let us look first at this requirement of a center for praxis, and then see how it also relativizes itself if it is to remain healthy. If we would *be* personal and social beings, and even more if we must take a role in liberating action, we must stand somewhere and act from some basis. We need a ground for the apprehension and understanding of reality—a ground that undergirds our choices, our critiques of the status quo, our policies. We need a ground for the values and eros that fuel and drive toward justice, and for the confidence and hope necessary for consistent action. We need criteria for the judgments essential both for reflective construction and for liberative doing; and we need priorities in value if we would creatively and actively move into the future. All this is as true of the pragmatic humanist as of the theologian—for both reflection and action.

There seems to appear here as a requirement of authentic being a relationship, on the one hand, to some stable and assumed, and in that sense, *absolute* standpoint, a participation in it, and commitment to it. But, on the other hand (and here is where the polar side of the dialectic appears), in order to avoid repeating in ourselves the same oppressive religious absolutism we confront, there must at the same time be a deep apprehension and recognition of the *relativity* of our standpoint. A dialectic or paradox combining and interweaving both one part absoluteness and two parts relativity, *a relative absoluteness*, represents a posture essential to public and political praxis, again whether humanistic or theological.

With regard to praxis in the other larger area of plurality—namely, the new interrelationships of religions to one another—the same dialectic or paradox, this interweaving and mutual dependence of apparent opposites, appears. As we have seen, in the face of the parity of religions it is almost impossible at the moment to formulate a theological resolution of the doctrinal dilemmas and contradictions involved. The interplay of absolute and relative—of being a Christian, Jew, or Buddhist, and *affirming* that stance, and yet at the same time relativizing that mode of existence—both stuns and silences the mind, at least mine. But again praxis, now in the form of dialogue between diverse positions, pushes and lures us into the middle of a maze we still can hardly enter intellectually. Just as we do in creative political action, so now in "doing" dialogue we embody and enact this paradox—and we do so most fruitfully step by step. That is, on the one hand, we do not relinquish our own standpoint or starting point: What is dialogue if our Buddhist partner ceases to be Buddhist or we cease to be Christian? Nor on the other hand do we absolutize our own standpoint—lest no interchange take place at all. On the contrary, we relativize it radically: truth and grace are *also* with the other, so that now ours is only *one* way. And yet we remain *there:* embodying stubbornly but relatively our unconditional affirmations. Or, in reverse, we qualify our acknowledged relativism by participating in our quite particular but still stoutly affirmed perspective. Again, it is in praxis that we uncover a *relative absoluteness*.

What to reflection is a contradiction, to praxis is a workable dialectic, a momentary but creative paradox. Absolute and relative, unified vision and plurality, a centered principle of interpretation and mere difference, represent polarities apparently embodiable in crucial practice despite the fact that they seem numbing in reflective theory. Thus reflection must not, because it cannot, precede praxis; on the contrary, it must be begun on the basis of praxis. The basic principle of such theory based on praxis is that what is necessary to praxis is also necessary for reflection and theory—though the reverse is not true.

Nevertheless, reflection is important and must be begun. Let us, therefore, start our reflections with this dialectic or paradox uncovered as the heart of praxis in relation to plurality—namely, political liberation and dialogue—and let us then push it reflectively outward toward theory, toward theology. I suggest we use this paradigm within praxis—the dialectic of infinity and the finite, of the absolute as *relatively* present in the relative—as now the clue to the center of theological understanding: to the interpretation of our relation to the sacred on the one hand (our religion), and on the other, as the key to reflection on that to which we are related, to the absolute as it manifests itself relatively in the relative, to "God." Recall: the structure of praxis is our most helpful clue to the structure of being as we now seek to reflect on it.

The infinite manifests itself in the particular, the absolute in the relative—and the aroma of *each* pervades all we do and think. Is this principle or insight new? Is it not the heart of Hegel, even of Kierkegaard? Is it not what Whitehead meant when he spoke of an infinite mystery hovering over and relativizing any system of rational coherence? Is it not what Dewey pointed to when, amid perpetual flux and relativity, he lifted up a method that was not relative and did not change? Is it not what Tillich pointed to with his concept of the *true* symbol that relativizes and sacrifices itself in pointing beyond itself; or Niebuhr who orchestrated the theme of a mystery deeper than any revealed or reflected scheme?

How is our situation different from, more radical than, what is addressed in their thinking? Each of them saw clearly the dialectic of infinity and manifestation, of absolute and relative, of unconditioned mystery and conditioned meaning. The difference is that each of them, true to their cultural and religious epoch, saw their own particularity, their concrete scheme of meaning, be it theological or philosophical, as somehow privileged, as final, as less relative than the others, as *the* clue to the mystery that transcended it—whether it was Hegel's or Whitehead's logos, Dewey's expanded scientific method, or Tillich's and Niebuhr's revelation. But an objective and universal rational order turns out to be a *Western* logos, and this defies an awareness of the plurality and relativity of cultures, and so of all logoi. And the claim to a final and definitive revelation defies the plurality and relativity of religions. No cultural logos is final and therefore universal (even one based on science); no one revelation is or can be the universal criterion for all the others (even, so we are now seeing, Christian revelation). Mystery is here more encompassing because the particular center, the concrete principle of meaning, now is *itself* relative, one among other centers. This is the new situation, and again it seems to stifle any philosophy grounded on a universal logos or any theology based on a universally valid revelation.

And so we return to our dialectic incarnate in unavoidable praxis: the infinite manifests itself in *relative* relativities, the unconditioned in *conditioned* concretion. Liberating theologies and dialogue are based on this. But can we *think* as well as act on this new basis? Let us turn this over: these manifestations are particular and relative, agreed. But despite this, they also participate in and manifest the absolute or the infinite. The infinite *is* in the concrete, the absolute is unavoidably in the particular—that is, it cannot be approached except through the particular and the relative. But therefore the particular and the relative are not completely relative, for neither praxis nor reflection can be without absolute ground and meaning. A symbol or a criterion points beyond itself and criticizes itself if it would not be demonic; but it also points *to* itself and *through* itself if it would not be empty, and if we would not be left centerless. The dialectic works *both* ways: relativizing the manifestation on the one hand, and so all incarnations of the absolute, and yet manifesting as well *through* the relative an absoluteness that transcends it—otherwise neither liberating praxis nor creative reflection would be possible.

I suspect that our wider culture, and so academia, will soon—but by no means yet—have to deal with this same dilemma: the relativism and yet the continued affirmation of Western forms of scientific, historical, and social consciousness—as the AMA is having to deal with acupuncture and Detroit with Toyota! We are now in the very middle of this in theology. How are we to understand Christian revelation and promise as our affirmed ground of life, of political praxis and reflection, but *as relative*, as one among other manifestations and grounds?

We must, then, not be ashamed to start with our particularity, our relativity—for no universal standpoint, cultural or religious, is readily available to us. But we must incorporate into the theological elaboration of these particular symbols a new and pervasive realization and expression of their relativity, a new and deeper speaking and not speaking at once. Thus I will attempt, as best I now can, to express this dialectic—or paradox—of infinity and manifestation, of absolute and relative, in one of its *Christian* or particular forms. I am content thus to remain with the particular (within the Christian), for I cannot escape all particularity. Just as any vision of plurality is itself qualified by the affirmation of a *relative* center, so each apprehension of infinite meaning is qualified by and expressed through particular symbols. There is for us no universal standpoint.

In Christian symbols—as in the historical events that were their occasion and inspiration—there is a *relative* manifestation of *absolute* meaning. They are true and yet relatively true; they represent a particularization of the absolute, and yet are relative, and so only one manifestation. The relative here participates in and manifests the absolute. As relative it thus negates and transcends itself. It is final and yet not the only one; it is definitive and yet so are other ways. These are paradoxical assertions. Are these paradoxes impossible—that is, contradictory—and so cancel each other out? Or are they strange windows to an even stranger mystery, and so keys or clues to renewed theology? If the latter, then they represent challenges to what are two conventional but false dichotomies. (1) "The absolute is lost if its expression becomes relative." The response to this assertion is that relativity and absoluteness can possibly coexist in reflection as they do in praxis. (2) "The relative loses all participation in and communication of the absolute if it is relative to others, if there *are* others." Again, to respond: possibly a series of manifestations can coexist on the same level and with genuine validity. At least it is this that seems to me now existentially and theologically possible, as it is in any sane, liberating, and humane praxis.

Let me mention some further theological elaborations of this fundamental dialectic. (1) The infinite can be seen as God—and yet God-as-symbol can also be recognized as transcended by an infinite mystery, a mystery consequently pervaded by nonbeing as well as being (as the Cross might remind us), and so a mystery truly but relatively manifest as God but also made particular and concrete in other ways through other symbols. (2) Correspondingly, the infinite is revealed as absolute love, as *agape*—that is, christologically. Here is a truth, yet a truth whose vehicle of manifestation, that whereby it is known and apprehended, is relative—and yet true. What is here truly apprehended, acknowledged, and witnessed to may also be expressed through other media and by means of other symbols (for example, the Bodhisattva). (3) The infinite mystery is, finally, understood as redemptive power and promise, and truly so understood—and yet the grace there known far transcends the bounds of its own manifestation to us and is creatively present in symbols derived from other manifestations. To understand God in relation both to a mystery that transcends God and to the nonbeing that seems to contradict God; to understand revelation in relation to other revelations that relativize our revelation; to view christology and gospel in relation to other manifestations of grace; anthropology in relation to *anatta* (no-self) and identity—this is the heart of our present baffling but very exciting theological task.

Perhaps the secret here is like the secret of existence itself—that is, existing with inner strength and outer liberating power: to hold on with infinite passion to both ends of the dialectic of relativity and absoluteness. Perhaps if one keeps these poles together in a synthesis, such a posture for theological reflection may seem possible, as it is already acknowledged to be possible in political action and in dialogue. If such a relativized theology seems, as it certainly will to its cultural critics, a foolish and illogical impossibility, then let them remember that they will face tomorrow the same baffling dialectic as Western consciousness appropriates to itself its own destined travail of relativity. Meanwhile, let us not forget that the present flood of relativity is balanced by the stern demands for liberating praxis and for creative theory.

PART II

The Theologico-Mystical Bridge: Mystery

4

Idolatry

In Comparative Perspective

WILFRED CANTWELL SMITH

Many years—indeed, many decades—have passed since I last used the word "idolatry", either in print or, so far as I am aware, even in speaking. My reason for rejecting it as a term has been a conviction that the conception that it usually communicates is one that distorts what it purports to name. The word "idol", too, from which it comes, is normally illegitimate. On the latter, and specifically on "idol-worship", my last published remark, twenty or thirty years ago, was: "No one has ever worshipped an idol. Some have worshipped God in the form of an idol; that is what idols are for." (Even regarding what is mis-named cow-worship, I have also remarked: "The Hindu reveres the cow that he sees, not the cow that we see".)[1] Much though I admire some of Bishop Heber's other hymns, such as his widely used "Holy, Holy, Holy", yet I have certainly objected to the lines that run, "The heathen in his blindness bows down to wood and stone", ever since I came to recognize that in that situation it was the missionary, rather, that was blind. Of course, I have not been alone among Christians in feeling restless with the attitude set forth in that type of wording. I once had occasion to trace the gradual modification or outright replacement of those lines or of the stanza in a sequence of versions of the hymn appearing in editions of certain twentieth-century denominational

---

Some editorial conventions used throughout the rest of this book are not used by Professor Smith, for his own good reasons.—ED.

hymn-books on this continent. (Another line in the same verse had originally affirmed, of the Asian mission field, that nature there is beautiful and "only man is vile". Later versions have emended this to read, "only sin is vile".[2])

Much of the Christian Church has come to recognize that its nineteenth-century attitude to other religious communities was wrong[3]. One should not dismiss it as at the time ridiculous or stupid: it grew out of compassion and noble concern, and only later came to be recognized instead as arrogance. It was virtue misguided by misunderstanding, distorted by misapprehension. (May we be in that same situation to-day in other matters—or some among us, still in this matter?)

Yet misguided it was. I repeat: Much of the Church now recognizes that its former attitude to other religious communities was wrong. It has been slowly wrestling with the question of what will be involved in setting it right; what new attitude may legitimately replace that old one. Yet it is not merely a nineteenth-century aberration that has got us into trouble, or that needs radical revising. Much more serious and central is the Old Testament source of the error, perpetuated firmly in the New. The inherently pejorative quality of our concept "idol" is built into the Christian inheritance from the Jews, and from St. Paul. (Jesus himself never used the term.) Of the almost dozen Hebrew words translated as "idol" in the King James Authorized Version and the Revised Standard Version, several mean, basically, "iniquity", "vanity", "thing of nought", "object of terror", "horror", "a cause of trembling", "a cause of grief", "abominable"[4]; and words like "defile", "pollute", "abomination", "sin", "abhor", are regularly linked with the word "idol" in the phrase where it occurs. Similarly "idolaters", in the New Testament, appears along with "covetous", "extortioners", "hatred, violence", "liars"; as in "dogs . . . and idolaters"[5].

Christian (and Jewish) failure to understand, let alone to appreciate, what is going on in the spiritual life of communities served by images, is integral to the Bible, and to our tradition. Indeed, the error was a failure to recognize that anything at all was going on spiritually. As a result, the concepts developed have signified the material objects involved but have omitted the transcendent dimension that was their primary significance. The particular concept that we are considering definitely implied an absence of that dimension. The mistake was important, and has had serious historical consequences. It is comparable to the Biblical mistake as to the date and fashion of the creation of the planet earth, whose historical consequences have recently also proven major. The Church has wrestled firmly with the one, and is beginning now with the other. (In both cases, the wrestling met internal opposition.)

Christians have often been accused of being, and have come to recognize themselves as indeed having been, arrogant and disdainful in their fundamental metaphysical view of other religious practitioners. For centuries it was Jews who paid the chief price for this profound Christian error, and the Church has fortunately become repentant, to a considerable degree, about its resulting horrendous treatment of the Jews over the ages. Nonetheless the irony has not been widely recognized that it was in fact from the Jews that Christians learned this arrogance and disdain, this rejection. It was from their Jewish legacy that they inherited this false judgement on outsiders[6]. The "Noachite covenant", which is sometime supposed to represent a Jewish thesis of universal salvation, in fact explicitly excludes idolaters (and therefore most of the human race). The distorted and distorting interpretation of the place of forms and images in human religious life, and specifically the forms and images of other communities than one's own, is integral to both the Jewish and the Christian religious traditions, and has done untold damage on the human scene through the centuries. (It has been integral also to the primary version of the Islamic tradition; and the rest of the world is beginning to pay the price for modern Muslims' reverting to the traditional Jewish-Christian-Islamic stance on outsiders' spirituality—after a good while when in their case this negative view of idolatry was to some extent modified in the widespread Sufi movement.)

My awareness in this general area, begun by my travelling outside of Christendom and as an undergraduate at home, was heightened when I lived for some years in India with friends from among its various communities, and it was then given intellectual depth when as a graduate student learning Persian I was introduced to Sufi interpretations. My education in this particular realm was furthered by two things that I learned more recently in my study of Hindu life. One is the ceremony called *pratistha* (this word is used also for the enthronement or coronation of a political ruler) or *pranapratistha,* for the consecrating or sacralizing of an image. Before this ceremony has been performed in any particular case, the image is indeed the wood or stone of which the Bishop of Calcutta wrote in his hymn (but with nobody bowing down to it); after the ceremony has sacrally invited the god or goddess (him- or herself a form [*sic*] of the higher divine; of God, we would say) to take up his or her presence in the image, and has consecrated it, it serves the worshipper as the locus—or: as a locus—of the deity; the consecrated image becomes a potential focus of his or her devotion. It is thus formally true, not merely substantially so, that that worshipper worships not the "idol", but God in that form, called "idol" by those who do not understand. (I was pleased to find my earlier remark, made before I became aware of this procedure, herein corroborated!) There is a counterpart ceremony by which, if required, the image may be deconsecrated. After that, the material itself may be discarded (without the uncouthness that seems to be communicated by signs that one occasionally nowadays sees in our cities where demographic and other patterns have changed, announcing "Church For Sale". Such signs mean, rather: building, previously serving as a Church, for sale).

The other help that I received from Hindu sources arose from my coming across a verse in the *Yogavasistha*[7] which says, of the Transcendent (of Brahman; of God, we would say), "Thou art formless. Thy only form is our knowledge of Thee". To me, this has proved a brilliant and immensely illuminating perception: one of the theologically most discerning remarks that I know. Our knowledge of God is always partial, of course; Christian theologians have known that, and the more profound they were, the more vividly they have recognized it. God does not reveal theologies; He reveals Himself, She reveals Herself, It reveals Itself. Every theological system or idea is a response. It is finite, is mundane, is a human construct. Yet theologies may serve as channels introducing those who ponder them, and especially those who subscribe to them, those who see their significance, to a truth that in turn is more than human; more than finite; to God.

Theologies are conceptual images of God.

Like other images, each may be less or more worthy of its Subject. Like other images, each may be of no spiritual significance or truth to outsiders, may not be for them a locus of transcendent transparency. This verse, however, goes further: it speaks not of our overt theological statements, but of our knowledge. Whether articulated in a great or in an unsophisticated conceptual pattern, or not articulated, our knowledge of God—the intellectual's knowledge, and too that of the cobbler—is the form in which ideationally God appears to each of us, less or more richly.

No such form is either final or complete. No such form is negligible.

The ideational itself is of course only one type of form, among others, in which transcendence is apprehended by, is communicated to, human beings. It is a particularly important form, no doubt, for those of us who are intellectuals.

Knowledge, here, is not to be confused with fancy. It is not that our ideas of God are all equally translucent. Only insofar as they are valid (so far as they go) may they be called knowledge. Yet even at that level they remain particular, finite, of this world. It is wrong for our intellects to absolutize their own handiwork.

With recognition of all this goes a deeper sense of truth, and a clearer appreciation of the way that human beings apprehend and express it. In modern comparativist times, we are pushed to a more adequate view of conceptualization and of language, especially of statements; to a "human" view of truth[8]. This view holds that statements are not true or false; that truth and falsity—more accurately, approximations to truth, less or more remote—are qualities not of statements but of what they mean, to those who utter and hear them, or write and read them: qualities of the awareness that they induce in persons. Such awareness regularly varies, for any given statement, certainly from century to century and from civilization to civilization, often from person to person and indeed, in major matters, over the course of an individual person's lifetime.

Persons live their lives on this earth, and in time. This means that they live them in a context that is mundane. They live them to some degree also in terms of a concomitant fact: that at the same time and in addition[9] they are in relation to a reality that transcends time and space and ourselves. We live at an intersection of time and eternity, to use one particular vocabulary. We live, at least potentially, in the presence of God, to use another. Our awareness of the transcendent dimension of our lives and of our world varies. For some persons or groups, for some moments or eras, it is more vivid, more genuine, more profound, than for others. As a student of the religious history of the world, I observe that despite the variation, radical unawareness of that transcendent dimension has been and is rare.

There has ever been a problem, however, as to how to express—in concepts, in art, in institutions, in activity, in other ways—and how therewith to nurture, that relation to what is more than mundane. Human beings have observably produced, and cherished, a vast number of ways of doing this. These have been in response, one may say, to the transcendence that has entered their lives. Yet historically it is noticeable that these expressions have been in response also in each case to a complex of mundane considerations, conscious or unconscious. Taking a cue from our *Yogavasiṣṭha* verse, one may suggest that a work of plastic art, an institutional structure, Handel's *Messiah,* a theological system, are all forms mediating less or more well between humankind and God, or from another perspective we should say between God and humankind. Often the most salient mediation is membership in a given community.

To see things so is not to adjudge that all forms are equally valid or effective or acceptable. It is to suggest that there is no fundamental difference in principle between a doctrine and a statue. (There may be considerable difference between their effectiveness in moulding the course of history—for good and for ill.) An artist is not necessarily further from the truth than is an intellectual. The saint, or indeed the humble moral member of the community, may be closer than either the artist or the intellectual. Some statues are magnificent works of art and embody profound insight; others are crude, or awry. (Moreover, some persons or groups may at times nonetheless see more in—through—what seems to be the crudest art.) Similarly with theologies. Both theology and art proffer relative apprehensions of the Absolute.

The upshot of all this is that I long felt that we had good reason to dismiss "idolatry" as a concept. As an interpretation of others' religious life, it simply would not do. Its characterizing of what it has purported to describe has been doubly in error: it has been intellectually wrong, and morally wrong. For it misunderstands what those involved are in fact involved in. And its built-in denigration of them as persons or communities is grossly arrogant, repugnantly insensitive.

To employ the words of my subtitle: in comparative perspective, the term "idolatry" appeared to be ruled out.

My choosing the term, nonetheless, as title for my presentation here might seem, therefore, surprising. At least, it was so to me. The choice represents a new sense of two matters, which I shall endeavour to explain. Rather than our dropping the term altogether, in comparative perspective it may indeed be seen as serving a new purpose.

First, there is here something not unusual in religious affairs: namely, that while participants in a given group vision may be limited or awry in their apprehension of the life of outsiders' communities, their discernment regarding matters within their own group may be sharp—because of that very vision. Further, their unawareness that certain concrete items are symbols for others may or indeed will lead to their failure to appreciate those items' role; yet they may in turn employ those same concepts in a transferred, and therefore recognizedly symbolic, fashion in relation to themselves. Christians have failed to sense what is going on in a foreign community served by what they call "idols", and they accordingly use the term literally to denote for those outsiders the external form. Such Christians have used the same term metaphorically, however, to connote a phenomenon in their own community, describing not its empirical condition but its spiritual overtones.

My immediate proposal is to suggest that in its metaphorical sense, our words "idol" and "idolatry" might prove helpful. One could say more firmly that they can prove indeed helpful in this second, transferred, usage. Let me explain.

Since the Western traditions mistakenly imagined that those whom they called idolaters had no transcendent reference, and specifically that the images had none, the word "idol" came to mean secondarily human attachment to some mundane thing without any such reference, or instead of it. Accordingly, putting one's faith in, giving one's allegiance to, material wealth, or worldy fame, or sensual pleasure, rather than to God or to spiritual pursuits, has by Christians, Jews, and Muslims been called a form of idolatry. In a similar way treating the sacraments, for instance, or any holy thing, as if it were merely magical rather than spiritual, as if its significance or power lay in itself rather than in its relation to God, has also been called a form of idolatry. (In pre-ecumenical days, many Protestants used to imagine that for Roman Catholics the crucifix or the rosary simply served as an idol; while Catholic leaders would themselves say that this was a potential danger for Catholics insufficiently sensitive to the cosmic divine action represented by these sacramentals, or to the divine presence mediated through it. Comparably, Protestants, who ideally are invited to hear God speak through the Bible[10], are potentially prey to bibliolatry—idolatry of the Bible—insofar as they think of the Bible not as pointing to God and opening up for us a way to approach and know Him/Her/It and His will and Her love for us and Its self-giving to and in us, but as if the Bible itself constituted an absolute.)

"Idolatry", by definition, in its literal usage denigrates one's neighbour by leaving out the transcendence of his or her position. Yet by the same token, in its metaphorical usage the word may prove helpful for oneself by calling attention to the danger of leaving it out.

I am not here suggesting that other people, or other communities, are always virtuous, while one is oneself always wicked, or one's own group is so. Morally, this would be perhaps a preferable stance to its more traditional contrary, which has through much of their history plagued the three Semitic world traditions: that we are right, they (more recently, you) are wrong; more stridently, that we are saved, you are damned. Apart from moral considerations, however, such self-deprecatory humility is not theoretically right. Rather, my thesis is that all of us on earth are prone to an error, one that Western theology, unfortunately, has tended at times to bless: the error of identifying with the divine, with the truth, with the final, with transcendence, the particular form in or through which we have been introduced to it, by way of which It or He or She has come into our particular lives—rather than relating that form to It/Him/Her, subordinating it, relativizing it in relation to the Absolute that it serves.

We come now to the heart of my presentation. Twenty-some years ago I wrote *The Meaning and End of Religion,* of which the thesis in a nutshell was that, seen in world-history perspective, what have been called the religions of the world are indeed parts of this world, are temporal, contingent, mundane, while their primary significance lies in their role as mundane intermediaries between humankind and God. Their two component elements, which I dubbed cumulative tradition and faith, play a role in this supremely significant matter. I might now speak rather of three component elements, counting community as in significant ways distinct from tradition, rather than subsumed under it, with participation in community as a major element. Traditions, and communities, have the demonstrated capacity to elicit and to nurture faith, the term that I gave—misguidedly, some have said; but the wording is of secondary importance—to that relation of human beings to God. The particular argument can, of course, be disputed (though few have disputed it directly). Certainly some have resisted my suggestion made with it that we should drop the concept of a variety of "religions". What is substantial, however, implicit in that work and explicit now in this presentation, is that it is a mistake to identify one's own "religion" or tradition with God, or with absolute truth; to regard it as divine, rather than as an avenue to, or from, the divine.

All the various religious movements of the world, Christian and other, have been constructed, and have kept being constantly re-constructed and modified, by human beings—in response (in part) to something that transcends the movement and that they have recognized as transcending it. I have no urge to contend that religious people have not been helped, year by year, in this constructing and re-constructing by what Christians call the Holy Spirit (though they have also been limited at each point by their own finite capacities and misguided by a variety of other intertwining considerations that have impinged).

For Christians to think that Christianity is true, or final, or salvific, is a form of idolatry. For Christians to imagine that God has constructed Christianity, or the Church, or the like[11], rather than that He/She/It has inspired us to construct it, as He/She/It has inspired Muslims to construct what the world knows as Islam, or Hindus what is miscalled Hinduism, or inspired Bach to write the B Minor Mass or Ramanuja to write his theological commentaries, or Pañcapana (if it was indeed he) to build Borobudur—that is idolatry.

The forms that have been called idols can in fact be very good things, I have argued. All the above have indeed been good things (even though the mundane elements in "Christianity" and "Islam" and "Hinduism" are many and some of them have been deeply deleterious). It would be wrong to call them idols. To mistake them, however, for God Himself, or mistakenly to elevate any one of them to some divine status, is to commit the fallacy of looking at the window rather than through it to God, and giving to it the honour, dignity, deference, due only to God.

Each "religion" is an "idol" in the best sense of the word, if one were going to use these words at all. Exclusive claims for one's own is idolatry in the pejorative sense.

To return to the particular question of theology, earlier raised. Theologies, we observed, and each specific doctrine, are conceptual images of God. Thus even for those few nowadays who do not make the recent error of reifying their religion, it is nonetheless easy to idolize the conceptual content of a theological position or tenet. Ironically, theologians themselves have sometimes emerged as prone to this, regarding as definitive the theoretical dimension of Christian truth. This is perhaps particularly the case since the Enlightenment, which began by recognizing the transcendent role of Reason in human life; its heirs have tended to identify the rational with the true, rather than as a great mediator of truth. For intellectuals, the rational is probably its greatest mediator. Some intellectuals, even, would in this fashion absolutize—idolize—the role of rational *propositions*—a still lower form of the rational. Certain theologians have absolutized not only Christian theology as such, but even particular doctrines within it. This elicits the derogatory sense of the word "dogmatic". Such an understanding of doctrine or dogma is a clear instance of an idolatrous attitude, in the negative sense, towards an image, in this case a conceptual image.

Surely those of us who theologize know that doctrines are human products, made by us (so that for us it is a bit silly, let alone, idolatrous, to treat them as final). They are not themselves transcendent, though we may hope and strive that they may serve to communicate or to mediate truth, which *is* transcendent.

For Christians to see Christ as divine is a perception (put then in conceptual terms): a perception that their own personal experience, and two thousand years of Church history, elicit and confirm. It is, however, impossible to *perceive* him as the sole such mediator; although one can hold this as a theological proposition, inferred by logic from what one does see. One cannot perceive the non-divinity of Krishna, or of the Qur'ān. (That these are not forms of God for oneself one may know. Whether they are or are not for other people one has to ascertain by investigation.) To believe that other groups' forms are *not* divine is a purely doctrinal construct. To hold that Buddhist, or post-Biblical Jewish, life is not the locus of God's salvific activity, fully comparable to God's activity in Christian life, is a sheer man-made* hypothesis. The

---

*The editors of this volume objected to my use of the term "'man-made" here. I am not aware, however, of any woman theologian who has formulated this doctrine, so as to have us think of it as woman-made. Some women have held the doctrine, once it was propounded by male theologians; and hold it to-day. Yet might one not feel permitted to hope that as women participate more fully and creatively in the on-going theological process of the Church, a more compassionate position on the matter, one advocated by both men and women, will become standard?

position has—inescapably—no direct grounding in reality. The doctrine of the divinity of Christ is a conceptual form of Christians' knowledge of God. The doctrine of other religious patterns' non-divinity is an intellectual formulation of ignorance: an ignorance of the life of those for whom those patterns are rich[12].

We may repeat, then, our previous assessment, but relating it this time specifically to doctrinal matters. Every positive theology, Christian or other, and each positive doctrine, is an "idol", in the best sense of the word, if one were to use that word at all. Exclusive or final claims for one's own doctrine, or for any, is idolatry in the pejorative sense.

Our conclusion, then, is this. In comparative perspective, one sees that "idolatry" is not a notion that clarifies other religious practices or other outlooks than one's own; yet it can indeed clarify with some exactitude one's own religious stance, if one has previously been victim of the misapprehension that the divine is to be fully identified with or within one's own forms. Christians have been wrong in thinking that Hindus are formally idolaters. We would do well, on the other hand, to recognize that we Christians have substantially been idolaters, insofar as we have mistaken for God, or as universally final, the particular forms of Christian life or thought.

Christianity—for some, Christian theology—has been our idol.

It has had both the spiritual efficacy of "idols" in the good sense, and the serious limitations of idolatry in the bad sense.

CHRISTOLOGICAL COROLLARY

It has been widely felt that the divinity of Christ is centrally at stake in the pluralism debate; even, that this is the crucial matter. The divinity of Christ is not, however, at issue in these discussions. In fact, in some ways it could become a serious distraction to the question before us. For their conviction, or recognition, of Christ's divinity is what prevents many Christians, they have felt, from recognizing as a divine fact—metaphysically valid, acceptable in the eyes of God—what they cannot avoid recognizing as a human fact: namely, the pluralism of the world's spiritual life. For they are imprisoned in the fear that to do so would mean a surrendering of their precious treasure of Christ as Himself divine.

Of course, there are others, both inside and regretfully outside the Church, who are deeply restless, in modern times, at what they regard as this untenable, this outdated, dogma. We would contend that the fear of the one group, and the restlessness and disparagement of the other, are both overcome in a sound pluralistic awareness. (After all, pluralism recognizes and comes to terms with diversity within, as well as among, religious groups.)

To begin at one extreme: some might feel that the general orientation set forth in this presentation would, if adopted, involve a notion that Christ would then be thought of as an idol. Now any *doctrine* about the nature of Christ is a conceptual image. The *figure* of Christ is another matter, though not unrelated. An in some ways comparable question, canvassed of late, is whether it be appropriate to consider the doctrine of Christ incarnate as a myth. This too might be thought to be engaged here.

It is not evident that these matters impinge on our present concern: pluralism. The questions, as I have suggested, no doubt are related to our outlook; yet the answer that one gives to them affects perhaps only obliquely the central focus of this essay, on Christian relations to other forms of faith. Let us consider these points.

First, has the figure of Christ served as—has it been—an idol through the centuries for Christians? Obviously, the answer depends on what the word "idol" is understood as meaning. As we have seen, the prevalent usage of this term has been to designate something conceived by the speaker to be mundane and not transcendent. Normally, the speaker's further implication is that the worshipper, in turn, mistakenly conceives it as transcendent and not mundane. In standard Christian orientations, Christ has been held explicitly to be not one or the other, but both. Indeed, a deal of highly serious thought has gone into, and a deal of rich inference—theoretical, affective, and practical—has been drawn out of, the affirmation that Jesus of Nazareth as the Christ was and is simultaneously very God of very God and also flesh of our flesh, bone of our bone. I have complained above that Christians (along with Jews and Muslims) have failed to recognize that Hindus, for example, perceive what these Near Eastern religious movements call "idols" as in fact simultaneously both also; and that therefore it has been an error to employ this derogatory term to characterize these communities' religious practice and piety. It may be that both Christian theologians and academic intellectuals will come to use the word "idol" in a changed meaning, to designate Hindu and other such forms once they have fully recognized that in fact those forms indeed are, and are perceived by worshippers as indeed being, materially mundane and at the same time substantially transcendent or the locus or channel of transcendence. If this happens, then certainly Christ should be spoken of as an idol too.

This development in vocabulary does not, however, appear to be happening. What seems to me more likely is that the term is on its way out, as too contaminated by its original meaning, traditional usage, and residue of connotations to be any more useful. It should be used in relation to all traditions, or to none. This is the fundamental point.

Some Christians would like to retain the term "idolatry" in its pejorative sense only—so deeply has its negativity become ingrained—as a stick with which to beat immoral things like Nazism and other over-weening nationalism. This, however, is like telling anti-Semitic jokes about non-Jews on the grounds that they are making a forceful and isolatedly valid moral point. To say that Nazis are like Buddhists simply will not do.

Of course, there have been times when the Christian emphasis on the human, or on the divine, of the two natures in the hypostatic union of Christ was particularly heavy, almost to the exclusion of the other and therefore of the confluence. The main thrust, however, has been precisely on the point that here the divine and the human, the transcendent and the mundane, meet. Christians have tended to speak of this as a 'mystery', which is of course neither unreasonable nor unhelpful; yet such a phrasing is in danger of falling victim to and perpetuating the modern-Western propensity to perceive the spiritual as separate from the rest of our life, even as a bit odd. One might find it more reasonable and more helpful to rejoin most of the rest of the human race in seeing transcendence as closely interwoven with, for human beings a fundamental and standard part of, the everyday; and recognizing the irreligious or insouciant, rather, as something deviant, virtually bizarre. Human life, even more than the universe at large, is indeed mysterious. Yet should that not be, not a private persuasion, but the starting point of all our intellectualizations—in science and everywhere else?

I myself certainly see the figure of Christ in the piety of hundreds of millions of Christians over the centuries as a form in which transcendence, God, has participated in our lives (and/or vice versa: a form in which we have participated in its life). In fact, it would seem to me obtuse for anyone to fail to see this, and silly to deny it (for any perceptive Muslim, for example, or atheist). I speak as an historian. (As an historian also of language, I recognize the problem here of vocabulary, for either affirming or denying this.) More specifically, Roman Catholics speak of the Real Presence of Christ in the Eucharist. Personally I would be more inclined to speak of the real presence of God in the lives of those with faith participating in the Eucharist, a presence mediated through that rite or in the interaction between the persons and the rite; but to pursue that matter here would take us too far from our present task. In any case, I am certainly impressed by, for instance, Ramanuja's, or for that matter the Bhagavad Gita's, insistence on the real presence of God in all religious forms—some would add, for the devotee—and indeed in some fashion in all the created or objective world. However that be, the important point is that transcendence, God, is—has been, historical observation may affirm—really present not only in the Eucharist but in much of for instance Bach's music or in the giving of a cup of cold water and other moves or movements of justice and compassion, or in community or in systems of ideas—to differing degrees for various people at different times. (No one, so far as I recall, has ever argued that all religious forms are always equally effective; that God is equally successful every day in all His/Her/Its attempts to bring human beings into salvific relation to Himself/Herself/Itself.)

The problem, for our present topic, pluralism, is not with whether the figure of Christ has served as a form in which God has entered history and been active within it. It is certainly not with *how* this has been done. Rather, our concern is with whether this has been and is one form among others. Some Christians have insisted, or have wished to hold, that there have been, are, no other forms; or, less logically, no forms other than this one plus certain further forms derived from or subordinately related to this one (e.g., the doctrines of the

Westminster Confession; the beads of a Christian rosary; a particular Sunday morning service; membership in the Roman Catholic Church . . .). Other Christians would concede—recognize—that there have been other forms, around the world and over the centuries, yet would urge a category difference between the instance of Christ and all the others.

I myself—after studying the history of the Islamic and the Christian movements and having friends in both groups—am not able to think of any reason that one might reasonably have for denying that God has played in human history a role in and through the Qur'ān, in the Muslim case, comparable to the role in the Christian case in and through Christ. That, of course, could be discussed (preferably, with those familiar with the facts). In any case, my thesis is that the germane issue here is not how one perceives Christ, or the figure of Christ, and how one formulates that apprehension conceptually; but rather, how in relation to that, one perceives and characterizes God's other activities over the course of human history.

One might call it idolatrous of Christians to regard the figure of Christ as divine insofar as they do not sense the role of the Holy Spirit in that understanding. *Mutatis mutandis* for Muslims with the Qur'ān. In the case of Islam, outsiders can readily see that the modern world is in danger of suffering from the consequences of such idolatry. Christians themselves, and the West generally, have been slower to see the damaging consequences in their own case.

No doubt, some Christians have understood Christ Himself, or various Christian authorities, as saying that God has acted effectively only in this one case, or surpassingly so. It is equally true that some Muslims have understood the Qur'ān or various Islamic authorities as saying much the same thing in their case. A claim to uniqueness is not unique. Its incidence is simply one of the significant facts of which the modern mind takes note before theorizing about religious or spiritual matters. It is, of course, true that Christ is unique. It is also true that the Qur'ān is unique, or K'ung Fu-tse. (This question of uniqueness has been further considered in our note 12.)

The notion "idolatry" means, or at least has meant: to treat, mistakenly, something mundane as if it were divine. (The Islamic counterpart concept involves not only *ṣanam* and *but-parasti* but *shirk*.) Since in actuality religious life proceeds symbolically, with various mundane things serving particular groups or persons for centuries as symbolic representations or channels of the divine, perhaps our question might be said to become: does a given person, or group, at a given moment, or era, fail to recognize the symbolic as symbolic, and therefore treats it as if it were itself divine, rather than as mediator.

More nuance than this, however, is requisite. A better question might be: to what extent is such an error being made in a particular instance. For actually the dividing line has normally not been sharp, to make it a yes-or-no affair; it is a matter, rather, of degree. Socrates held that we always choose what we think to be good, though we be often mistaken. In our terms here: whatever we deem good is always to some extent for us an idol of what is truly The Good. (Since nothing actual is ideal, it is wrong to confuse one's views with absolute truth, or one's judgements with absolute value.) One need not necessarily agree with the Socratic view of all our human choosing; yet we may recognize that in religious life over the centuries and around the globe people have regularly had a sense of transcendence, of God's presence, in and through the symbolic forms, as well as at times—commonly: at the same time—seeing those forms themselves as embodying God.

Traditionally, Christians would modify the Greek-derived position above to hold: nothing actual is ideal, except Christ. (Muslims: except the Qur'ān.) Still more nuanced, then—and some would judge, better—would be a thesis that one might call intermediary: that one or another or all such forms are God-given. The Bhagavad Gita propounds, and at sustained systematic length the Hindu theologian Ramanuja, for instance, affirms, that God graciously condescends actively to take the form, however petty, that His worshipper treats as housing Him. Historically, Christians have tended to hold that their own forms—Presbyterian or Roman Catholic or more generally Christian—are given by God, others' forms are not (Jews and Muslims similarly). Thus idolatry might along these lines come to be understood more fully as meaning: to treat (mistakenly, would one wish to add?) something mundane as if it were itself divine, as well as seeing—feeling, worshipping, obeying—the divine Itself through and beyond that form. (Thus Tillich speaks of symbols as "participating" in what they symbolize; although personally I find that inadequate.)

Our point here is that there are, and in practice certainly there have been, many ways of interpreting doctrinally what is going on in the spiritual life either of humankind at large or more narrowly within one's own community. (Christian theologians, for example, have differed among themselves.) Whichever of the ways one chooses, it is delinquent not to be ready to relate it to other positions elsewhere on earth.

Whether the doctrine of Jesus Christ as the Son of God Incarnate is to be viewed as a myth is, as noted, a comparable problem. Again the answer of course depends on what the term "myth" is taken to mean. For some, it is drastically unacceptable because for them the term is again pejorative. In this "myth" case, however, present-day Christians have inherited the concept not from the Bible or the religious tradition, with the concomitant emotional strength of connotation that such inheritance imparts, but from nineteenth-century pre-critical (pre-historical, pre-pluralist) Enlightenment rationality. Nonetheless the force of that heritage is by no means to be under-estimated, though it be less for those of us as intellectuals who are rationally critical within that tradition. Like many historians of religion, I myself am one of those for whom the term "myth" is not inherently pejorative. Yet I recognize that there are others for whom it has primarily or only negative connotations, or even denotation. I have a higher sense of the cosmological status of myth than do many. Moreover, as earlier suggested, I have a lower sense of the cosmological status of propositions than do most; certainly than do most modern anglophone philosophers. Although truth is in my perception eternal, there is no proposition, and no myth, that is not historical, contingent. The capacity of either of these to approximate to truth—more strictly, to communicate to human beings an approximation to truth—is always a function of time and place, and of the particular persons or groups involved. Also historical, even relatively recent, is the rise of clearly distinguishing, indeed of mounting a stark contrast, between myths and prosaic ("true") propositions; and the wide adoption and sense of the importance of that distinction or contrast.

Also historical, but much more recent, of our own day, is that some intellectuals and theologians are beginning to recognize myths as myths in a laudatory sense, and specifically to regard the doctrine of God incarnate in Christ as mythic in this laudatory sense. At least, they are beginning to perceive that it would be helpful, and even that it may have become requisite, that we do so—in principle, all of us. Along with that would have to go the concomitant recognition that historically myths can communicate approximations less or sometimes more close to truth than do or can propositions. That many, inside and outside the Church, should see the incarnation and other doctrines in this way could be a great step forward in a number of cases. Among those inside, the number of cases is perhaps growing in which it would be such a step forward, for themselves and even more so in their relations with their neighbours; among those outside the Church, it would surely be so for all concerned. (For world peace, this development may even be requisite. *Mutatis mutandis* for the Qur'ān.)

I leave these matters aside, however, since the important issue for our purposes here remains that of whether one applies such orientations to the religious life of all communities, or instead endeavours to exempt one's own, giving it a privileged status or supposing that God has given it that. There have been many ways of understanding the particularities of any given tradition, of turning perceptions into theses (in the Christian case, whether Christological, eucharistological, or whatever). We cannot settle disputes among them here. *Nor need we.* Rather, we both can and need recognize that whichever way one adopts, it applies comparably for other traditions.

NOTES

1. These two remarks appeared as follows. On "idols": *The Meaning and End of Religion* (New York: Macmillan, 1963) p. 141 (same page in the various 1978 editions); (New York: New American Library [Mentor Books], 1964; London: New English Library, 1965) p. 127. On "cows": *Questions of Religious Truth* (New York: Scribners, and London: Gollancz, 1967), p. 17. The conviction has been fairly common in the Muslim Sufi tradition for centuries. Recently I was delighted to find it set forth in virtually the very words (*sc.* their Arabic equivalent) of my '63 comment, by—surprisingly—the nineteenth-century Muslim political activist and North African resistance leader—and mystic—the amîr 'Abd al-Qâdir (ibn Muḥyî-d-Dîn al-Ḥasanî). Not only did he write that God appears (*ẓahara*) to Christians—finitely, particularly—in Christ, to Zarathustrians in fire, and so on, and "to the worshipper of every thing in that thing, be it stone or tree or animal or the like, in such a way that worshippers do not worship the particularized finite forms in and of themselves; rather, they worship what is manifested (*or:* what is revealed—*mâ tajallâ*) to them in that form, of one or other of

the characteristics of the true God—who transcends! . . . Thus the object of worship for the entirety of worshippers is one and the same" (*Mawqif* 246). Moreover, this writer is led into this exposition by his striking interpreting of what is widely known as the first assertion of the Muslim so-called "creed", "There is no god but God". This is often read, rather, with exclusivist emphasis. 'Abd al-Qâdir cites it directly from a Qur'ân verse (directly from God Himself, as it were); and affirms it as meaning that it is always God that is manifested, however limitedly, in every god. (The mistake, he says, is to imagine that He is particularized therein.) *There is no god that is other than God.* See al-Sayyid al-Amîr 'Abd al-Qâdir al-Jazâ'irî, *Kitâb al-Mawâqif, fî al-taṣawwuf wa al-wa'ẓ wa al-irshâd* ([Damascus:] Dâr al-Yaqzah al-'Arabîyah [1911], 2nd edn., 1966), 3 vols., pp. 560–61 (= vol. 2, but the volumes are paginated consecutively). There is a French translation: Emir Abd el-Kader, *Écrits spirituels, presentés et traduits de l'arabe par Michel Chodkiewicz*, Paris: Éditions du Seuil, 1982, where this *mawqif* is selection 29, pp. 131–34.

2. For some of the details, see my *Meaning and End* . . . ; of the 1963 and the various 1978 editions, note 43, p. 313; of the 1964 and '65 editions, pp. 320–21.

3. This statement applies chiefly to Church leadership, not only in the liberal ("mainline") Protestant Churches but also in the Vatican; and especially to intellectuals and serious theologians. Some would note, against our observation, that a sizable, and perhaps growing, number of ordinary Church members are currently re-affirming, at times with some vehemence, the old-time exclusivist stance. Over against this development one must reckon the uncounted number of those who have abandoned the Church for reasons that include their discerning Christian intolerance as intolerable. Further, one must recognize that if the exclusivists become dominant in the Church, countless more persons will leave it.

4. For the King James Authorized Version, the fourteen words are *âwen, êmah, ēl, 'lîl, gillûl, ḥammān, miphleçeth, çîr, ṣemel, shiqqqûç, t'rāphîm*, and various forms of the root '-ç-b. (Cf. Robert Young, ed., *Analytical Concordance to the Bible*, Edinburgh, 1879, and many subsequent editions; mine is the 22nd American edition [Grand Rapids: Eerdmans, 1973], where the relevant entry is p. 507. It is not, however, fully accurate: for instance, Ezekiel 18:15 has been missed, and some verses show only one of two appearances.) Of these Hebrew terms, three derive from notions of 'forming, fashioning'; one is of unknown etymology; the other ten are from roots signifying "trouble, sorrow, wickedness", "terror, dread", "to shudder", "worthlessness", "detestable", and so on (cf. Brown-Driver-Briggs, *Lexicon* [Oxford: Clarendon, 1906, and many subsequent revised editions], s.vv.). In the Revised Standard Version, a few of these words are, or are occasionally, rendered differently (e.g., *ḥammānîm* as "images", II Chron. 34:7), but in most cases "idol" is retained and indeed the English term is used on the whole somewhat more often than in 1611. Thus it similarly replaces a few times the earlier "(graven) images" (e.g., Isaiah 40:19), and equally often replaces "vanity" (e.g., II Kings 17:15); once (Ezekiel 43:9) the newer version proffers "idolatry" for the former quite straightforward "whoredom" (for *zenûth*—a word that occurs also, in the identical context, two verses earlier and is there rendered by the RSV as "harlotry").

5. The last is from Revelation 22:15. The term occurs otherwise in the New Testament at I Cor. 5:10, 5:11, 6:9, 10:7, Eph. 5:5, and Rev. 21:8.

6. This has been noted, also, by outsider observers. For example: "The Jews first invented the myth that only one religion can be true"—Sir Sarvepalli Radhakrishnan, *The World's Unborn Soul: an inaugural lecture delivered before the University of Oxford*, Oxford: Oxford University Press, 1936, p. 10.

7. *Yogavâsiṣṭha* 1:28. I have used the following text: *Srîmad-Vâlmîki-Mahârṣi-*

Praṇîtaḥ Yogavâsisṭhaḥ, Sanskrit text with the commentary *Vâsisṭhamahârâmânay-anatâtparayaprakâsa.* Ed. Vâsudeva Lakṣmana Pansîkar. 2nd edn. (Bombay: Tukârâm Jâvajî), 1978. Part 1, p. 144.

8. Cf. my "A Human View of Truth", *Studies in Religion/Sciences religieuses,* 1 (1971): 6–24, reprinted in John Hick, ed., *Truth and Dialogue: The Relationship between World Religions* (London: Sheldon, 1974) (= *Truth and Dialogue in World Religions: Conflicting Truth-Claims* [Philadelphia: Westminster, 1974]), pp. 20–44 (cf. pp. 156–62). Cf. also my introduction to the Propædia, Part 8, "Religion" ("Religion as Symbolism") in *The New Encyclopædia Britannica,* pp. 498–500; and other writings, from *The Meaning and End* to *Faith and Belief.*

9. To phrase the situation in this fashion is imperceptibly to take sides in a question of priorities; a question that many thoughtful human beings throughout history have answered differently from this. Or we may say: to use this wording is to make a concession to the current secular or secularized conviction, which sees the mundane as the primary, if indeed not the sole, dimension of human life. It would be asking perhaps too much from modern readers to say, " . . . this is in addition to their being in relation . . . ".

10. By both Luther and Calvin, among others.

11. This too I contended twenty-some years ago in my *Meaning and End of Religion;* for instance in its remark, "God . . . does not reveal a religion, He reveals Himself" (1963, 1978, p. 129; 1964, 1965, p. 117), and nothing in my observations or listening since has done anything but confirm that view. In this present study I have added that God does not reveal theologies.

12. One has to recognize that historically many Christians have derived considerable spiritual strength and emphasis from their conceptualization that they have been accorded quite special treatment by God, available to no one else in like measure (or in any measure); that the Church constitutes a decidedly chosen people. The case is similar with Muslims, and others. The positive aspects of this erstwhile notion have in modern times become quite overbalanced by the negative. Whatever its import in the past, its way of formulating the perception that various groups have of their place in the universe has become a millstone around our necks and must be thrown off—valid though the perception on which it was based, or the transcendent ground of that perception, in part be. This particular way of formulating one's grateful awareness that one's relation to God is (as it is always) special is to-day morally intolerable, politically disastrous, and theologically awry. Nonetheless, the widespread role of such exclusivist ("we/they") thinking in past human religious (and other) history requires study. For an understanding of the human condition, the theory's many forms have been too important to be shunted aside as without significance—even, religious significance.

5

The Cross and the Rainbow

Christ in a Multireligious Culture

STANLEY J. SAMARTHA

I

Although most Christians today are unwilling to take a totally negative attitude toward neighbors of other faiths, there seems to be a good deal of hesitation on the part of many to reexamine the basis of their exclusive claims on behalf of Christ. The place of Christ in a multireligious society becomes, therefore, an important issue in the search for a new theology of religions.

Theological claims have political consequences. This is particularly true in contemporary India where the exclusive claims made by any one particular community of faith affect its relationships with members of other communities of faith. Such claims make it difficult, if not impossible, for persons belonging to different religious traditions to live together in harmony and to cooperate for common purposes in society. Such claims, open or hidden, also raise basic theological questions concerning God's relationship to the whole of humanity, not just to one stream of it. Thus both historical pressures and theological imperatives demand a reexamination of all exclusivist claims.

Through the incarnation in Jesus Christ, God has relativized God's self in history. Christian theologians should therefore ask themselves whether they are justified in absolutizing in doctrine him whom God has relativized in history. Today's questions regarding the relationship of Jesus Christ to God are very different from those asked in earlier centuries. In many ways, they are new questions that need new solutions. These new solutions, however, must be theologically credible, spiritually satisfying, and pastorally helpful.

A process of rejecting exclusive claims and seeking new ways of understanding the relationship of Jesus Christ to God and humanity is already underway. From what may be described as "normative exclusivism," Christians are moving toward a position of "relational distinctiveness" of Christ, *relational* because Christ does not remain unrelated to neighbors of other faiths, and *distinctive* because, without recognizing the distinctiveness of the great religious traditions as different responses to the Mystery of God, no mutual enrichment is possible.

Such efforts toward a new Christian theology are taking place in India. Christian theological reflection in India obviously cannot be carried on in isolation and must take into account what is happening in different parts of the world church, but at the same time Indian theologians cannot go on as if, in the long centuries of religious life in India, there had been no theological reflection whatsoever on issues of interreligious relationships. More precisely, the Hindu response to religious pluralism should become a part of Indian Christian theological reflection. Thus, the interplay of these two factors—the ferment within the world church and the experience of religious life lived pluralistically in India—provides the context for the following reflections.

II

During the last two decades significant changes have taken place officially in Christian attitudes toward neighbors of other faiths. The well-known declaration of the Second Vatican Council, *Nostra Aetate* (1965), is regarded as "the first truly positive statement" of the Catholic Church about other religions.[1] Founded in 1948, the World Council of Churches moved rather slowly and somewhat reluctantly on this issue until, in 1971, it accepted an "interim" policy statement on other faiths. After nearly a decade of hard work, often marked by controversy, the WCC accepted in 1979 a theological statement and adopted a set of *Guidelines on Dialogue*, "welcoming the degree of agreement and mutual understanding represented by it among those who held different theological views." With regard to neighbors of other faiths, the statement said: "We feel able with integrity to assure our partners in dialogue that we come not as manipulators but as fellow-pilgrims."[2]

These attitudes are indeed strikingly different from those the Christian church persistently held during previous centuries. It is precisely at this point, however, that there now seems to be considerable hesitation as to what steps the church should take next in a continuously pluralistic world. It looks as if, having opened the door slightly, Christians are afraid that the strangers, long kept outside, might indeed turn out to be fellow pilgrims after all. What if the forbidden frontier turns out to be a welcoming threshold?

Since the mid-1960s there have indeed been many developments both in the Catholic Church and in the churches affiliated with the World Council of Churches. But many internal tensions have also developed. There are Catholic scholars who feel that the tensions regarding other religions are rooted within the official magisterium:

The failure adequately to explain what Vatican II means, and to square it either with Scripture or with the strong theological tradition that has seen other religions as idolatrous is serious. Unless the magisterium can do so convincingly, it will be under fire.[3]

Catholic scholars in India also feel that there is now a stalemate in interreligious dialogue, with participants repeating the same alternatives in various combinations, unwilling to move ahead.[4] Pope John Paul II convoked an extraordinary Synod of Bishops "to relive in some way the extraordinary atmosphere of the ecclesial communion during the Council [Vatican II]" and "to foster a further deepening and acceptance of Vatican II in the life of the church, especially in the light of new demands."[5] Inasmuch as some of the new demands are precisely in the area of relationship with neighbors of other faiths, one would hope for a more decisive turn in the attitude of the Catholic Church.

Within the World Council of Churches, given the variety and complexity of its membership and the very different theological positions represented within its wide spectrum of opinions, the tensions are even stronger, though not always openly articulated. With the many Evangelicals represented within the fellowship of the World Council of Churches, there is an unavoidable tension between mission and dialogue; yet the problem is even more complex than it appears, for there are tensions *within* the perceptions of mission itself and of dialogue itself. "Though it might *seem* that the tension between 'mission' and 'dialogue' has been resolved," writes Allan R. Brockway, "the real tension remains."[6] The massive studies now underway in ecumenical and evangelical circles on "Gospel and Culture" are important, but they can also become a way of avoiding the challenge and invitation of other religions by diverting resources toward a topic on which a great deal has already been said.[7] What is the substance of *culture*, particularly in Asian societies, without its *religious* dimensions? An essay on the elephant without reference to its ivory is incomplete, and can even be positively dangerous. Even though the theological issues have already been identified and questions for the study of other faiths formulated, there seems to be great reluctance to move ahead.[8]

With regard to conservative Evangelicals, it is difficult to talk about *next* steps when even the *first* steps have not been taken. One cannot ask a door to be opened *wider* when it is already latched from within, and chained. Given the evangelical assumption of the inerrancy of the Bible, it is hardly likely that any positive approach toward neighbors of other faiths will emerge in the coming years. Evangelicals' recent talk about "dialogue" with its *seeming* openness to members of other faiths is misleading. Dialogue is understood by them as a means to communicate the message. "The dialogic method is necessary if those who witness to Christ are to engage the minds of their listeners."[9] In "true" dialogue and encounter, it is claimed, "we seek both to disclose the inadequacies and falsities of non-Christian religions and to demonstrate the adequacy and truth, the absoluteness and finality of the Lord Jesus Christ."[10] It is the *instrumental* use of dialogue rather than its *intrinsic* worth as a living way of seeking new relationship in the household of God that is emphasized.

There are many reasons why, in this matter of interreligious encounter, Christians are unwilling to move beyond the positions they have already taken. Sometimes political and economic factors influence the attitude of one religious community toward others. Quite often, unexamined ideological assumptions prevent Christians from critically examining their traditional positions. But the major reason for the present impasse is the unresolved theological tension within the consciousness of the church about other religions.

To ask theological questions about this matter is to go to the very roots of our pluralistic existence today. To truly confront these questions, the study of religions has to be shifted from a *missiological* to a *theological* framework, particularly in our theological colleges and seminaries. The question is not *what* to do with so many other religions that claim the loyalty and devotion of millions of followers in the world, but *why* are they so persistently present providing meaning and direction to the lives of millions of our neighbors. What does this mean theologically—that is, for our understanding of God and God's relationship to the whole created *oikoumene*, of which Christians are not the only citizens? Can it be that plurality belongs to the very structure of reality? Or can it be that it is the will of God that many religions should continue in the world?

These are difficult questions indeed, and it may take a long time for the church to arrive at clear and unambiguous answers to them. The Western church took quite some time to come to terms with Copernicus and Darwin, with Freud and Jung, with science and technology, and is still struggling with Marx and Mao. The challenge and invitation of other religions may take even longer to elicit firm and clear answers. But beginnings have to be made lest the church look like a fortress to be defended rather than the household of God where strangers and sojourners can become fellow citizens.

III

In contemporary India a radical change in the Christian stance toward neighbors of other faiths is both an existential demand and a theological necessity. It is desperately needed when the unity and integrity of the country are in danger of being torn apart by forces of separation that are often influenced by the claims and counterclaims of diverse religions. And yet the search for new relationships between different religious communities is not just a matter of political adjustments or a redistribution of economic resources. Deep down, it is a theological question seeking to relate different responses to the Mystery of Truth.

By blaming the highly visible religious communities for the political and social ills of the country, one avoids a serious discussion about the spiritual and theological resources available within religions for the critical renewal of community life. No one would deny that religions have exploited persons and have contributed to much of the social injustice in India (as well as in other countries). In the struggle for a just society, established religions have often been on the side of the rich and the powerful, not that of the poor and the oppressed. Religions have been unable to tame political passions and, quite often, have added religious fuel to political conflagrations. Yet recent studies on communal clashes between Hindus and Sikhs (after the assassination of Mrs. Indira Gandhi) have brought out the point that religion "is not the *causative* factor but the *instrumental* factor in such clashes . . . it is made to appear as the causative factor."[11]

A secular "emptying" of religions in light of the role of religion in the real or imaginary ills of society would lead to a tremendous loss of creative power. It is very necessary to accept "the normative plurality" of India's life, and to provide space for dialogue between religious, linguistic, and ethnic groups. The contemporary contribution of India as a civilization to the meaning and content of democracy could be in the way India tolerates this initial babel of multicultural encounters that can lead to the creation of new communities, myths, and languages. The acceptance of plurality can well be an answer to fascism.[12]

Through long centuries of pluralistic existence India has developed a particular attitude toward religious dissent. A systematic and sympathetic study of this mood of "tolerance" is yet to be made.[13] But a few "moments" in India's long history can be profitably noted.

Already in the Vedic period about 1500 B.C.E., Brahmanism tried to solve the clash between the One and the many by suggesting that while *Sat* (Truth, Being) is One, sages call it by different names. It was not by eliminating the gods or by conquering them but by relating them to the One, and therefore to each other, that they were held together in a structure of difference rather than similarity. The One was greater than any of the gods or even the sum total of the gods. And even when the distinctiveness and legitimacy of different gods were recognized within an existential relationship, the ontological substance remained above and beyond the gods. Without recognizing and accepting this Mysterious Center (the *Satyasya Satyam*—The Truth of the Truth), genuine plurality is impossible.[14]

It took many centuries for Brahmanism, and later on for Hinduism, to "overcome" the challenge of the Buddha who rejected the authority of the Vedas, the superiority of the Brahmins, and the necessity of the sacrificial ritual. Now, however, the Buddha is "co-opted" into the Hindu structure of the *avataras*.[15] Later on, the *sampradāyas* (traditions connected with Vishnu, Siva, and Sakti) within Hinduism were held together in a larger framework, despite the tensions caused by different kings who followed different *sampradāyas*.[16]

If one takes a leap across the centuries, one encounters moments when Islam and later on Christianity, armed with their exclusive claims and allied with military, political, and economic power, rudely intruded into India's delicate balance of relationships. This created deep disturbances within Indian consciousness, the consequences of which are with us even to this day. The Hindu arguments against any claim of "uniqueness," "finality," or "once-for-allness" for one particular way are well known. Westerners, together with Indian Christians, are familiar with the English works of Ram Mohan Roy (1772–1833) and S. Radhakrishnan (1888–1975) on this subject.[17] The "Neo-Hindu" emphasis on the equality of all religions (*sarva dharma samanvaya tattva*) was probably more a *political affirmation* of the relationships between different religious communities at a time when political tensions were developing in the country rather than a *theological statement* on the relationships between religions. Perhaps, therefore, one should not attach too much theological significance to this emphasis. On the other hand, there is a body of writings in Sanskrit and other Indian languages that reflects more strongly the tolerant mood and feelings of the people in general; these writings remain a closed book to those who restrict themselves to the English language.[18]

It is worthwhile to note these orthodox Hindu arguments because they are influential even to this day. Basing themselves on two principles—*mataikya*, the unity of all religions, and *matavirodha*, their noncontradictoriness—the pandits advanced three arguments against the claim of Christian superiority. First, the plurality of religions is "intrinsic and purposeful" because of *dharma*. The basic differences in humankind make it natural and inevitable that there should be plurality, not singularity, in religion. In other words, plurality is rooted in the diversity of human nature itself. Secondly, there is the principle of *adhikāra* which may be translated aptitude, competence, eligibility, which makes plurality necessary. Birth is never accidental. It is the result of *karmic* repercussions. Therefore one is born in a particular religion because of the *sādhana* (discipline) possible for that particular person. Thirdly, this *adhikārabheda* (differences in aptitude or competence) is not a matter of choice but is a "given" element, even the will of God, and it allows persons to choose different *mārgās* (paths or ways). God defines one's *adhikara* by the attraction (*ruci*) one feels toward a certain *mārgā*. Hindus are Hindus rather than Christians because they have aptitude and eligibility only for their *dharma* and not for Christianity. Therefore the question of superiority or "uniqueness" of any one *dharma* over others does not arise. Criticism of one religion based on criteria derived from another is unwarranted. Conversions are unnecessary. The Hindus are not asking Christians to give up *their* commitment to God in Christ. Rather, they are pleading with Christians not to ask Hindus to give up *their* commitment. One should note that these arguments, so different from the later "neo-Hindu" affirmation of the equality of all religions, are *echoed* even to this day and have a *pervasive* influence on general Hindu consciousness.

Perhaps it is worthwhile to recall an even more recent moment in the history of India just after the nation's political independence (1947). Despite fresh memories of how their country was divided on religious grounds and torn by massive human sufferings, Hindus as the majority community were generous toward their minority neighbors—Muslims and Christians. In the Constituent

Assembly, working on a Constitution for the Republic of India, Loknath Mishra introduced an amendment that would delete the words "to propagate" from the Article on Fundamental Rights: "to profess, practice and propagate" one's religion (Article 25:1). During the debate, such well-known leaders as Pandit Lakshmikant Maitra, T. T. Krishnamachari, K. M. Munshi (vice-chancellor of the Bhavan University), and several others argued for retaining the words "to propagate" as a recognition of a fundamental right of minority communities. Without the support of Hindu leaders, the clause would have never passed. Soli Sorabji, a distinguished jurist, remarks, "One cannot but be struck by the broadmindedness and the spirit of tolerance and accommodation displayed by the founding fathers of the majority community towards their Christian brethren."[19] In no other country, therefore, does the claim for the "uniqueness" of one particular religious tradition or the assertion of the "normativeness" of one particular faith over others sound so rude, out of place, and theologically arrogant as in India. Such assertions contradict India's whole ethos and tear at the fabric of interreligious relationships so carefully woven during centuries of conflict, tension, and massive sufferings by the people.[20]

IV

In this context of ongoing life in India where Christians live and work together with neighbors of other faiths, where a deep-seated *theological* toler-ance coexists with *social* intolerance and is sometimes mixed with outbursts of *political* intolerance, can a christology be developed that is free from the burdens of the past but is unmistakably Christian and recognizably Indian?

Any attempt to formulate such a christology should take into account at least two factors that have emerged out of India's long history of multi-religious life. One is the acceptance of a sense of Mystery and the other the rejection of an exclusive attitude where ultimate matters are concerned. Mys-tery is not something to be used to fill the gaps in rational knowledge. Mystery provides the ontological basis for tolerance, which would otherwise run the risk of becoming uncritical friendliness. This Mystery, the Truth of the Truth (*Satyasya Satyam*), is the transcendent Center that remains always beyond and greater than apprehensions of it or even the sum total of those apprehensions. It is beyond cognitive knowledge (*tarka*) but it is open to vision (*drişti*) and intuition (*anubhava*). It is near yet far, knowable yet unknowable, intimate yet ultimate and, according to one particular Hindu view, cannot even be described as "one." It is "not-two" (*advaita*), indicating thereby that diversity is within the heart of Being itself and therefore may be intrinsic to human nature as well.

This emphasis on Mystery is not meant as an escape from the need for rational inquiry, but it does insist that the rational is not the only way to do theology; the mystical and the esthetic also have their necessary contributions to theology. Mystery lies beyond the theistic/nontheistic debate. Mystery is an ontological status to be accepted, not an epistemological problem to be solved. Without a sense of Mystery, *Theos* cannot remain *Theos*, nor *Sat* remain *Sat*, nor can Ultimate Reality remain ultimate.

In religious life, Mystery and meaning are related. Without a disclosure of meaning at particular points in history or in human consciousness, there can be no human response to Mystery. The history of religions shows that these responses are many and are different, sometimes even within a particular religious tradition. Quite often these differences are due to cultural and historical factors. Although each response to Mystery has a normative claim on the followers of that particular tradition, the criteria derived from one response cannot be made the norm to judge the responses of other traditions.

One strand of Hinduism, for example, has described this Mystery as *sat-cit-ānanda* (truth-consciousness-bliss). This is one way of responding to Mystery in a particular cultural setting that is very different from that of the early Christian centuries. Christians believe that in Jesus Christ the meaning of this Mystery is revealed in such a way as to constitute a revelation of God and to provide a way of salvation for all human beings. The doctrine of the Trinity, which describes God as Father, Son, and Holy Spirit, is an attempt to make sense of this Mystery through the meaning disclosed in Jesus of Nazareth, identified with Christ, and using categories from Greek thought alien to the Indian context.

Both the terms "Brahman" and "God" are culture-conditioned. One could as well use the term Mystery, which may be more acceptable. In this case the two statements—namely, that "Brahman is *sat-cit-ānanda*" and "God is triune, Father, Son, and Holy Spirit"—could be regarded as two responses to the same Mystery in two cultural settings. One cannot be used as a norm to judge the other. The limitations of language are obvious here. Feminist theologians have already objected to the "maleness" of the trinitarian formula; if cultural obstacles could be overcome, they might be persuaded to accept the Hindu notion, which avoids this problem. In any case, neither *sat-cit-ānanda* nor Trinity could, in linguistic terms, adequately describe the inner ontological working of Mystery. One could ask, therefore, on what grounds can it be claimed that the trinitarian formula offers a "truer" insight into the nature of Mystery than does *sat-cit-ānanda*? At best, the two formulations can only be symbolic, pointing to the Mystery, affirming the meaning disclosed, but retaining the residual depth.

No one could have anticipated in advance the presence of God in the life and death of Jesus of Nazareth. There is an incomprehensible dimension to it. That Jesus is the Christ of God is a confession of faith by the Christian community. It does indeed remain normative to Christians everywhere, but to make it "absolutely singular" and to maintain that the meaning of the Mystery is disclosed *only* in one particular person at one particular point, and nowhere else, is to ignore one's neighbors of other faiths who have other points of reference. To make exclusive claims for our particular tradition is not the best way to love our neighbors as ourselves.

If, then, human responses to the *revelation* of Mystery are plural and are articulated in different ways, the same observation applies to the experience of *salvation* as well, and to the manner in which it is articulated by followers of different religious traditions.

In multi-religious situations such as in India, the notions of "salvation" and of what we are saved from are understood differently. This is to be expected. The question here is not whether there *may be* plural ways of salvation. In multireligious situations the fact is that there *are* plural ways of salvation, experienced and articulated in different ways. Both the context and expression of salvation are different. When the questions asked about the human predicament are different, the answers are bound to be different. How can it be otherwise? Already in the New Testament salvation through Jesus Christ was experienced and interpreted differently by the Aramaic-speaking Jewish Christians, the Hellenic Jews of the diaspora who were much more open to other peoples among whom they lived, and the non-Jewish Christians such as the Greeks, Syrians, and Romans who had no part in the Jewish "history of salvation." And yet, there was no doubt about the root of this experience of salvation in Jesus Christ.

Whereas Christians use the term "sin" to describe the human predicament, Hindus might use *avidyā* (ignorance) and Buddhists *dukkha* (sorrow) as the condition from which deliverance is sought. The notions of *moksha* and *nirvana* as the ultimate goals of deliverance are conceived differently, as also the *sādhana*s, the ways of discipline, advocated as necessary to attain these goals. In addition, today one must also take into account the desperate desire of millions of human beings for salvation of a different kind—namely, liberation from oppression, exploitation, and injustice. In this context, many feminist Christian theologians decline to accept as normative the notion of a revelation and salvation through a male person that excludes more than half of humanity.

Where alternative ways of salvation have provided meaning and purpose for millions of persons in other cultures for more than two or three thousand years, to claim that the Judeo-Christian-Western tradition has the *only* answer to all problems in all places and for all persons in the world is presumptuous, if not incredible. This is not to deny the *validity* of the Christian experience of salvation in Jesus Christ, but it is to question the *exclusive* claims made for it by Christians, claims that are unsupported by any evidence in history, or in the institutional life of the church, or in the lives of many Christians who make such claims. If salvation comes *from God*—and for Christians it cannot be otherwise—then possibilities should be left open to recognize the validity of other experiences of salvation.

The nature of Mystery is such that any claim on the part of one religious community to have exclusive or unique or final knowledge becomes inadmissible. Exclusiveness puts fences around the Mystery. It creates dichotomies between the divine and the human, between humanity and nature, and between different religious communities. It leaves little room for the nonrational elements in religious life—the mystical and the esthetic, rituals and symbols, prayer, worship, and meditation. It is not surprising that very often Christian theologians ready to discuss religious "ideas" with others feel extremely uneasy when it comes to matters of "worship" or art in interreligious meetings (*satsang*—fellowship of truth). Further, those who make open or hidden claims of exclusiveness find it impossible to live together with neighbors of other faiths except on very superficial social levels. A one-way, exclusivistic "proclamation" is like a stone hurled into a flowing stream. It makes a little splash, and then remains submerged, and makes no difference whatsoever to the waters flowing past it. Someone might even pick it up and hurl it back to where it came from.

Very often, claims for the "normativeness" of Christ are based on the authority of the Bible. Exclusive texts are hurled back and forth as if just by uttering texts from scriptures the problem is settled. The authority of the Bible is indeed important for Christians. In the multireligious situations, where there are other scriptures whose authority is accepted by neighbors of other religious traditions, how can the claims based on one particular scripture become the norm, or authority for all? Here, too, the plurality of scriptures is a fact to be accepted, not a notion to be discussed.

But there are even more important factors to be recognized. For example, what does one make of the fact, hardly recognized by Christian theologians, that none of the revelations on which Christians theologize today took place in a West European context or were written down in a West European language? Recent studies in the ontology of language point out how precarious it is to depend on texts and translations when it comes to the question of authority in matters of faith.[21]

Even notions of "authority" are different when it comes to interpreting holy scriptures. To the Hindu and the Buddhist, the authority of the scriptures does not depend on the *writtenness* of the text, but on *hearing* and *seeing* the word (*Śabda*). Texts are indeed important. But a Hindu or Buddhist would reject the notion that through the study of texts one can encounter the truth behind them, or that merely by quoting texts one can encounter the truth within them, or that merely by quoting texts truth is communicated to hearers. Knowledge of God is not something to be *dis-covered* through the study of written texts. It is to be *re-covered* through *hearing*. The holiness of words is intrinsic. One participates in it not through understanding but through reciting and hearing it.

The Western notion of editing an *original* text is an intrusion into Eastern situations. One has to go behind the written texts to the *sound* of the Word, recited and heard over long periods of time by the community, in order to see how words have functioned religiously in matters of faith. This question of hermeneutics in multireligious situations needs careful study. In India, around 35–32 B.C.E., Buddhists were the first to commit their sacred oral texts to writing. Attempts are now being made by Indian Christian biblical scholars to study Hindu and Buddhist hermeneutical theory as it has developed over the centuries, and to work out the implications of Eastern hermeneutics for the Indian Christian theological enterprise.[22]

If the great religious traditions of humanity are indeed different responses to the Mystery of God or *Sat* or the Transcendent or Ultimate Reality, then the *distinctiveness* of each response, in this instance the Christian, should be stated in such a way that a mutually critical and enriching *relationship* between different responses becomes naturally possible. Exclusiveness regards universality as the extension of its own particularity and seeks to conquer other faiths. Inclusiveness, though seeming generous, actually co-opts other faiths without their leave. Both exclusiveness and its patronizing cousin inclusiveness may even be forms of theological violence against neighbors of other faiths and, when combined with economic, political, and military power, as has often happened in history, become dangerous to communal harmony and world peace. It is not without significance that only after the second world war (1945), when, with the dismantling of colonialism, new nations emerged on the stage of history and asserted their identity through their own religions and cultures, that both the Vatican and the World Council of Churches began to articulate a more positive attitude toward peoples of other religious traditions, although both church bodies remained reluctant to recognize the *theological* significance of these other faiths.

In moving beyond exclusiveness and inclusiveness, Christians must come to a clearer grasp of the uniqueness of Jesus. The distinctiveness of Jesus Christ does not lie in claiming that "Jesus Christ is God." This amounts to saying that Jesus Christ is the tribal god of Christians over against the gods of other peoples. Elevating Jesus to the status of God or limiting Christ to Jesus of Nazareth are both temptations to be avoided. The former runs the risk of an impoverished "Jesusology" and the latter of becoming a narrow "Christomonism." A theocentric christology avoids these dangers and becomes more helpful in establishing new relationships with neighbors of other faiths.

A theocentric (or Mystery-centered) christology is not a new fashion. The Bible continually emphasizes the priority of God, and Jesus himself was theocentric. In recent years, within the Indian and the broader world church, discussion of this question has begun. The issues were earlier hinted at or articulated by certain Christian theologians in different parts of the world. Both in the Catholic Church and in the churches affiliated with the World Council of Churches, new dimensions of this christologico-ecumenical issue are taking shape. On one level, the discussions seem to be within a parochial Christian ecumenical framework, seeking to accommodate different Christian viewpoints. On another level, however, the implications of these new christological insights go far beyond the narrow confines of Christians to the deeper and larger ecumenism that embraces the whole of humanity. In discussions in different parts of the world, a new hermeneutics is developing, a hermeneutics willing to read and hear biblical texts about Jesus in ways quite different from those of the West.

In the West, the International Theological Commission appointed by the pope admits no distinction between christology and theology. And yet it states that "*confusion* between christology and theology results if one supposes that the name of God is totally unknown outside of Jesus Christ and that there exists no other theology than that which arises from the Christian revelation." The commission thus opens the possibility of recognizing theologies other than Christian. The statement goes on to call the church to cooperate with others in order "to participate in building a civilization of love."[23]

Also in the World Council of Churches, fresh discussions have started on "the inner core" of its basic credal affirmation that "the Lord Jesus Christ is God and Savior." Throughout the council's history, questions have been raised about the adequacy of this formulation. On the one hand, New Testament scholars have pointed out that the statement identifying Jesus Christ with God goes beyond the witness of the New Testament. On the other, Catholic and Orthodox theologians have felt that the statement is narrowly "christomonistic" and needs a full-fledged trinitarian emphasis. More recently, additions have been made to the original phrasing.[24] In the present discussion, two factors have become important: the christological question is being raised against the background of renewed dialogue with adherents of other faiths and of cooperation with persons of secular convictions who are struggling against the forces of death and destruction. The ontological equation of Jesus Christ with God would scarcely allow any serious discussion with neighbors of other faiths or with secular humanists.[25]

Throughout the Bible the priority of God is taken for granted. The affirmation that God is the creator of all life and of all humanity puts Christians and their neighbors of other faiths together at the very source of life. God breathes life into humanity (Gen. 2:7) and in doing so entrusts to it responsibility for all created life (Gen. 2:15). God lets men and women share in the divine power to create life (Gen. 4:1). Life is God's gift, and human beings have the duty and responsibility to cherish and guard it.

This belief in the ontological priority of God is also taken for granted by Jesus Christ and his hearers in the New Testament. He started his ministry by declaring that "the time is fulfilled, and the kingdom of God is at hand" (Mark 1:14). New Testament writers emphasize God's initiative over and over again. "God so loved the world that he gave his only begotten son" (John 3:16). "God was in Christ reconciling the world to himself" (2 Cor. 5:19). God set forth in Christ "a plan for the fulness of time, to unite all things in him" (Eph. 1:10). "And when all things are subjected to him, then the son also will be subjected to him who put all things under him that God may be all in all" (1 Cor. 15:28). This acknowledgment that God is the Creator and Redeemer of all life enables the entire world, the whole of humanity, to be included in the struggle for life and to feel responsible for its preservation and its continuation. God, in the sense of *Sat* or Mystery or the Transcendent or Ultimate Reality, is the ultimate horizon over the ocean of life. God's covenant with all humanity, of which the rainbow is a timeless symbol, has never been abrogated.[26]

A theocentric christology provides more theological space for Christians to live together with neighbors of other faiths. "Christomonism" does not do full justice to the total evidence of the New Testament, nor does it give sufficient emphasis to the trinitarian dimension of the Christian faith. It tends to minimize the work of the Holy Spirit in the lives of others. The Orthodox rejection of the *filioque* clause in the description of the procession of the Holy Spirit in the Nicene Creed—that is, its insistence that the Spirit proceeds from the Father and *not* from the Son—has far-reaching ecumenical significance. To draw attention to these points is not to minimize the centrality of Jesus Christ in Christian faith, but to put him more clearly into the structure of trinitarian faith. New insights contributed by biblical studies and research on the great christological councils of the church (Nicea 325 C.E. and Chalcedon 451 C.E.) help us better understand how God is in Jesus Christ and how Jesus Christ is related to God. Christocentrism without theocentrism leads to idolatry.

A theocentric christology provides a basis for retaining the Mystery of God while acknowledging the *distinctiveness* of Jesus Christ. It makes commitment to God in Jesus Christ possible without taking a negative attitude toward neighbors of other faiths, and at the same time it offers a more comprehensive conceptual framework for dialogue with these neighbors. Removing the *threat* implicit in one-way proclamations, it offers an *invitation* to all to share in the abundant riches of God. It makes dialogue a normal way of relationship between persons of different faiths instead of artificially contriving to make it a mode of communication. It helps to shift the emphasis from a *normative* to a *relational* attitude toward neighbors of other faiths. New relationships may have to be sought through recognizing *differences* rather than through seeking *similarities*. It helps avoid the dichotomies between "we" and "they" or those on "the inside" and those on "the outside."

The theocentric circle includes the christocentric circle. It makes it possible to recognize the theological significance of other revelations and other experiences of salvation, a point that for many Christian theologians is frightfully difficult even to admit. Theocentrism allows for an evolving quest for the meaning of Jesus Christ in which neighbors of other faiths can also participate, as in fact they already do, thus opening for Christians undreamt-of possibilities of enriching others and being enriched by them. Further, theocentrism grounds cooperation not on expediency, but on *theology*, providing a vision of participating with all human beings in God's continuing mission in the world, seeking to heal the brokenness of humanity, overcoming the fragmentation of life, and bridging the rift between nature, humanity, and God.

V

Exclusive claims isolate the community of faith from neighbors of other faiths, creating tensions and disturbing relationships within the larger community. But when the *distinctiveness* of a particular faith is stated in a manner that avoids open or hidden exclusiveness, then meaningful *relationships* between different communities become possible. This has been happening throughout the history of different religions in the multireligious life of India. It is unfortunate that Christian theologians, including Indians, have failed to recognize the significance of such relationships for the shaping of an emerging theology of religions.

Perhaps one reason for this failure is the stranglehold of propositional theology and its methodology on the minds of most Christian theologians. This is not to minimize the need for and the importance of serious, rational theological work; rather, it points out that to exclude the cultural, the mystical, and the esthetic from the experience of interreligious relationships is to seriously impoverish theology. Such a claim is based on an understanding of theology as critical reflection on God's relationship to humanity and nature, history and the cosmos.

Nowhere else than in India, perhaps, is the importance of the esthetic more manifest, for here we find that the distinctiveness of Jesus Christ is expressed through art by persons who do not necessarily belong to the visible Christian community. India might well be the only place where persons of other faiths, without crossing over the visible boundaries that separate them from Christians, have related themselves to Jesus Christ through art, thus breaking down the walls of exclusiveness. These artists, standing outside the confines of institutional Christianity, make evident that it is not the dogmas and doctrines about Christ or the institutions of the church that have touched the heart and mind of India, but the life and teachings of Jesus of Nazareth, his death and resurrection, the illumination he has brought into the Mystery of God, and the transforming power he has introduced into human life, as he invites all persons to move from self-centeredness to God-centeredness. He is indeed *jivan-muktā,* one who is truly liberated in life, and therefore able to liberate others.

Visitors to India are often struck by the responses that followers of other faiths have made to Jesus Christ through the religious dimensions of art— literature, poetry, and drama in the different languages of India (including English), as well as painting, movies, and television. Jesus Christ seems to move beyond the structures of the church, with its dogmas and doctrines about his person, in order to establish new relationships with adherents of other faiths. There seems to be an "unbaptized *koinonia*" outside the gates, which the church is most reluctant to recognize or even talk about. One must indeed be careful not to exaggerate such phenomena. But neither should their importance be minimized nor their theological significance for developing new relationships with neighbors of other faiths be rejected rudely and hastily.

Over the centuries there have been many examples of this influence of Christ beyond the confines of the church. Among the more recent ones is Manjeshwar Govinda Pai, a noted Hindu poet who won the national award for literature some years ago. His well-known and lengthy poem *Golgotha* is marked by literary beauty, depth of religious perception, and a sensitive understanding of the crucifixion of Jesus Christ.[27] Muliya Keshavayya, a Hindu lawyer, wrote a drama on the life of Christ with the title *Mahā Chētana* ("Great Energy"), bringing out the compassion of Christ toward the poor, and the power of his cross and resurrection.[28] Gopal Singh, a well-known Sikh scholar and diplomat, wrote a poem entitled *The Man Who Never Died*.[29] The poet has the risen Christ speak these lines:

> But, he said unto those that believe
> that nothing dies in the realm of God—
> neither seed, nor drop, nor dust, nor man.
> Only the past dies or the present,
> but the future lives for ever.
> And I am the future of man.
> To me, being and non-being were always one.
> I always was and never was![30]

Many Hindu and Muslim artists have been inspired by themes in the life of Jesus Christ, particularly his sufferings, death, and resurrection. According to Jyoti Sahi, a noted Christian artist, Indian Christian art was initiated not by Christian, but by Hindu artists. For example, there is the well known painting of the Last Supper by Jamini Roy of Calcutta. More recently, well-known Hindu and Muslim artists like Hebbar, Panikker, Hussain, Khanna and others have painted many themes from the life of Christ.[31] All this might well be regarded as "signs" of the increasing "traffic across the borders," helping to develop new relationships between persons of different religious communities and bringing out new meanings in christology.

There can be no exclusiveness in art. By evoking feelings of reverence and joy and gratefulness, it transforms human feelings and gives to those who participate in it a sense of inner peace, *shānti*. It liberates persons from feelings of possessiveness. Some of these examples, and there are many more, make it clear although Christianity belongs to Christ, Christ does not belong to Christianity. This kind of art by Hindu or Sikh or Muslim neighbors mediates the mystery of Christ to Christians in new ways, different from those of the West, and builds deeper relationships between members of different faiths. This form of art should be regarded as at least one of the new ways of bringing out the relational distinctiveness of Jesus Christ, the theological implications of which have yet to be worked out. To ignore it would be disastrous to future interreligious relationships.

When theological debates end in sterile apologetics, when social relationships between different religious communities become superficial or degenerate into sullen coexistence, when economic sharing becomes a matter of profit and loss, and when political cooperation in the life of a nation becomes difficult, if not impossible, because of narrow communal interests, quite often it is esthetic experience that provides the bridge for deeper relationships between persons of different faiths. It does not always happen, and when it does indeed happen, it is mostly by the few on behalf of the many. Nevertheless, art combines truth and grace and, in generosity of spirit, through color and sound and symbol and image, it mediates Mystery to a broken humanity. Through participation in art focused on Christ and the experience of enjoying it, the walls of exclusiveness are broken down and new relationships established between persons of different faiths in the larger community.

NOTES

1. Karl Rahner, "Basic Theological Interpretations of the Second Vatican Council," in *Concern for the Church* (New York: Crossroad, 1981), pp. 81–82.

2. *Guidelines on Dialogue* (Geneva: World Council of Churches, 1982), pp. iv, 11.

3. William R. Burrows, "Tensions within the Catholic Magisterium about Mission and Other Religions," *The International Bulletin of Missionary Research*, 9 (1985) 3. The same point is made by other Catholic scholars. Paul Knitter remarks that "Christians should seriously consider whether this opening has been toward more abundant life or has now arrived at dead ends" ("Roman Catholic Approaches to Other Religions: Developments and Tensions," *International Bulletin of Missionary Research,* 8 (1984) 53.

4. See *Jeevadhara*, vol. 9, no. 65, September–October 1981 (Theology Centre, Kottayam, India). The whole issue is on "Inter-Religious Dialogue Today." See also John B. Chethimattam, "Christian Theology and Other Religions," *Jeevadhara*, 8 (1978) 352–66.

5. Quoted in "The Extraordinary Synod" (editorial), *Vidyajyoti*, 49 (1985) 106.

6. "Questions after Vancouver," *Ecumenical Review*, 36 (1984) 184, emphasis added.

7. See *International Review of Mission*, vol. 74, no. 294, April 1984. The entire issue is on the theme "Gospel and Culture."

8. See *Guidelines on Dialogue*, pp. 12–13, for a list of concerns and study questions. It must be pointed out, however, that the WCC Working Group on Dialogue, in its March 1985 meeting, decided to launch a substantial study extending over a period of four to five years on the theological significance of other faiths.

9. Arthur F. Glasser, "A Paradigm Shift? Evangelicals and Inter-Religious Dialogue," *Contemporary Theologies of Mission*, Arthur F. Glasser and Donald A. MacGavran, eds. (Grand Rapids: Baker Book House, 1983), p. 206.

10. John Stott, "Dialogue, Encounter, Even Confrontation" in *Faith Meets Faith: Mission Trends No. 5*, Gerald H. Anderson and Thomas F. Stransky, eds. (New York: Paulist Press, 1981), p. 168.

11. Asghar Ali Engineer, "Bombay—Bhiwandi Riots in National Political Perspective," *Economic and Political Weekly*, 19 (1984) 1134ff. "Communalism is a modern phenomenon with medieval trappings to enhance its national appeal. The use of medieval symbolism ensures a relative autonomy to it . . . and creates the illusion in the minds of common people about the causative efficacy of religion in the whole conflict" (p. 1136). Muslim, Hindu, Sikh, and Christian writers, political scientists, sociologists, and theologians have emphasized this point, which should not be forgotten lest religions be blamed for all the ills of Indian society. See also Kishan Swarup Thapar, "Genesis of Partition," *Mainstream* (New Delhi), August 18, 1984, pp. 10ff.; S. Tasmin Ahmed, "Second Thoughts on Secular Democracy," ibid., pp. 15ff.; Nirmal Srinivasan, "Majority Communalism versus Minority Communalism: Is It a Threat to Indian Secularism?," *Religion and Society*, 30 (1983) 138–46 (Christian Institute for the Study of Religion and Society, Bangalore). Bipan Chandra in a major study clarifies "the misconception of religion as the sole determinant of communalism" in *Communalism*

in Modern India (New Delhi: Vikas Publishing House, 1984), p. 165. "Communalism was the false consciousness of the historical process of the last 150 years because, objectively, no real conflict between the interests of Hindus and Muslims existed. . . . Seeing religion as the main inner contradiction in social, economic, and political life was certainly an aspect of false consciousness" (ibid., p. 167).

12. Rajni Kothari and Shiv Vishwanath, "Moving out of 1984: A Critical Review of Major Events," *Mainstream Annual: India, 1984* (New Delhi), January 1985, no. 305, p. 31.

13. See the long footnote by Wilfred Cantwell Smith in *Faith and Belief* (Princeton University Press, 1979): "The famed 'religious tolerance' of Hindus, their acceptance in principle of pluralism as something not merely inescapable but right and proper, has become explicit as a formulated affirmation only gradually and especially perhaps in relatively recent times. . . . The spirit of recognizing religious life as polymorphic is, however, ancient in India" (p. 215). See also Hajime Nakamura, *Ways of Thinking of Eastern Peoples*, Philip Wiener, ed. (Honolulu: East-West Center Press, 1978), p. 170: "Generally speaking *we cannot find in any Indian religion the conception of the 'heretic'* in the sense of Western usage."

14. In its original context it was a problem that arose within the Brahmanic consciousness, although even to this day this solution is suggested as a way out of tensions between different religions. The full text reads: "They call him (*Sat*) Indra, Mitra, Varuna, Agni, or the heavenly sun-bird Garutmat. / The seers call in many ways that which is One; / they speak of Agni, Yama, Matarisvan" (*Rig Veda*, I, 164, 46). In another well-known verse, when the sage Yajnavalkya was asked: "How many gods are there, O Yajnavalkya?," the long answer leads the student through the many to just the One—and yet, not just the One, but the One without a second (*Ekam Evādvitīyam. Brihad*, III, 9, 1–9, and *Chandogya*, VI, 2, 1–3. See *Sources of Indian Tradition*, Theodore de Bary, ed. (New York: Columbia University Press, 1958), pp. 5ff.

15. See Lal Mani Joshi, *Studies in the Buddhist Culture of India* (Delhi: Motilal Banarsidas, 1977), pp. 177–78. There are others who maintain that the ideas of Buddhism are not original but are dependent on Hinduism, e.g., T. M. P. Mahadevan, *Gaudapada: A Study in Early Advaita* (Madras: Madras University Press, 1960), pp. 84, 226. Radhakrishnan argues that what the Buddha did was "to democratise the lofty teachings of the Upanishads" (S. Radhakrishnan, *Indian Philosophy*, vol. I, [London: Allen and Unwin, 1931, 2nd ed.], p. 471). Although it is extremely difficult to reconstruct past relationships between different religious communities, and one should be careful not to exaggerate the "tolerance" of Hindus, it remains true that when two Chinese travelers, Fa-Hein (5th century C.E.) and Hieuen-Tsang (7th century C.E.) traveled in India they reported that Buddhism was flourishing in northern India with several kings as its patrons. In spite of continuing tensions, "Mutual toleration of prevailing faiths was the general rule of the country during the Gupta period" (7th century C.E.) (*History and Culture of the Indian People*, vol. 3, R.C. Majumadar, ed., [Bombay: Bharatiya Vidya Bhavan, 1964], p. 397).

16. The *Bhagavad Gita*, faced with the possibility of many *mārgās* (paths to God), suggested that those who worship other gods, in reality worship Krishna alone, but *not properly* (IXX:23) or worship him but *unknowingly* (IX:24). Does not this remind one of certain Christian attitudes today? The *Gita* goes even further. Krishna says, "Whatever form any devotee wishes to worship, I make that faith of his steady" (VII:21). Also, "in whatever way persons approach Me, in the same way do I accept them" (IV:11). If Christians can speak of the "unknown Christ of Hinduism," the Hindus too

can talk of the "unknown Krishna of Christianity." See Daya Krishna, "Religion and the Critical Consciousness," *New Quest* (Bombay), July-August, 1978, p. 144.

17. Perhaps one has to reassess the lasting effect of the movement led by Ram Mohan Roy in this last regard. Mulk Raj Anand, the noted novelist, remarks that the Samaj movements led by Ram Mohan Roy, "passed over the ocean of Hinduism and produced some ripples but no deep currents" (quoted by Guru Dutt in an article entitled "Will Hinduism Survive?," in *Bulletin* [Institute of World Culture] [Bangalore], 5 [1985] 1ff.).

18. In recent years, much valuable research of Sanskrit works has been done. See, e.g., the excellent work by Richard Fox Young, *Resistant Hinduism: Sanskrit Sources on Anti-Christian Apologetics in Early Nineteenth Century India* (Leiden: Brill, 1981). In the year 1839 John Muir, a servant of the East India Company, published a volume in Sanskrit entitled *Mataparīksa*. It consisted of 379 terse lines in the form of a dialogue between a guru and a *sishya* to prove the superiority of Christianity as the only way. Three conservative Hindu pandits took up the challenge and published their answers, also in Sanskrit, because at that time Sanskrit was still the language of scholarship and theological discourse. These were *Mataparīksasīksā* (1839), by Somanatha (Subaji Bapu); *Mataparikṣottara* (1840) by Harachandra Tarkapancanana; and *Śastratāt-tvavinirnaya* (1844–1845) by Nilankanta Goreh. This exchange was a genuinely theological and philosophical debate reflecting a serious attempt to come to grips with the central claims of Christianity and the mood of Hinduism. It was probably far more influential on the minds of people than the English controversy between Ram Mohan Roy and the Serampore missionaries.

19. In an article entitled "Politics" in the *Illustrated Weekly of India*, January 27–February 2, 1946, p. 34. The Constituent Assembly was formed on December 9, 1946. The draft constitution, prepared by the committee headed by Dr. B. R. Ambedkar, was submitted to the Assembly on February 21, 1948. The amendment to delete the word "propagate" was forcefully pressed by Loknath Mishra on the ground that "religious propagation had been responsible for the unfortunate division of the country into India and Pakistan and that its incorporation as a fundamental right would not therefore be proper" (ibid, p. 34).

20. Lest this be misunderstood as an uncritical exaggeration of Hindu "tolerance," it should be pointed out that there are Hindu organizations that indeed manifest a decidedly "intolerant" attitude toward other religions. The Arya Samaj, the Rama-krishna Mission, Rashtriya Svayam Sevak Sangh, the Vishwa Hindu Parishad, and many others are not particularly tolerant of Muslim and Christian efforts to convert Hindus. Earlier, Hindu violence was directed at Jains, particularly in the 8th century C.E. See Burton Stein, *Peasant State and Society in Medieval South India* (Delhi: Oxford University Press, 1980), p. 80; Romila Thapar, "Syndicated Moksha?," *Seminar: The Hindus and Their Isms* (New Delhi), no. 313, September 1985, pp. 14-22. There has indeed been violent and intolerant resistance to Islam and Christianty, but these were often defensive reactions against both the religious and political implications of conversions. I have drawn pointed attention to these movements in some of my writings, such as "Indian Realities and the Wholeness of Christ," *Missiology*, 10 (1982) 301-17; "Dialogue and the Politicisation of Religions in India," *International Bulletin of Missionary Research*, 8 (1984) 104ff.; "Dialog statt Kreuzzug," *Evangelische Kommentar*, February 1985, pp. 75–77.

21. See Charles H. Craft and Tom N. Wisely, eds., *Readings in Dynamic Indigeneity* (Pasadena: Wm. Carey Library, 1979), pp. 259f.; Jacques Derrida, *Writings and Differences*, Alan Bass, tr. (University of Chicago Press, 1978), pp. 280ff., Paul

Ricoeur, *Essays in Biblical Interpretation* (Philadelphia: Fortress Press, 1980), p. 4.

22. See *Seminar on Non-Biblical Scriptures*, D. S. Amalorpavadass, ed. (Bangalore: National Biblical-Catechetical-Liturgical Centre, 1974), p. 707. I have just completed a manuscript on "The Search for New Hermeneutics in Asian Christian Theology" (59 pp.), drawing attention to the attempts being made in diffferent countries in Asia to shake off dependence on Western hermeneutics and work toward a more relevant Asian Christian hermeneutics. See also Gopinath Kaviraj, *Aspects of Indian Thought* (Burdwan: University of Burdwan, 1967), pp. 41 ff.; G. Kashikar, *Preface to Rigveda Samhita* (with the commentary of Sayana), N. S. Sontakka and G. Kashikar, eds., vol. 4, (Poona: Poona Vaidika Samsadhan Mandala, 1946); Thomas B. Coburn, "Scriptures in India: Towards a Typology of the Word in Hindu Life," *Journal of the American Academy of Religion*, 52 (1984) 435ff.

23. The International Theological Commission appointed by the pope in 1969 has brought out two volumes on this matter: *Select Questions of Christology* (1980), and *Theology, Christology, Anthropology* (1983), both published by the Publications Office, United States Catholic Conference, Washington, D.C. The quotations given above are from *Theology, Christology, Anthropology*, pp. 3 and 11.

24. The full text now reads: "The World Council of Churches is a fellowship of churches which confess the Lord Jesus Christ as God and Savior according to the Scriptures and therefore seek to fulfil together their common calling to the glory of God, Father, Son and Holy Spirit." See "Ecumenical Foundations: A Look at the WCC Basis," *One World* (Geneva), no. 107, July 1985, p. 11.

25. Vol. 37, no. 2 of *Ecumenical Review*, April 1985, is devoted to a discussion of the WCC basis. Two writers, Konrad Raiser and Werner Loeser, S. J., draw pointed attention to the need to take into account the dialogue with persons of other faiths in this connection. Raiser describes this as one of the two "crucial challenges" (p. 18) and Loeser observes that the most central question here is "that of the picture of God" (p. 237). Thomas Stransky goes even further in calling for "a basis beyond the basis." He repeatedly refers to Jesus Christ as "Lord and Savior" rather than "God and Savior" (p. 21).

26. A far more careful and systematic exegesis of related texts within a new hermeneutical framework is called for here. New Testament scholars identify five texts in this connection: Titus 2:13; John 1:18; John 5:20; Romans 9:5; and 2 Peter 1:1. In the text from Titus the use of a single word in the original Greek alters the meaning: "the appearing of the glory of *our* great God and Savior Jesus Christ." The alternative reading, equally justified on the basis of the Greek text, would be: "*our* great God and *our* Savior Jesus Christ." Even Paul with his radical christocentrism is extremely careful in his christocentric statements. He reminds the Corinthians, "You belong to Christ, Christ belongs to God" (1 Cor. 3:23). "The total Christian faith, as reflected in the New Testament, is essentially and primarily theistic, that is to say monotheistic, and secondarily Christological" (F. C. Grant, *Ancient Judaism and the New Testament* [New York: Macmillan, 1959], p. 130). For a fuller discussion, see A. W. Martin, " 'Well Done, Good and Faithful Servant?' Once More the W.C.C. Basis," *Journal of Ecumenical Studies* 18 (1981) 251–66. Referring to "the continued use of a seemingly heretical formula," Martin asks: "Is it time to retire the formula with the judgement of more or less 'well done'?" (p. 266).

27. Manjeshwar Govinda Pai, *Golgotha* (Mangalore: Baliga and Sons, 1948). It was written in Kannada, the language of Karnataka, one of the southern states, spoken by about 36 million persons.

28. Muliya Keshavayya, *Mahā Chētana: A Drama on the Life of Christ* (Mangalore: Kodialbail Press, 1976).

29. Gopal Singh, *The Man Who Never Died* (London: Macmillan, 1969). The poem has also been published in German translation.

30. Ibid., p. 77.

31. Jyoti Sahi, "Trends of Indigenisation and Social Justice in Indian Christian Art," *Indian Journal of Theology*, 31 (1982) 89–95. See also Masao Takenaka, "Christian Art in Asia: Signs of Renewal," in *Asian Christian Theology*, Douglas J. Elwood, ed. (Philadelphia: Westminster Press, 1980, rev. ed.), p. 169.

6

The Jordan, the Tiber, and the Ganges

Three Kairological Moments of Christic Self-Consciousness

RAIMUNDO PANIKKAR

*Does one need to be spiritually a Semite or
intellectually a Westerner in order to be a Christian?*

THE DILEMMA

In this chapter, I should like to present a general picture of what I have been doing and saying for almost half a century regarding the question of what it means today to be a Christian.[1] Recognizing that my experiences and encounters are too numerous to recall,[2] and leaving aside strictly theological problems, I shall limit myself to a more general philosophical description of the present Christian situation.[3] If it is true that humankind is facing a mutation in our times, contemporary theological reflection can no longer legitimately proceed with its usual categories. The problems are different; the very questions, let alone the answers, need rethinking. This is what has prompted me to call not for a Vatican III but for a Second Council of Jerusalem. For this we need a certain vision of the state of the world and a certain inner-Christian perspective. I shall limit myself here to the latter.

The history of the Christian tradition in its relation to other religions could be symbolized by the three sacred rivers in the title of this chapter. Jesus was baptized in the Jordan, the *Hâ Yârdên,* the *Nahr al-Urdunn.*[4] The waters of the

Jordan cannot be washed away from the Body of Christ—that is, from Christians.[5] Christian tradition shows an indelibly Jewish origin. Jesus, the apostles, and the evangelists were all Jews. Without a certain Jewish spirituality the Gospels are incomprehensible. By spirituality I understand a set of *basic attitudes* prior to their manifestation in *theories,* or their unfolding in *praxis.* So we face a question: Can there be a single universal spirituality—that is, a basic human attitude that is both universal and concrete? Does a Jewish-based spirituality offer such a possibility? Is the Jordan *the* river, as the Egyptians called the Nile?

Such theoretical questions have to be considered in light of the twenty centuries of Christian history equally marked by the waters of another sacred river, the Tiber, *il Tevere.* Peter and Paul died on its shores. There, too, they had a historical resurrection. Without Rome, Christianity is also incomprehensible, even in its anti-Roman aspects. The Mediterranean is the Christian sea, the *mare nostrum,* "our sea." Present-day Christianity is a more or less harmoniously blended complex of Jewish heritage with Helleno-Roman-Gothico-Western elements. My point here is that we should neither overlook nor absolutize this fact. Christianity is the religion of these two rivers. We cannot do without them. But must it remain so?

If *spiritually* Christianity cannot dispense with Judaism, *intellectually* it would collapse without its connection with the Tiber, which I take as the symbol of the mentality of the West, however broad and multifaceted this mentality may be.

The question today is whether these two rivers delimit Christian theological boundaries or whether one should cross another Rubicon, this time not to defeat Pompey but to reach peacefully the Ganges. The question is twofold: Must Christians recognize that they cannot—and should not—conquer the world, because they represent only one phylum in human history, and thus should not claim the universality of being the only true religion? Or is there something specifically universal in the christic fact: Is Christ a universal symbol? In exploring these questions, I refer to the *Gangā* not only because of my familiarity with it, but also because it seems an apt symbol. The Ganges has many sources, including an invisible one; it disappears in a delta of innumerable beds, and has seen many religions born on its banks. Yet by no means should the metaphor imply an Aryan bias. Every country has its rivers, and most of them are sacred. The *Mā Gangā,* the motherly river of the Ganges, is taken here as the symbol, not just for Hinduism, Buddhism, Jainism, Sikhism, and primordial religions, but for all other traditions of Asia, Africa, and Oceania, which represent not only other spiritualities but also different mentalities.[6]

Christian theology does not make much sense to those mentalities. Not only the Bible, but most Christian presuppositions and ways of thinking are foreign, if not simply bewildering, to the non-Abrahamic traditions. I must insist on this. Although hardly 10 percent of the world speaks fluent English, and although Christians are a minority on the planet, English-speaking people are prone to assume that what they want and think represents universal patterns. A number of cultures are caught in such a universalizing syndrome.

So we have two possible answers, both legitimate. Which answer we favor is more than just an individual's religious decision. Which answer the Christian body as a whole will favor is a political decision of immense historical consequences. Reality is not just given once and for all. The future of religions depends also on how the different traditions understand themselves and what kind of decisions are taken. Christianity is also what Christians make—or will make—of it. Politics and religion must be distinguished, but they cannot be totally separated.[7]

The first response will say that Christians should not claim universality. Christians should let the rivers of the world flow peacefully without pumping Christian waters into them or diverting their beds to the Dead Sea or the Mediterranean. They should not cross another Rubicon and inundate every country in the world. Christianity is considered as one religion among many, and Jesus, ultimately, the savior only of Christians. The relationship with other religions will have to be dealt with as an interreligious problem, like international affairs among sovereign states. In this case Christianity preserves its identity by differentiation.[8] Christianity is unique because it is different. And this difference should be preserved. Tolerance, mutual respect, and good neighborliness are not at stake here. At stake is only the claim to universality of a certain Christian tradition.

According to this first answer, Christians should acknowledge the other traditions each in its own right. Unlimited growth is cancer and so would be an ever growing single Christian religion all over the world. The rivers should preserve their separate identities and so should the religions. The waters of the *Ganga,* or of the *Huanghe* or the *Nahr an Nil* (Nile), this first answer will say, contain too many salts (or pollution, if you want) and are too far away (philosophically, theologically, humanly) to be able to mix with the Christian rivers without producing major chemical and physical transformations. It is better, then, to keep them separate.

The second, probably still the most common, answer will say that the claim to universality is inherent in Christianity. Christianity is seen here as a privileged phylum called upon to unify the world, to "convert" the other cultural and religious streams into a Christian *Amazonas,* watering the entire planet—in the process of which, of course, Christianity itself will have to change into a still more universal religion. With what right, this second answer argues, should we stop the growth of this Christian dynamism? Is it not the temptation of every revolutionary movement, once its leaders achieve power, to suffocate any further evolution? Has Christianity succumbed to such a temptation? Until now Christians have absorbed syncretistically the "good things" of the Mediterranean religions. Why cannot they do something similar with other religions?

The dilemma is this: many Christians will feel that they are betraying their deepest beliefs if they give up the conviction that the christic dimension of their faith is meant to be universal. On the other hand, an increasing number of

Christians are becoming dimly but painfully aware that the claim to universality is an imperialistic remnant of times that should be past, and that most followers of other religions feel this claim as a threat—and an insult—to their beliefs.

The present study will ambitiously try to solve this dilemma by showing that the rivers of the earth do not actually meet each other, not even in the oceans, nor do they need to meet in order to be truly life-giving rivers. But "they" do meet: they meet in the skies—that is, in heaven. The rivers do not meet, not even as water. "They" meet in the form of clouds, once they have suffered a transformation into vapor, which eventually will pour down again into the valleys of mortals to feed the rivers of the earth. Religions do not coalesce, certainly not as organized religions. They meet once transformed into vapor, once metamorphosized into Spirit, which then is poured down in innumerable tongues. The rivers are fed by descending clouds, and also by terrestrial and subterranean sources, after another transformation, that of snow and ice into water. The true reservoir of religions lies not only in the doctrinal waters of theology; it lies also in the transcendental vapor (revelation) of the divine clouds, and in the immanent ice and snow (inspiration) from the glaciers and snow-laden mountains of the saints.

My contention will be that the christic principle is neither a particular event nor a universal religion. What is it then? It is the center of reality as seen by the Christian tradition. But this vision is only the Christian vision, not an absolutely universal one. It is the *christic* universal vision. I shall pursue this metaphor, trying to show that no religious tradition has a monopoly on the living waters of the rivers (salvation) and that we should not water down the tenets of any authentic religion in order to reach religious concord.[9] Elsewhere I have developed the *pars pro toto* effect inherent in this problematic.[10] My metaphor does not stand for the transcendent unity of all religions in an unqualified way. It goes in this direction, but I should not like to confuse the actual rivers with chemically pure water. Each water is different, as is each religion—each river carries its proper salts and micro-organisms. Nor should we forget that the waters undergo a transformation (of death and resurrection—into water, snow, and again water), which alone allows them to go on fertilizing the earth.

Religions are not static constructs. No religion should fear to let its water evaporate when the climate becomes unbearably hot. The clouds will restore the waters when the heat of polemics and waves subside. Put in another way: not only is each water unique, but also every river contributes its shape, taste, and beauty to the religious world, which is the entire world facing its ultimate destiny. The meanders, ghats, ports, bathing spots, quiet ponds, quick cascades, tranquil and stormy waters belong also to the religious phenomenon. Whatever the "essence" of religion may be, living and actual religions are not essences, but concrete, powerful, and dangerous existences. Religious rivers are much more than chemical H_2O.

My method cannot be purely deductive. It has to be also empirical and historical. For this reason, before drawing any conclusions, I shall try to indicate, on the one hand, the historical stages of Christian self-understanding and, on the other, a theological interpretation of these stages.

THE FIVE HISTORICAL PERIODS

Affirming the present-day recognition that theological understanding of the Christian phenomenon is a function of temporal, contextual, and many other parameters, we can understand why Christians have not always interpreted the christic fact in the same way. The self-understanding of Christians throughout history can be summed up in five historical periods, although each of them is still permeating the others. For this reason, I call them not chronological but kairological moments of Christian history.[11]

The Periods

1. *Witnessing* represents the prevalent Christian self-consciousness of the first centuries. The early Christians did not imagine that they formed a new religion. Rather they witnessed to those living words heard at the Jordan and confirmed by the resurrection. They witnessed to a fact that transformed their lives and, although soon interpreted in different ways, remained a kind of transhistorical event. They were not living exclusively in history. Eschatology was an ever-present factor. They could fearlessly face death. They were martyrs, witnesses to an event. Fidelity was paramount. This conviction was dominant roughly until the fall of Rome under Alaric in 410, or the death of St. Augustine in 430. The true Christian was a martyr.

2. *Conversion* represents the next moment. The world was becoming "Christian," but the climate was still "pagan." Slowly, Christians did establish themselves as a societal and even political reality. Yet they were aware that the Constantinization of Christianity had its pitfalls. True Christians had to distinguish themselves from the "world." One becomes a real Christian not so much because one adheres to an official religion but because one undergoes a change of heart. *Conversio morum* (a change of lifestyle) is the monastic slogan. The authentic Christian may tamper with the emerging political order or be allured by Christian social power, but the real criterion is style of life, purity of heart. To be a Christian means to be converted to Christ. True Christians follow the monastic calling. But by now Christianity has developed not only a specific set of doctrines, but also rules of political allegiances. The Christian understanding is that now Christians form a religion, even a state, the emerging empire. This religion is not inimical to other religions, especially those far away, but conversion slowly acquires political connotations. Entire peoples are converted and carry with them the basic attitudes of their respective ways of life. This was the fate of a great part of the peoples of Europe. This state of affairs lasted until the Middle Ages, although it suffered a convulsion in the clash with Islam. This clash elicits a new attitude.

3. *Crusade* characterizes the Christian self-understanding during this new period extending from the eighth century until well past the fall of Constantinople in 1453, probably until the defeat of the Turkish power at Lepanto in 1571. Christendom is firmly established. There are struggles and inner tensions among Christian princes, but nothing shapes Christian life more than the threat from Islam. It was almost a collective obsession. Spain falls quickly under Muslim dominion after the battle of Guadalete in 713, and the south of France is also "invaded." Charles Martel is hailed as the savior of (Christian) Europe, but Jerusalem and the holy places "fall" under Muslim domination. Vienna is threatened. The Christian empire has to assert itself. The danger is felt everywhere. Often Jews are scapegoats of Christian frustrations. The Christian has to be a soldier, a crusader, a "militant," a word that will be used until our times. The superiors of the new religious movements are no longer called fathers, abbots, or mothers, but generals—and the movements become "orders." *Militia Christi* (army of Christ), either in the most literal sense of becoming a crusader, or in the most lofty interpretation of becoming a Jesuit, represents the main attitude of this period.

Protestantism presents a similar feature: Christianity is a demanding enterprise; it requires courage, faith, decision. You have to be a Christian chevalier. You need to be a hero; you have the sacred duty of conquering or reconquering for Christ the life within and the world without. One should not compromise with the world. Faith alone suffices. Islam, which is felt as a threat (partly providential, as a warning not to become lukewarm), becomes the image of all other religions.

Christianity begins to develop the idea of being the only true religion. The others are false. To be sure, *vera religio* (true religion) is a consecrated phrase, but the meaning shifts from true religiousness to the only true and salvific institutionalized religion. This attitude lasts for centuries. But, at a certain moment, something new happens in Christendom—that is, in the *Sacrum Romanum Imperium Germanicum* (the Holy Roman German Empire). A new continent is "discovered" in 1492. This changes the scene: Christendom as a world order slowly collapses, and Christianity as a religion emerges.

4. *Mission* then becomes the dominant feature until the end of the modern age. The thrust to conquer is irresistible. But the religious justification of the conquest of America cannot be that of a crusade. The Amerindians could neither be called a threat, like the Muslims, nor were they accusing Christians of anything. The *conquista* could be justified only if they were to be made Christians. Salamanca is boiling with theological discussions. Bartolomé de las Casas defends the *Indios*. Francisco de Vitoria tries his best, but the triumphant ideology is that Christians have the duty—in a word, the *mission*—to proclaim, convert, and thus to save the Amerindians. This ideology spreads steadily. The true Christian is a *missionary.* The meaning of the word, again, extends from literally going to preach to the "infidels" to mystically offering oneself for their salvation, giving an example to the world. Thérèse de Lisieux,

secluded in her Carmelite convent, sees—and fulfills—her life as a missionary. Mission theology is the most elaborated theology.[12]

Nevertheless, in contact with other peoples of the world, Christians discover that these new religions contain treasures of spiritual values, and a theological reflection sets in. The names of Matteo Ricci and Roberto de Nobili recall this approach, but many such efforts were stifled because Christian institutions found them threatening to the dynamism of the times—that is, to the political expansion of the European states, which, because they declared themselves Christian, could not allow other interpretations that might undermine their power. The dispute over the Chinese rites is well known. In short, Christianity has a world mission. Christians still pay and pray for the missions. Even political embassies are called missions up to our own times and the name becomes universally accepted. But two world wars, a hundred million war-deaths in our century, and the independence of some one hundred fifty new states mark the end of this period. Many Christians realize that they can no longer "missionize" other peoples. We enter into the contemporary age.

5. *Dialogue* is the new catchword after the dismantling of the colonial political order. There is a trend now toward indigenization, inculturation, greater respect for other religions, and attempts at a new interpretation of the christic fact. Many Christians no longer want to conquer, not even to convert; they want to serve and to learn; they offer themselves as sincere participants in an open dialogue—although with understandable mistrust on the part of their partners, as anybody conversant with past history can well understand. Christians are beginning to say that dialogue is not a new strategy, but an open process of mutual enrichment and better knowledge of each other. Christendom has little prospect, Christianity is in crisis, but the Christ-symbol remains effective. Christianness emerges on the sociological plane.

To be sure, the Christian somehow retains all five traits. There is something of a *witness* in all Christians, and they will feel uneasy if they are not somewhat better than non-Christians (*conversion*), if they do not have the courage to confess their faith (a militant, a *crusader*), and do not sense the burden and responsibility of caring for the whole world (*mission*). Now discovering that they are not alone, Christians open up to *dialogue*. We are just at the beginning of a new spiral of the interaction between Christians and the peoples of other belief systems.

The Lessons of History

We should situate our reflections within the respective historical contexts. The first period is still nurtured by the waters of the Jordan. The Old Covenant is felt to be paramount. Spiritually, Christians are Semites. The three following periods are nourished by the waters of the Tiber. Christians are intellectually European, still linked primarily to Mediterranean cultures. Across the Atlantic there are only colonies in the historical sense of the word, despite the fact that after half a millennium of more or less independent existence, the Americas present features of their own.

Only the fifth attitude is no longer content to simply export Mediterranean culture. It aspires to bathe, together with other believers, in the waters of the Ganges and all the other rivers of the world. Christians discover that those rivers are real rivers that do not belong to them. It is a new sociological situation, despite some remarkable exceptions in the past.

These exceptions do merit some brief mention, for the contemporary attitude of dialogue is a kairological moment not totally absent in other periods. We can refer to Minutius Felix, the disputes of Barcelona and Toledo, Ramón Lull, Bernard of Clairvaux, Nicholas of Cusa, and, in more recent times, Brahmabandhav Upadhyaya and John Wu, among many others. All these figures attest that the felt need for dialogue is not brand-new. On a more popular level, an existential exchange has always existed where populations of different religious allegiances live side by side. In Kerala, for instance, animists, Hindus, Christians, and Muslims have lived for centuries in a relatively positive symbiosis.

We may now draw some lessons from this historical survey.

The *first* lesson history makes us aware of is that all our disquisitions are dependent on a temporal factor—that is, on historical circumstances. Were it not for the fact of the political decolonization of the world, we would not be speaking the way we are today. Dialogue has not sprung out of pure speculation. It has been almost forced upon Christians by circumstances. Praxis conditions theory. Yet it is also wisdom to make a virtue out of necessity.

The *second* lesson should be one of liberation, from both a narrow unidimensional supernaturalism and a sheer dialectical materialism. The change in Christian attitudes is neither solely the fruit of a providential God guiding a particular people, nor is it merely the result of cynical calculations on the part of institutional churches hoping to remain in power and continue dominating purses and consciences. Both factors—and still others—may be at work. Although historical circumstances impel us toward certain attitudes, this does not preclude the possibility that these circumstances are the fruit of still other forces acting in history; nor is a divine factor necessarily excluded, though it is certainly not a deus ex machina. The Spirit of God, to use traditional language, should be distinguished but not separated from the spirit of the times. History explains the *how,* not the *why.* In other words, history shows the triumph of neither the best (blessed by divine Providence) nor the most cunning ("blessed" by sheer power). In the view of the *Bhagavad Gita,* Dharmakṣetra and Kurukṣetra belong to each other; or, to speak with the gospel, wheat and the tares must grow together.

The *third* lesson invites us to the relativization of all our endeavors, including our theological and intellectual achievements. Our critical attitude toward ideologies of the past suggests that we ourselves are not an exception, and not essentially better off. We are also situated within a limited and ultimately provisional framework—"just for the time being," which is our being in time.

We are as much a passing phase as our ancestors were. If we have to beware of ethnocentrism, we should equally guard against chronocentrism.

The *fourth* lesson stresses the creativity and freedom of authentic theologizing. Theology does not merely repeat past doctrines or only draw implicit consequences from them. It also creates something new. Its decisions and insights can be momentous; they can strike a new direction that is not a mere "development" of an already existing dogma. There are mutations and there is freedom in the real world. Theology is not only exegesis, it is also praxis, not simply a matter of drawing conclusions, but also of establishing new premises and creating new situations. In other words, the history of Christian self-understanding is not a logical unfolding of premises; it is the fruit of a series of factors, many of which are free movements of the human and divine spirit.

To sum up: the criterion for the next step is not a logical continuation of the previous ones. It presupposes them, but is not necessarily contained in them. Life is more than logical unfolding—even more than evolution.

History also teaches us the proper way to approach our topic. In order not to lengthen this chapter unduly, I shall only enunciate some methodological principles.

Methodological Reflections

1. A Christian reflection on Christian self-understanding has to take three factors into consideration:
   a) the original sources of Christian self-understanding
   b) the interpretation of such sources by tradition
   c) the personal experience of and new reflection upon these sources and tradition

The art of theology consists in blending these three factors into a convincing harmony.

2. A Christian interpretation of the christic fact today needs to be concerned about the following:
   a) not to commit apostasy—that is, not to sever itself from the very tradition it wants to continue
   b) not to dilute the tradition into an amorphous common denominator, not even for the sake of tolerance or the ecumenical spirit
   c) not to neglect a thorough knowledge of other traditions. Christian self-understanding has to be open to other religious experiences, and belief-forms (and systems), to be willing to listen to them, to learn from them, and even to incorporate anything that appears to enrich or deepen Christian interpretation, to be ready for a mutual transformation. This interreligious fertilization may produce a new awareness and even, eventually, a new form of religious consciousness or religion

3. The method has to be dialogical,[13] and it is to be applied:
   a) among religions themselves—in this case, Christianity and the other religions of the world

b) within the very heart of one's own religion—in our case, among the different sorts of Christian understandings and theologies

c) within the inner recesses of the theologians themselves, or the persons engaged in such an enterprise. It is an intimate religious exercise.

I shall not elaborate on any of these points, for I hope that this essay itself is an example of such a methodology.

THE THREE GEO-THEOLOGICAL MOMENTS

The Rivers

The christic fact has been understood so far as essentially historical. Thus, the analyses of the five kairological moments, above. But it is also transhistorical. The christic event is not something of the past only or of the future only. It belongs also to the order of the heart, of the personal life of the believer. It has a sui generis contemporaneity and, in a way, transcends time and space without abolishing the spatio-temporal framework. It is theological. It prompts reflection on the given data in the light beaconed by its own tradition, as well as in the light from other lighthouses—although everything is always filtered through our own optical glasses. The three geo-theological moments are also kairological: they are intertwined; each is present in the other. And yet the respective moments appear with major force at precise points in the temporal manifestation of christic consciousness.

History and tradition are *loci theologici* (sources of theological activity). Any contemporary theological reflection that ignores the new context is methodologically flawed. Neither dogma nor Christian self-understanding are ahistorical and ageographical facts. Geography as much as history is a human as well as a religious category.

If the five facets of Christian self-understanding described above have developed along historical lines, the following three theological moments follow a religio-geographical pattern. If the christic phenomenon of the third century is different from that of the twentieth century, there is a similar difference between the Christian experience along the Tiber and along the Ganges. My potamic metaphor is more than a geographical nicety. It is also a theological category. Whether Christianity is universal or not, the Christian interpretation of life in an African desert is different from one in a Scandinavian city. We have been much more sensitive to history than to geography.

We should be fully aware that the geography of Christianity cannot be reduced to the Jordan of Palestine, the Tiber of Italy, or the Ganges of India. Not only are the fauna and flora on the shores of the many rivers of the world different, but also humans and their religiousness are different. The geo-theological coordinates are not Cartesian and neutral geometrical parameters; they impinge on the very nature of humans and their beliefs. The "geography of religions" is still an unexplored discipline. Furthermore, geography and history are intertwined.

The Tiber, for instance, is not only the Tiber of Rome. Rome is also Byzantium, and for centuries Moscow was the third Rome. Also, the Italian city itself encompasses, as it were, three Romes: that of the caesars (Christian or not), that of the popes (with or without temporal power), that of the people Yet I shall consider the Tiber to be representative of this second period of Christian geography.

What follows is, necessarily, only a sketchy overview.

1. *The Jordan: Water, Faith, Event, Religiosity, Upwardness—Exclusivism.* Jesus is the Christ. This is perhaps the shortest formulation of Christian belief. Although the meaning of Christ is polysemic, the origins of this formulation were very closely linked to the Jewish understanding of the Messiah, despite the reservations that Jesus himself seems to have had with this title. In the grammatically synonymous titles that are used, there is a shift of meaning: "Anointed One," "Messiah," "Christos," "Christ," and, of course, "Jesus Christ."

This Christian self-understanding is intimately linked—in both continuity and confrontation—with the Jewish Bible. Circumcision is abolished, thus creating a break with Judaism. But it is "replaced" by the baptism of *water*—which was, however, Jordan water. Those waters baptized Jesus, the son of Mary, the Son of Man. They are holy waters because the Spirit of God broods upon them. Water is the symbol for initiation: it cleanses, runs, is in polarity with fire, comes from wells and rivers, but also from high above and deep below the earth, bringing death and resurrection. But there is only one Jordan. Not everybody is initiated. *Exclusivism* is lurking here, although all water, we shall be told later, is Jordan water.

The Christian is the Man* of *faith*. This faith is centered on the person of Jesus. Theological discussions, therefore, will have to elucidate who this Jesus is. The central point, however, is not so much his nature, but the reality of his *event,* especially the resurrection. This event is first of all a historical fact in the life of Jesus: the condemnation of a Palestinian by the legal, religious, and political authorities of the times. We are embedded in history and personal history, and so fidelity to his person is central. The teachings of this young rabbi, even though most of his sayings might have been said before, are fascinating; his example has an irresistible attraction.

Christians, in spite of the warning of the angels at the ascension, still look up to heaven. They have a "religious" attitude that permeates their lives, a particular *religiosity,* not a religion. They look *upward* to the risen Christ.

---

*Editors' Note: Dr. Panikkar has requested that the editors keep his particular usage of "Man." He explains: "Neither *purusa,* nor *anthropos,* nor *homo* (and Romance derivatives), nor *Mensch* in Indo-European languages, nor analogous words in other cultures, stand for the male alone. I would not want to give males the monopoly on humanness (from *homo*) nor would I want to contribute to the fragmentation of 'Man' (the knower) by accepting the fragmentation of knowledge when dealing with that being which stands between heaven and earth and, different from other entities, knows it.—No discrimination! As I have explained elsewhere, 'wo-man' can be a derogatory expression, for it betrays male domination (and 'feminine' submission)."

Eschatological hopes are predominant. His resurrection will reveal and effect *our* resurrection.

It is a privilege to come under the influence, spell, grace of Jesus. It is something special, which confers a dignity; a source of joy, it is also a burden. The Jordan, to continue with my potamic metaphor, has a particular power, as the Jewish scriptures knew. "Are not Abana and Pharpas, rivers of Damascus, better than all the waters of Israel? Can I not wash in them and be clean?" exclaimed Naaman, the commander of the King of Aram's army, to Elisha, the prophet of Israel (2 Kings 5:12). In other words, uniqueness, privilege, and even *exclusiveness* do not create any insurmountable problem in a hierarchical world. Christians are few, and even fewer are the saved.[14] In a hierarchical context there is nothing repellent about a certain exclusivism.

This first moment corresponds to the first historical period, described above—that of *witnessing*.

It is obvious that the central theological problems here will hinge on the identity of Jesus Christ—christological and trinitarian issues.

2. *The Tiber: Fire, Belief, Institution, Religion, Introversion—Inclusivism.* But is the Jordan the only sacred river? Is not baptism also of *fire*? Fire burns the old and it spreads afar. It purifies, but also destroys. Christian identity today cannot be reduced to the experience of the first generations and overlook the cultural and religious constructions that twenty centuries of Christian life have produced. We are dealing here with the second, third, and fourth periods mentioned above—*conversion, crusade,* and *mission,* spanning well over fifteen centuries of Christian history.

The Christian is committed to a certain worldview, which is expressed in a set of *beliefs*. To be a Christian does not mean just to profess fidelity to Christ; it also entails adherence to Christian society, be it called church or beliefs. Splits and schisms, once well established, also develop their own orthodoxies. Christianity becomes an *institution*. The sense of belonging together becomes highly institutionalized. The ideal is Christendom, the Christian Empire, Christian civilization. When it begins to collapse around the sixteenth century, it is replaced more and more by Christianity as *religion*.

The Jordan is a geographical and mystical river. Its waters are baptismal waters. The Tiber is a historical and political river. Its waters flow into the Thames, the Seine, the Paraná, and the Potomac. Its waters carry a theology, a well-structured vision of the world, even if broad and flexible. They are the waters of Christian civilization past and present. Christendom and Christianity as its successor are not just private affairs. The Christian waters flow everywhere; they irrigate all the fields of a civilization that claims to encompass the entire world. A variety of contemporary names—John Paul II, President Reagan, Queen Elizabeth, General Pinochet, philosophers Maritain and Gilson, theologians Barth and Lonergan, and historians Toynbee and Heer—could be added here. All these persons endorse a belief in the superiority of Christianity. This belief does not prevent one from acknowledging the greatness of others and the failings of Christians; yet, as will be argued, such acknowledgments are according to the values of Christianity and under the authority of Christ.

Christianity has become so powerful and universal, so convinced of its mission, that it does not feel the need to look outside except to learn and to improve itself. *Inwardness* is one of its features, be it mystical, religious, or political. Within Christian revelation, doctrine, praxis, and way of life, one finds all that is needed for a full human life as well as for judging other religions and cultures. This is the kind of *introversion* I am referring to: in ourselves we find the whole truth. Theology is turned *inward*. We want to find in ourselves, in our own tradition or revelation, the answers to all theological issues. We may speak about the others, we may revere them and integrate them into our system, but it is still *we* who perform the task. Here is one example: when for the first time in church history an ecumenical council not only recognized that other religions have a right to exist but even praised them, as happened in *Nostra Aetate* of Vatican II, no need was felt to invite representatives of these religions to speak for themselves. Catholic experts felt sufficiently confident to speak on behalf of others. The Tiber was enough.

A tight theological case is made to defend a certain kind of Christian *inclusivism*. The Christian religion represents the culmination of religious evolution; it stands for universal values and claims a sort of universality. In brief, Christianity does not need to despise others but it certainly considers itself superior.

Anima naturaliter christiana, "anonymous Christians," "fulfillment theology," "servants of humankind," "the realm of nature and grace," or in more secularized ways, "democracy," "global civilization," "world government," "one world market," "universal human rights," are all expressions of the same syndrome. All the rivers carry the same water. But ultimately it is "our" water, even if the canoes going up or down the stream do not know it.

To be sure, there are many Christian institutions, churches, and theologies. Often they struggle among themselves for power, or for a better understanding of their theological issues (internal or ecumenical), or for better ways of dealing with other religions of the world. Within such diversity, we detect the same kind of language. Can we call it the Western logos? Christians become irritated at such a qualification, for the logos, they say, is universal (although it can only be "our" logos). If not the Tiber itself, the waters of the Tiber are everywhere. That is why we need *fire* and *inwardness*.

Efforts at greater openness within this inclusivistic attitude are praiseworthy: there is the notion of an invisible Christianity, a cosmic Christ,[15] a universal pneumatic church, a God who makes sense also for Buddhists, and a law that does not exclude *nómos, dhamma, karma,* or *li.* The ideal is a "universal theology of religion" or, in more scientific terms, a unified field theory.[16] This Tiber is indeed longer than the Mississippi.

As long as Christianity remains invisible, Christ unknown, the church spiritual, God ineffable, the law unwritten, and theology undone, there is no quarrel. *Homo loquens tamen* (Man is but a speaking being), and we cannot speak language as such, nor practice religion as such. We have to speak a particular language and practice a particular religion. Christian universality then becomes suspect and collapses—unless. . . .

Unless it is felt that the Christian phylum is so privileged that it absorbs all the others and becomes the only *Amazonas* for the entire world. This is the case in the many new forms of revivalism and fundamentalism. In all such phenomena, preoccupation with self-identity is central.

It is also clear that the main theological problems here will hinge on who Christians are and what their destiny means: problems of ecclesiology, grace, salvation, relationship to other religions, and, in general, orthodoxy.

3. *The Ganges: Earth, Confidence, Religiousness, Dimension, Outwardness—Pluralism.* We face now the challenge of a "theology" for a postcolonial era. It corresponds to the above-mentioned fifth attitude of dialogue. A dialogical theology posits what it is talking about only when the subject matter—and obviously the language—has been found in common or created in the dialogue itself. The very agenda of the dialogue should be worked out in the dialogue itself. In other words, Gangotri is only one of the sources of the Ganges (the Sarasvati is an invisible one) and the delta is no longer a river, nor even "Indian" territory. The sources of our Ganges are the snow of the mountains and the clouds of the skies. None of them are actually water.

The symbol here is *earth*—that is, secularity (*saeculum*), or the kingdom of justice here on earth, which entails the readiness to collaborate with all others, even if we disagree with them. There is no planetarian consciousness, but there is a special awareness of the other(s) and a certain inclination to welcome without suffocating them—that is, to accept without comprehending. We trust. We have a higher *confidence* in our common destiny than the certainty (security) placed on our logos. Christian identity begins to appear neither as defending a certain culture nor as belonging to an institutionalized religion, but as living a personal *religiousness*—that is, a sort of religious attitude that constitutes a *dimension* of Man, one factor of the *humanum,* one aspect of the divine.

Christians are no longer worried only about themselves, but are also open to others, and to the world at large: *outwardness*. This moment is characteristically *outward*bound, not in order to go out and conquer, but to be in relationship. It is an attitude that sees oneself in relation to others, and others in relation to oneself. I do not call it openness, so as to keep the balance with the other two moments. An example may clarify what is meant. The Christian theology of the second moment tended to emphasize the newness of the Christian message and to defend identity by difference, thus affirming that love of one's neighbor, the doctrines of Trinity, grace, and so forth, were all specific and unique contributions of Christian revelation.[17] Whatever the particular cases may be, the third moment will feel more comfortable if it discovers that all those doctrines and sayings are humanity's common good and that Christianity simply incarnates the primordial and original traditions of humankind.

What I am saying is this: neither exclusivism nor inclusivism represents the proper attitude of this third moment. I am talking about *pluralism*.

Before elaborating the positive aspects of this new moment, which I call Christianness, I should review some of its negative features (which will lead us, like Moses, up to the borders of the Promised Land). I am speaking of the possible incommensurability of ultimate worldviews.

I have often argued that, properly speaking, comparative philosophy is not possible, because the necessary standpoint from which the comparison is to be made already belongs to a definite philosophical view.[18] Something similar can be said about comparative religion.[19] Unless we assume that reason (ultimately "our" understanding of reason) is the neutral, universal, and sufficient criterion for evaluating religions, we cannot assume at the outset that all religious traditions can be justly and truly measured with the same *metron*. Each religious tradition, as a relatively complete system of self-understanding, segregates its own parameters. A fruitful dialogue has to agree on the parameters to be used in the dialogue itself, otherwise there is only talking at cross-purposes. Simply stated: What do we mean by the very words we use? The talk about meaning of words precedes, conditions, and also constitutes dialogue.

The consequence of this is that religious traditions *may be* incommensurable—they may not have a common measure that can adequately evaluate them. And in point of fact, they are mutually irreducible—until some agreement has been reached or established. A realistic assessment of the present state of affairs is that religions, and even theologies, often consider themselves mutually incompatible.

And we do not necessarily need to resolve our intellectual frustration by postulating an intellect for which all, absolutely all, is intelligible. This hypothesis only begs the ultimate question. It pretends to answer the *why* of Being, and in so doing it makes Being subservient to the *why*, to logos, to consciousness. We may logically say that all that an infinite or supreme intellect encompasses is intelligible. There are no limits to an infinite intelligence: all is intelligible to it. But unless we identify Being with consciousness, we cannot logically show that there could not be Being that could not be known.

One might object that if such an infinite intelligence could not know all, it would not be infinite. We might respond that an infinite intelligence is infinite qua intelligence, but does not need to be infinite qua Being, unless we already assume that Being and intelligence ultimately coalesce—which is precisely what is under discussion. This simply implies that there may be facets of reality opaque to the light of the intellect. I shall return to this point when dealing with the notion of pluralism.

If the problems of the two previous moments were christologico/trinitarian and ecclesiologico/soteriological, the theological problems here will hinge on the issues of humankind and how Christians can help solve them. This does not mean that these problems are merely political or economic, or only a matter of justice. They are also anthropological, for Man has gained a peculiar self-understanding. They are also cosmological—that is, concerning the vision of the world and of history.

It is over against this historical and geo-theological background that we can situate the specific challenge and problems of a pluralistic Christian self-understanding for our times. Following are some features that may be helpful in elucidating our question.

Attitudes: Christendom, Christianity, Christianness

I begin with a question of vocabulary.

The word "Christian" can be the adjectival content of Christendom (a civilization), of Christianity (a religion), and of Christianness (a personal religiousness). During the period of the so-called Christian culture of the high Middle Ages, one could hardly be a Christian without belonging to Christendom. Until recently, one could hardly confess oneself to be Christian without belonging to Christianity.

Now persons increasingly envisage the possibility of being Christian as a personal attitude without adhering either to Christendom or to Christianity as institutional constructs. I speak here of a personal, not an individualistic, attitude. "Person" always implies community. The Christian attitude is ecclesial, which does not mean ecclesiastical, which, in the current sense of the word, is synonymous with a large traditional organization. *Ecclesia* (church), strictly speaking, implies an organism, not an organization. An organism needs a soul, life. An organization requires an idea, a rationale.[20]

The distinction is important. To be a Christian as a member of Christendom belongs mainly to the past and to the dreams of some for the future, but it does not constitute a problem for the majority of theologians. Still, the spirit and the reality of Christendom has neither disappeared nor can it be totally abolished from Christian consciousness. It belongs both to human nature and to Christian dynamism to build "reservations" where the Christian ideal can become fully incarnate in the smallest details of life. In the past such reservations were called the Christian empire, or the Christian nation, later religious orders, and in modern times, sects or movements. All are ambivalent—and not totally obsolete. Yet the christic fact cannot be exhaustively identified with what we call Christendom. There is also Christianity and Christianness. There are many mansions in the Father's house!

We also have Christianity. To be a Christian as a member of Christianity amounts to belonging to one religion among many. It may be more or less pure than others. It would, however, represent not only an abuse of language but an abusive language to denounce other religions as false or incomplete. The problems of Christianity as religion are different from the issues of Christendom as a full-fledged social organization. Some hundred years ago Catholics who opposed the "divine right" of the pontifical states were excommunicated. Those who denied the right to torture heretics also incurred excommunication. No Catholic Christian today feels obliged to obey the rules, laws, and injunctions of the medieval and renaissance popes. Such obligations belonged to Christendom, not to Christianity.

I should add a remark here similar to the one regarding Christendom. Papal nuncios belong to Christendom, yet they still exist, and their function may have some historical justification. Canon law is still valid and pontifical encyclicals still carry their authority—to give some Catholic examples. But they no longer exhaust the ways of being Christian, nor of being Catholic.

A third facet emerges powerfully in our times. To be a Christian can also be understood as confessing a personal faith, adopting a Christlike attitude inasmuch as Christ represents the central symbol of one's own life. I call this Christianness. In German it might be called *Christlichkeit,* or *cristianía* in Spanish. It does not need to be interpreted as an exclusively historical fact. It is just a *factum*—that is, something we make and at the same time is not made only by us. Elsewhere I have made a similar distinction: Christianity, Church, Christ, referring respectively to the social aspect of religion, its sacramental dimension, and its mystical core.[21] The last-named could be called the christic principle.

Let me give some examples from the Roman tradition. The use of contraceptives is formally forbidden by the supreme authority of Catholic Christianity. Yet an enormous number of persons belonging to the Catholic Church ignore such a law and consider themselves "good Catholics." With divorce a similar situation is beginning to take shape in some countries. Also, there are some eighty thousand validly ordained Catholic priests who consider themselves such, in spite of having transgressed what they consider the unjust law of celibacy. Abortion, euthanasia, pacifism, capitalism, and communism represent similar conflicting situations. Can one be a communist and a Christian, a capitalist and a follower of the Gospel. . . ?

In a word, Christianness differentiates itself from Christianity as Christianity extricated itself from Christendom. The situation is certainly fluid. Each period is a period of transition, but there are epochs more saliently different than others.

One more example: the South and Central American grass-roots communities (*comunidades de base*) have spontaneously developed a Christianness that does not reflect existing Christianity. The Vatican has seen this clearly. Yet, institutionalized Christianity shows enough theological discrimination, common sense, or political prudence to know that it cannot alienate itself from one of the largest Christian continents. So it strikes a political compromise in order that Christendom, Christianity, and Christianness might not be split. The Christianness of the past century was mainly pietistic and individual. It could tamper with institutionalized Christianity without major tensions. Present-day Christianness presents a more personal and political commitment, and so poses a challenge to Christianity. Wisdom here, as elsewhere, consists in transforming destructive tensions into creative polarities.

Christianness should not be described in only a negative relation to Christianity. I have been saying all along that the three belong together and cannot be totally separated, although they have to be distinguished.

There is also a theological reason for this distinction. Many religions have sacred-legal scriptures. In the two monotheistic religions of the Abrahamic trunk, law is part of revelation itself (Torah, Qur'ān). One could incidentally and ironically remark that Marxism, as the fourth Abrahamic religion, shows also a similar respect for the Communist Party, which represents a secularized revelation. Not so with Christianity. Christianity has no law of its own. For many centuries the Bible for Christianity meant only the "Old Testament." The "New Testament" was not considered holy scripture.[22] Also, Christianity has no proper name for the Supreme Being. "God" is a common name (which for Jesus was his Father). All this suggests the possibility of a Christianness different from Christendom and Christianity.

To be sure, the mystics living in Christendom have always stressed Christianness, and the mystics living in Christianity have always been witnesses to the respect due to the legal structures without being imprisoned by them. Sheer rebellion or simply dropping out is not the christic solution. The example of Jesus Christ is too glaring. He is a denouncer and a protestor, even a transgressor, but not a runaway, a traitor. Peter had learned to obey God rather than Man, yet as a loyal Jew he did not wish to abolish circumcision—although he accepted being overruled by his colleagues and the Holy Spirit.

And in fact if we look back to history we find a score of Christians who believed they had reached Christianness after overcoming, not rejecting, Christendom and Christianity. Many simple and deep believers, but also Tertullian, Origen, Eckhart, Savonarola, Dante, Vico, Joachim of Fiore, St. Joan of Arc, St. John of the Cross, Erasmus, Kant, Hegel, and in our times Teilhard de Chardin and Padre Pio, Merton and Abhishiktananda, could be mentioned as examples.

In sum, the different interpretations of the gospel injunction "Look for the kingdom of God and its justice" could serve as a way of expressing this threefold structure of Christian consciousness. Referring to the well-known passage of Luke 17:21, the first attitude will understand "the kingdom" as a construct "among" us. The kingdom is also on earth and it has political connotations. The second will underscore the same Greek particle, *entos,* as meaning that the kingdom is "between" us, so that the cultural-communitarian aspect becomes paramount. The third, finally, will be inclined to interpret the kingdom to be "within" us, thus emphasizing the dimension of interiority. Something similar could be said about the interpretation of the word "justice": as mainly a political symbol, a doctrinal one, or an immanent reality. (Let it be recalled that the New Testament word *dikaiosyné* means both justice and justification.)

The sociological implications of these distinctions are important. There is undoubtedly in the world today a certain crisis of Christian identity. Although there are revivalist movements going back to the ideal of a modernized Christendom and other more theological tendencies striving for a reformed Christianity, there is a growing number of responsible persons struggling to articulate a genuine Christian confession without being totally conditioned by the historical burden of the past and by the doctrinal strictures of tradition. They do not sponsor a privatization of Christian identity, although sometimes they are almost forced to it. They sponsor an exteriorization of their Christian identity that is the fruit more of inner experience than of historical and doctrinal inertias. More or less consciously aware that the world is undergoing a mutation, they are attempting to live this change at its deepest—that is, at the religious level of their consciousness and consciences. In simpler terms, a substantial number of contemporary Christians want to be religious, believers, and even Christian—but without the "contaminations" that they feel have been attached to those names. They aspire to rediscover their roots in order to grow in another soil unspoiled by the manure of ancient times, the graftings of the Middle Ages, the pesticides of the modern age, and the radiation of modernity. This struggle for renovation is innate in the human being; it has always been so, but today it is taking on cosmic proportions.

To draw some explicit connections between these attitudes and our three rivers: if the spirituality of the Jordan is close to Christianity, and that of the Tiber to Christendom, the Ganges here stands as a symbol for Christianness[23]—although all similes should be taken with a Pascalian *esprit de finesse* (rather than *de géométrie*). My point is this: these three attitudes represent the complex Christian phenomenon of our times. Furthermore, the increasing awareness of Christianness offers a platform from which the dilemma of exclusivism or inclusivism may be solved in favor of a healthy pluralism of religions that in no way dilutes the particular contribution of each human tradition.

Problems

A. *Concrete and Universal versus Particular and General.* We need to distinguish, as I have elaborated elsewhere, between concreteness and particularity, universality and generality. The concrete can be universal, not so the particular. Something is concrete (my belief, parents, house . . .) precisely because it embodies the universal (faith, parenthood, habitat . . .). The universal is universal because it re-presents the entire field and not because it detracts from concreteness, as the general does. The universal is centered; it is turned toward its own center: *universus.* It is incarnated in the concrete. The Christian attitude is and should be concrete. It is limited, and yet it re-presents the totality. Like the very mystery of the incarnation, in the concreteness of one Man dwells the fullness of the divinity. I have called this phenomenon the *pars pro toto* effect (part for the whole). We see the whole through our window; we see and even are the *totum in parte* (whole in the part).[24] The concrete is the *pars pro toto.* The particular is the *pars in toto* (part in the whole). We *may* "sacrifice" the particular for the sake of the whole. We cannot do that with the concrete.

The modern geometrical mentality interprets the meaning of universal as the sum total of an elementary geometrical area constituted by contiguous parts.

One part, of course, one sector of a circle, cannot be the whole. This is not the traditional way of understanding universality. In Christian history, St. Augustine still literally translates "catholic," *kath' holon,* by *secundum totum*—that is, as the religiousness that for us is complete inasmuch as it provides all we need for our fulfillment and salvation. It is only with the geographical expansion of late and collapsing Christendom that Christianity as Catholic religion came to mean the spread of one single religion over all the earth.

But there is still more. Universal is not necessarily a quantitative notion. A drop of water may be equal to another drop of water, but it is not the second drop. They are numerically and factually different. They may contain exactly the same mass of water, but one drop is not the other, in spite of the fact that both are water, and that if it were not for the surface tension making them two drops in space and time, we could not distinguish them. Nevertheless, one individual mass of water is not the other. And yet if we abstract the quantity of water, both are just water, water indivisible (from within as it were). In other words, the water of the drop—not the drop of water—is both concrete and universal: it is both this water and simply water.[25] Christian scholastics used to speak of the *specular* character of the universe in the sense that each being, especially each human being, image and likeness of God, reflects, mirrors, represents the entire reality.

These distinctions bear christological implications. Christ, as the second Adam, stands for all humanity, and in a certain sense for the whole cosmos, says Christian tradition following Paul. *Minutis minuendis,* every person represents and is the symbol of all reality. The mechanistic worldview, prevalent in our times, is a great obstacle to reenacting this liberating experience. The problem of the universality of Christ and of Christian salvation would practically be solved if approached in the light of a more traditional cosmology. There is no question of competition, say, between Christ, Buddha, Krishna, or whomever. Nor is there question of separated constituencies. If Christian theology is carried on within the perspectives of Christendom or Christianity, such problems may arise. But Christian theology today cannot ignore Christianness. In this perspective the problem is not one of jurisdiction. Doctrines may differ, theologies may quarrel, institutionalized religions may discuss their spheres of influence, but the existential problem of human "salvation" is not one of deciding who has the passport to heaven, or which consulate or embassy has the right to issue such documentation. What we have to change is the very perspective of the question.

The universality of Christ would represent his transparency, his perfection. We are here within another cosmology, which dissolves the problem of singularity and universality.[26] We should not confuse the individuality of Christ with our individuation of him; his identity is not his (our) individuation.[27] Christ is unique, as any loved child is unique for its parents—*eminenter* (eminently), I may add.

Perhaps an example will help to clarify all this. The Ptolomeic conception of the solar system was exceedingly complicated. One of the advantages of the

Copernican revolution was that the new heliocentric system was much simpler. In one stroke an enormous amount of calculating became superfluous. I am suggesting something similar. As long as we entertain a mechanocentric conception and a geometrical notion of reality, a number of problems are exceedingly complicated and can hardly find any solution. Either Christians "stick" to their "Christ" and become exclusivistic, or they give up their claims, dilute their beliefs, and become, at best, inclusivistic. These two horns of the dilemma are equally unacceptable. The parallel Copernican revolution consists in shifting the center from linear history to a theanthropocosmic vision, a kind of trinitarian notion, not of the godhead alone, but of reality.[28] The center is neither the earth (our particular religion), nor the sun (God, transcendence, the Absolute . . .). Rather, each solar system has its own center, and every galaxy turns reciprocally around the other. There is no absolute center. Reality itself is concentric inasmuch as each being (each tradition) is the center of the universe—of its own universe to begin with. The theanthropocosmic insight (which sees the unity between the divine-human-cosmic) suggests a sort of trinitarian dynamism in which all is implied in all (each person represents the community and each tradition reflects, corrects, complements, and challenges the other).

B. *Plurality and Pluralism.* As I said above, our times seem ripe for a *pluralistic attitude*—for a plunge into the Ganges.[29] This attitude may be summed up in the following statements:

1. Pluralism does not mean plurality or a reduction of plurality to unity. It is a fact that there is a plurality of religions. It is also a fact that these religions have not been reduced to any sort of unity. Pluralism means something more than sheer acknowledgment of plurality and the mere wishful thinking of unity.

2. Pluralism does not consider unity an indispensable ideal, even if allowance is made for variations within that unity. Pluralism accepts the irreconcilable aspects of religions without being blind to their common aspects. Pluralism is not the eschatological expectation that in the end all shall be one.

3. Pluralism affirms neither that the truth is one nor that it is many. If truth were one, we could not accept the positive tolerance of a pluralistic attitude and would have to consider pluralism a connivance with error. If truth were many, we would fall into a plain contradiction. We said already that pluralism does not stand for plurality—a plurality of truths in this case. Pluralism adopts a nondualistic, advaitic, attitude that defends the pluralism of truth because reality itself is pluralistic—that is, incommensurable with either unity or plurality. Being as such, even if "encompassed" by or "co-existent" with the Logos or a Supreme Intelligence, does not need to be reduced to consciousness. The perfect self-mirroring of Being is truth, but even if the perfect image of Being is identical to Being, Being is not exhausted in its image. If the Logos is the transparency of Being, the Spirit is, paradoxically, its opaqueness. The Spirit is freedom, the freedom of Being to be what it is. And this is, a priori as it were, unforeseeable by the Logos. The Logos accompanies Being; it does not precede it; it does not pre-dict what Being is. It tells only what Being is. But the *is* of

Being is free. The mystery of the Trinity is the ultimate foundation for pluralism.

4. Pluralism does not allow for a universal system. A pluralistic system would be a contradiction in terms. The incommensurability of ultimate systems is unbridgeable. This incompatibility is not a lesser evil (that would be to judge only by the logos), but a revelation itself of the nature of reality. Nothing can encompass reality.

5. Pluralism makes us aware of our own contingency/limitations and the nontransparency of reality. It is incompatible with the monotheistic assumption of a totally intelligible Being—that is, with an omniscient consciousness identified with Being. Yet pluralism does not shun intelligibility. The pluralist attitude tries to reach intelligibility as much as possible, but it does not need the ideal of a total intelligibility of the real. It "knows" that we have to stop somewhere lest we corrode Being (the "originality" or independence of Being) by reducing it to (self-)intelligibility.

6. Pluralism, then, is not a mere symbol. It expresses an attitude of cosmic confidence (in the Spirit, which is not subordinate to the logos), which allows for a polar and tensile coexistence between *ultimate* human attitudes, cosmologies, and religions. It neither eliminates nor absolutizes evil or error.

7. Pluralism does not deny the logos and its inalienable rights. The principle of noncontradiction, for instance, cannot be eliminated. But pluralism belongs also to the order of myth. It incorporates myth, not, of course, as an object of thinking, but as the horizon that makes thinking possible. The myth is the locus of beliefs.

In view of the preceding description of pluralism, a Christian pluralistic attitude can subscribe to the following statements:

1. There is no single Christian self-understanding.
2. There is a plurality of them.
3. They cannot be put under one common umbrella as a supersystem.

(These first three statements are simply facts, hard as we may try to belie the third. From them follow other elements in a Christian pluralism.)

4. Different theologies can be recognized as Christian by their own self-affirmation. Their unity transcends the logos because one theology may consider the other incompatible with a Christian stance, and yet all declare themselves Christian. Their link is not a common essence but an existential fact. Yet their diversity does not contradict the logos, because we may find *each time* a formal common denominator. No theology, however, can be sufficiently described by some minimal doctrines, for the internal coherence of a theological system makes even such minimal "truths" dependent on their overall incorporation within a total picture; and inasmuch as the total pictures differ, the alleged common denominator is a sheer reductionist abstraction. All Christian theologies, for instance, may confer upon "Christ" a central role, but the meaning—and even referent—of this word may be radically different.

5. We cannot prescribe from one single perspective what the other Christian

views should be. This would amount to establishing ourselves as the ultimate criterion for Christian identity; it would destroy pluralism. Pluralism, we said, belongs to the order of myth.

6. A Christian pluralistic attitude has to be ready to be excommunicated by a nonpluralistic view without retaliating by declaring the other to be non-Christian. Pluralism undermines the rationale for power struggle.

7. Christian pluralism could accept as its motto: all that is not against us is for us. What does not contradict a concrete opinion cannot be rejected. And yet any rejection brings within itself the limits in which the rejection is valid. It is not absolute. The principle of tolerance is not based on the recognition of truth but on confidence.

8. Vis-à-vis the religions of the world, a Christian pluralistic attitude will affirm the Christian tenets, but without forgetting the limitation and contingency of the subject who formulates them. In other words, it will never proclaim: "The true belief is x." It will always confess: "I believe x to be true" (the true belief). The "I believe" cannot be severed from belief. Nevertheless, this does not prevent me from affirming that I believe that others are wrong and even that their views are so harmful that I may feel obliged to combat particular errors—although not as absolute evils.

9. The Christian pluralist will not affirm that there are many saviors. This is a nonpluralistic assertion. The pluralistic christological affirmation will begin—as with the Trinity (*Qui incipit numerare incipit errare* ["who begins to count, begins to err"], said Augustine)—by denying the meaningfulness of any quantitative individualization in the Mystery of Christ. The saving power—which Christians call Christ—is neither one nor many.

All this means that Christian self-understanding is a function of the all-embracing myth reigning at a particular time and place. This unifying myth is not constant. The myth-themes for our present situation may be summed up in the following conclusions.

CONCLUSIONS

A Christian reflection on religious pluralism and its implications for Christian self-consciousness can incorporate the following points into its agenda:

1. We should neither ignore nor neglect the past; we should respect traditional self-understandings, but should also submit them to appropriate (new) interpretations.

2. We should not be satisfied with merely exegetical approaches. We should allow for a possibly new Christian awareness.

3. The greatest change in Christian self-understanding is both the text and the context. The text is being enlarged by the incorporation of other sacred texts that until now have been excluded. In other words, the reflection on "the Christian economy of salvation" cannot ignore the existence—and the challenge—of the religions of the world. The traditional context was represented by the Tiber. The new context is that of the Ganges—that is, not the

context of Western history, but that of a present-day universal relevance. Obviously, the Ganges does not stand here for an exclusively Hindu river (the Jordan of Hinduism, as it were), but as symbol of the wider world.

4. The new context is not just a new territory added to the old one, nor is it the same territory seen in a new light. The new context entails both new elements, which were not there before, and a transformation of the old context. It is a new context that embraces, corrects, and supersedes the old, but keeps a certain continuity with it. Nevertheless, this new context is equally limited and concrete. It should not be identified with a sort of universal texture, which would amount to an antipluralistic homogenization of reality.

5. We should not identify the christic fact of *Christianness* with *Christianity* as religion, and much less with *Christendom* as civilization.

6. There is no need for one single view of Christ, however broadly it may be conceived. No single notion can comprehend the reality of Christ.

7. Religions may be incommensurable with each other despite some possible common traits. Each religion is unique with the uniqueness of every real being. But we should not confuse the autopsy of a religion with its living existence. This very incommensurability, like that of the radius with the circumference, does not preclude the fact that each religion may be a dimension of the other in a kind of trinitarian *perichoresis* or *circumincessio*. Each one represents the whole of the human experience in a concrete way.

8. Each religion expresses one concrete form of humanness. This does not exclude a possible divine shaping of the *humanum,* or religious degradation of it.

9. When religions encounter each other, they can mutually enrich each other and also destroy each other.

10. If Christians are able to extricate from their own religion the christic principle, this principle can be experienced as a dimension at least potentially present in any human being, as long as no absolute interpretation is given. This could equally be said of a similar principle in other traditions (Buddhahood for instance).

11. Christians may find in this christic principle the point of union, understanding, and love with all humankind and with the whole of the cosmos, so that in this concreteness they find the most radical human, cosmic, and divine communion with reality—notwithstanding other possible homeomorphic equivalents.

12. The Christian point of insertion is the kenotic experience of Christ, which entails acceptance of and openness to the Spirit.

I may say, then, that an awareness of the overall context of our world today leads to the recognition of a mutation in Christian self-understanding. This mutation is due to:

a) *Historical changes*: the passage from Christendom to Christianity and then to the christic attitude expressed in Christianness.

b) *Philosophical discernment* between the concrete/particular and universal/general—that is, the overcoming of the quantitative patterns of thinking.

c) *Cosmological revolution*: the worldview in which Christianity thrived can no longer stand critical scrutiny.

d) *Theological recognition* of the rights and values of other religions, and thus a healthy pluralism.

This implies a deep awareness of the christic fact or principle transcending sociological and religious constructs.[30] We accept slowly the emergence of a new Christian consciousness tied neither to Christian (Western) civilization, nor to Christian (institutionalized) religion. New communities may appear, even in traditionally non-Christian countries, and some may even shun the name "Christian" because the "Christian" label may be understood as a *mere* continuation of the past.

It is not a question of denying the civilizational aspects of Christians, or of minimizing the importance of organized religion. It is only a question of emphasizing the personal spiritual life, the discovery of the kingdom of heaven, the pearl, the wholeness of the Mystical Body, the communion with the divine, the interior, historical, and at the same time cosmic and transtemporal Christ. There have been times when it was dangerous to be a Christian, others in which it was advantageous. These two features are still very real today. But I am underscoring a third feature: it is difficult to be a Christian. It is difficult because it requires the personal discipline, the courage to face not only the profane world, but also the ecclesiastical institutions. Christianness stands for experience of the life of Christ within ourselves, insight into a communion, without confusion, with all reality, an experience that "I and the Father are One," that labels do not matter, that security is of no importance, and that reflection also is a secondary source (although a primary tool). It is with hesitation that I use the phrase "mystical experience," but perhaps there is no better way of saying it. Not without a certain bias I chose the mystical Ganges as the symbol. Was not this what Christ said? "Waters of eternal life"—from any river or sea. One has only to drink them.

I end this chapter with a personal note, which may shed light on the preceding analyses. I shall try to state my interpretation of Christ in a theanthropocosmic vision. I believe this interpretation follows the methodological principles of this essay, but in no way do I wish to suggest that it is normative, or necessarily representative, of Christian theology.

The mystery that is at the beginning and will be at the end, the alpha and omega by and through which all has to come into being, the light that enlightens every creature, the word that is in every authentic word, the reality that is totally material, completely human, and simply divine, which is at work everywhere and elusively present wherever there is reality, the meeting place at the crossroads of reality where all realms meet, that which does not come with fanfare and about which one should not believe that it is here or there, that which we do not know when we perform a good or an evil action and yet is "there," that which we are—and shall be—and which we were, that symbol of all reality not only as it was or is, but as it still shall freely be, also through our synergy, is what I believe to be the Christ.

If it is said that this symbol is too broad and universal, I would respond that if the circumcision of the body has been superseded, why should we not overcome the circumcision of the mind?

And I insist that with such a view of Christ I am not escaping the scandal of the incarnation and the process of redemption. I am not ignoring these historical facts. It is simply that I do not worship history, nor do I limit reality—not even human reality—to history, nor history to the Abrahamic history. Just as traditional theology speaks of a *creatio continua,* we could by analogy envisage a continuous incarnation, not only in the flesh, but also in the acts and events of all creatures. Every being is a *christophany.*

NOTES

1. From my "Sobre el sentido cristiano de la vida" *Arbor* (Madrid), no. 64 (1951), republished in my book *Humanismo y Cruz* (Madrid: Rialp, 1963), pp. 112–77, to my "Què vol dir avui confessar-se cristià" in *Questions de vida cristiana* (Montserrat: Publicacions de l'Abadia de Montserrat [no. 128/129] 1985), pp 86–111.

2. I should like to stress that although I have written extensively on these subjects, my praxis (talks, meetings, projects, activities, etc.) has been with me all along. In fact, what I have said and done may be more important than what I have written and published.

3. This essay should be understood against the background of previous publications of mine, such as:

a) *The Unknown Christ of Hinduism* (London: Darton, Longman and Todd, and Maryknoll, N.Y.: Orbis Books, 1981, rev. ed.);

b) *The Intrareligious Dialogue* (New York: Paulist Press, 1978);

c) *Die vielen Götter und der eine Herr. Beiträge zum ökumenischen Gespräch der Weltreligionen* (Weilheim: O. W. Barth, 1963);

d) *Religión y Religiones* (Madrid: Gredos, 1965);

e) "Ṛtatattva: A Preface to a Hindu-Christian Theology," *Jeevadhara,* 49 (1979) 6–63.

f) "Salvation in Christ: Concreteness and Universality, the Supername" (inaugural lecture at the Ecumenical Institute of Advanced Theological Studies, Jerusalem [Tantur], 1972). A shortened version of the first part was published as "The Meaning of Christ's Name in the Universal Economy of Salvation," in *Evangelization, Dialogue, and Development,* M. Dhavamony, ed. (Rome: Gregorian University Press, 1972), pp. 195–218.

4. Matt. 31:13; Mark 1:9.

5. We should remember that the expression "Body of Christ" traditionally meant the Christian people and only later the Eucharist. See F. Holböck, *Der eucharistische und der mystische Leib Christi* (Rome: 1941), and H. de Lubac, *Corpus mysticum* (Paris: Aubier, 1949); idem, *Méditation sur l'Eglise* (Paris: Aubier, 1954).

6. See, as an example, Hajime Nakamura, *Ways of Thinking of Eastern People* (Honolulu: University of Hawaii Press, 1985).

7. See my "Religion and Politics: The Western Dilemma," in *Religion and Politics in the Modern World,* P. H. Merkl and Ninian Smart, eds. (New York University Press, 1985), pp. 44–60. Mahatma Gandhi is reported to have said without the slightest hesitation, and yet in all humility, that: "those who say that religion has nothing to do

with politics do not know what religion means" (*An Autobiography or the Story of My Experiments with Truth,* M. Desai, tr. [Ahmedabad: Navjivan Publishing House, 1982], p. 420).

8. See my *Le mystère du culte dans l'hindouisme et le christianisme* (Paris: Cerf, 1970), pp. 37ff.

9. The last stanza of the *Rig Veda* (X, 191,4) is a hymn to religious concord.

10. "The Invisible Harmony: A Universal Theory of Religion or a Cosmic Confidence in Reality?" in *Toward a Universal Theology of Religion,* Leonard Swidler, ed. (Maryknoll, N.Y.: Orbis Books, 1987).

11. See my chapter, "Christianity and World Religions," in *Christianity* (Patiala: Punjabi University, 1969), pp. 78–127 (Guru Nanak Quintcentennial Collection Series), where these five periods are explained at greater length.

12. The ground-breaking book by Paul Knitter, *No Other Name? A Critical Survey of Christian Attitudes toward the World Religions* (Maryknoll, N.Y.: Orbis Books, 1985), is sponsored by the *American Society of Missiology Series* (no. 7). In the "Preface to the Series," W. J. Danker, the chairman of the committee, states: "Always the focus will be on Christian mission." And he specifies: "By 'mission' in this context is meant a cross-cultural passage over the boundary between faith in Jesus Christ and its absence" (p. xi). The title given to the collection of essays stemming from the SEDOS seminar on "The Future of Mission" (which gathered 102 persons from 45 Catholic religious families and six continents), in Rome, 1981, was *Mission in Dialogue,* M. Motte and J. R. Lang, eds. (Maryknoll, N.Y.: Orbis Books, 1982).

13. See my "Dialogical Dialogue," in *The World's Religious Traditions,* Frank Whaling, ed. (Edinburgh: T.T. & Clark, 1984), pp. 61–72 (volume in honor of Wilfred Cantwell Smith).

14. In a still unpublished paper of mine, "Das Heil der Welt," I have tried to show how this idea was common to all salvation-religions. It is, after all, the law of nature: one among millions of spermatozoa becomes a human individual; one among millions of living species becomes human, one among millions of plants becomes an animal, and so on. Only a few of the peoples of the world are Christian and even fewer become divinized, saved, realized.

15. I should point out that when I used the rather ambiguous title "The Unknown Christ of Hinduism" for one of my early books, I was not referring to a Christ known to Christians and unknown to Hindus but to *The Unknown Christ of Hinduism*—and a fortiori of Christianity. See note 3, above.

16. For a representative statement of the contemporary North American debate, see Wilfred Cantwell Smith, *Toward a World Theology* (Philadelphia: Westminster, 1981).

17. The title of the otherwise wonderful book by Karl Prümm exemplifies what I am trying to say: *Christentum als Neuheitserlebnis* (Freiburg: Herder, 1939).

18. Raimundo Panikkar, "Religious Pluralism: The Metaphysical Challenge," in *Religious Pluralism,* Leroy S. Rouner, ed. (Boston University Studies in Philosophy and Religion, vol. 5) (University of Notre Dame Press, 1984), pp. 97–115.

19. Raimundo Panikkar, "Aporias in the Comparative Philosophy of Religion," *Man and World,* 13 (1980) 357–83.

20. See my "The Dream of an Indian Ecclesiology," in *In Search of an Indian Ecclesiology,* the Indian Theological Association, ed. (Bangalore: L.T.C., 1985), pp. 25–54.

21. See "Christianity and World Religions," note 11, above.

22. "Es ist bekannt . . . , dass das Neue Testament sich nirgendwo als 'Schrift' versteht, 'Schrift' ist ihm nur das Alte Testament, während die Christusbotschaft eben

'Geist' ist, der die Schrift verstehen lehrt" (K. Rahner and J. Ratzinger, *Episkopat und Primat* [Freiburg: Herder, 1961], p. 47).

23. In fact, many "ex" or "fallen" Christians who came as "converted" Hindus to Varanasi on the Ganges in the 1960s and 70s have in the 80s, after they returned to their homes, acquired a Christianness-identity.

24. See "The Invisible Harmony," note 10, above.

25. See my "L'eau et la mort. Réflexion interculturelle sur une métaphore," in *Filosofia e religione di fronte alla morte,* M. Olivetti, ed. (Padova: CEDAM, 1981), pp. 481–502.

26. See my "Singularity and Individuality. The Double Principle of Individuation," *Revue Internationale de Philosophie* ("Méthode et philosophie de l'histoire" [Hommage à Raymond Klibansky]), 111–12 (1975) 141–65.

27. See my "Salvation in Christ," note 3, above.

28. For clarity's sake I am forced to refer to other publications of mine: "Colligite Fragmenta: For an Integration of Reality," in *From Alienation to At-One-ness,* F. A. Eigo and S. E. Fittipaldi, eds. (Villanova University Press, 1977), pp. 19–91. Also "Der Mensch—ein trinitarisches Mysterium," in *Die Verantwortung des Menschen für eine bewohnbare Welt im Christentum, Hinduismus, und Buddhismus,* Raimundo Panikkar and W. Strolz, eds. (Freiburg: Herder, 1985), pp. 147–90.

29. See my "The Myth of Pluralism: The Tower of Babel—A Meditation on Non-Violence," *Cross Currents,* 20 (1979) 197–230.

30. See my essay "La religión del futuro—o la crisis del concepto de religión: la religiosidad humana," *Civiltà delle machine* (Rome), 27 (1979) 82–91, where of twelve points, the first states: "The problem of the future of religion is not that of the religion of the future," and the eleventh: "The future of religion is first of all a personal religiousness and not a single religious confession."

7

"I" in the Words of Jesus

SEIICHI YAGI

I

In the contemporary theological scene of Japan, if we ask how Christians can and should understand Buddhism, we would do well to look to the thought of Takizawa Katsumi (1909–1984).[1] He distinguished between what he termed the primary and the secondary contacts of God with the human self. The first contact is the unconditional fact that God is with each one of us, no matter what we are or what we have done, even though we are usually ignorant of this unity lying at the very ground of the self. Despite this ignorance, it can happen, by virtue of the primary contact of God with the self, that we are awakened to this fact. Then it becomes possible for the self to live in conscious accord with the will of God. Takizawa named this awakening the secondary contact of God with the self.

According to Takizawa, Jesus was a man who was awakened to the primary fact—that is, he attained the secondary contact, and he did this so thoroughly and completely that he became the model for other selves. This does not mean, however, that before the coming of Jesus, the primary contact of God with the human self did not exist; for Takizawa, the "event of Jesus" alone is not the exclusive ground of our salvation. Rather, Jesus was the person who in Hebrew tradition played the same role as did Gautama Buddha in the Indian tradition. The ground of salvation is the primary contact of God with the self, and this is the common ground of both Buddhism and Christianity.

I am in full agreement with Takizawa's perspective (though there are other aspects of his thought that I would question).[2] With his distinction between the two contacts and with his understanding of Jesus, he offers Christians possibilities of genuine dialogue with Buddhism that would go beyond Protestant superficial admiration of the depths of Buddhist faith, as well as beyond

Catholic efforts to use the method of Zen meditation without having to leave their sanctuary of Christian exclusivism.

In this essay I shall, for the most part, offer an explanation and interpretation of Takizawa's thought (without laying out his full understanding of the common ground between Christianity and Buddhism) as the basis for coming to a clearer understanding of the distinction between the self and the ego. This understanding will enable us, then, to grasp both the "person" of Jesus and the resurrection[3] in such a way that the signficance and uniqueness of Jesus will be both more existentially meaningful and at the same time more dialogically open to other religious traditions. In a sense, this essay is an example of how a dialogue with Buddhism might aid Christians in formulating a more *pluralistic* christology and theology of religions.

Let me begin with an examination of "I" in the New Testament.

II

In the light of "form criticism," accepted as the general approach to investigating the synoptic traditions, most scholars would respond negatively to the question whether Jesus had a "messianic consciousness." During the "new quest of the historical Jesus" of the 1950s and 60s, scholars explored the "self-consciousness" of Jesus from a new angle; many of them concluded that although Jesus did not understand himself as "messiah" or "son of man," the fact that he spoke and acted with an unparalleled authority, which surpassed even that of Moses, constituted the root of subsequent christology.[4] But unless I am mistaken, none of these scholars inquired deeply into the meaning of "I" in such statements of Jesus as "But I say to you. . . ." This "I" has many levels of meaning. We can ask, then, just what the "I" in the words of Jesus really means.

To answer that question, we can begin by considering certain analogies or parallels in Paul's writings. What is the "I," or the subject, in the words of the Apostle Paul? He states: "For through the law I died to the law—to live for God. I have been crucified with Christ. It is no longer I who live; Christ lives in me. And the life I live now in the flesh I live by faith in the Son of God, who loved me and sacrificed himself for me" (Gal. 2:19f.).

The "I" in Paul has a double structure. When Paul was "crucified with Christ," a change of subject took place so that Christ became Paul's ultimate subject. This does not mean, however, that the "ego" of Paul disappeared.[5] On the contrary, it was Paul's ego that believed in Christ, or more correctly, it was his ego that, aware of the reality of Christ in him, proclaimed that he believed in the Son of God who was, in this case, the object of his faith. In the words of Paul quoted above, Christ is both Paul's ultimate subject as well as the object of his faith referred to in the third person. So we can say that for Paul, Christ as the object of faith and Christ as the ultimate subject of the believer are, paradoxically, identical.

This corresponds to Paul's understanding of the person as consisting of the ultimate subject and the ego. As we shall see below, for Paul the ultimate subject and the ego are both one and two at the same time. They are one, for Paul states: "For I will not dare to speak that which Christ did not wrought *through me* to make the Gentiles obedient, by word and deed" (Rom 15:18). Paul's mission is his own work—none other than what he himself was doing. And yet it was also the deed of Christ who was working through him. We can say that Christ acted *as Paul* because Christ can work in history only through those who are aware of the reality of Christ. In this way, the ultimate subject and the ego of Paul are one.[6]

This same structure is implied in such passages as: "If any man think himself to be a prophet, or spiritual, let him acknowledge that the things I write to you are the commandments of the Lord. If he does not recognize this, he himself is not recognized" (1 Cor. 14:37f.; cf. 2 Cor. 5:20). Or: "Since you seek a proof of Christ speaking in me . . ." (2 Cor. 13:3). Note how the subject changes in the following words: "And to the married I command, not I, but the Lord, a wife must not separate herself from her husband. . . . To the rest I say, not the Lord: If any brother has a wife who has no faith, and she is willing to live with him, he must not deliver her" (1 Cor. 7:10–12). In verse 12, Paul's ego is clearly distinguished from the Lord. In verse 10, the relationship between the ego and the Lord is more complicated: "I command, not I, but the Lord." We might, of course, assume that Paul is here referring to some synoptic tradition (e.g., Mark 10:9). Yet if we consider that Paul generally does not depend on synoptic traditions but directly on the heavenly Lord (see Gal. 1:1; 1 Cor. 14:37f.), and especially if we attend to the remarkable statement "I command, not I, but the Lord," then it seems clear that we are dealing here with a unity between the Lord and Paul. The statement "I command, not I, but the Lord" means that Christ commands through him. Keeping in mind that Jesus Christ was Paul's Lord and that Paul was his servant, we see the double structure in Paul's self (or subjectivity). On the one hand, Christ is the ultimate subject of Paul, Paul's very self; on the other hand, the ego of Paul is clearly distinguished from the Lord. The two realities are both one and two.

In what follows, I use the word "self" in this sense: "Christ in me"—that is, the paradoxical identity of the divine and the human. Paul was aware that all his life-activities were the works of Christ (Phil. 1:21: "To me, to live is Christ"). Human life is at the same time divine. This is the case with the "self"—"Christ in me"—but not with the empirical ego. The ego is the locus where the self becomes manifest.

We can comprehend how important this expression, "Christ in me," was for Paul from the way it appears at decisive passages in his letters. It occurs in the account of his conversion: "[But when it pleased God] to reveal his Son *in me* that I might proclaim him in the Gentiles." The Greek *en emoi* should be translated "in me." Some contemporary theologians consider this revelation to be an interpersonal encounter between Christ and Paul, and not a moment of "enlightenment" (cf. 2 Cor. 4:6), and so they prefer to render *en emoi* as "to me."[7] But the same expression appears again in the very next chapter: "Christ lives *in me*" (Gal. 2:20). Both these expressions are closely related; it makes good sense that the Christ who was once revealed "in me" now "lives in me." Paul uses this expression in passages that express that which grounds his entire being.

Romans 7:17 offers a third example of Paul's use of "in me." Here he describes how the ego in general, including his own ego, is captive to the power of sin by standing under the law and not coming to faith. "It is no longer I who perform it, but sin that dwells *in me*." This passage stands as a kind of negative counterpart to Galatians 2:20: "It is no longer I who live, but Christ lives in me." So Paul's expression, "in me," merits serious attention; most contemporary scholars, however, prefer to focus their attention on the more "mystical" expression: "in Christ."

Paul's understanding of being "in Christ" reflects his notion of the person. As is well known, "in Christ" signifies the grace of Christ. God's gracious gifts are presented "in Christ" (1 Cor. 1:4).[8] Whoever is in Christ is a new creature (2 Cor. 5:17). Christians find themselves, so to speak, in the field of Christ's power, so that they can receive the gifts of Christ's grace. The beings in the field, like music formed in the heart, reflect the field. Or, the field expresses itself as the beings in it—as, for example, the church as the Body of Christ (1 Cor. 12). In this "expresses itself as" we see the unity of the human and the divine. This is the case, as we saw above, with the Christian life. When Paul says, "By the grace of God I am what I am" (1 Cor. 15:10), he is affirming that the grace of God given "in Christ" forms the ground of what he is—the ground of his being. We are dealing here with another paradoxical identity: Christ as the ultimate subject (Christ in) and Christ as the ground of being (in Christ) are identical. And so Paul can say, "I am what I am," In this case, "I" means first of all the ego that has become aware of the reality of Christ in him. Yet "I" signifies the whole person who is in the field of the gracious power of Christ, and at the same time the whole person whose ultimate subject is Christ working "in" and "through me." Christ and "I" are one in such a way that "I" am at the same time a servant of Christ in whom "I" believe.

Figure 1 may throw some light on what I have been talking about.

Figure 1

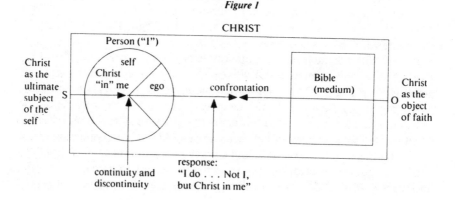

The person is in the field where Christ is at work ("I" in Christ), but at the same time, Christ lives "in me." Christ as the ground of my being is Christ as my ultimate subject. So now, Christ grounds all my life-activities ("To me to live is Christ": Phil. 1:21). In this way, then, Christ and the person are one. My living, though a purely human activity, is the work of Christ; or more precisely, the human is the human based on the activity of Christ, not separated from it. So the activity of the ego is based on Christ working in me—that is, the self (God working in the person produces both willing and performing: Phil. 2:13). On the other hand, Paul could make a clear distinction between "I" and Christ. Indeed, believers can always abandon their faith (Gal. 1:6). This is why Paul (we too) makes the distinction between his ultimate self ("Christ in me") and his ego. Between "Christ in me" and the ego there is both continuity and discontinuity. This is why we are still responsible for our decisions.

All of this makes for a rather complicated reality. Christ speaks to me, for instance, through the Bible. He encounters me personally. And so Christ is the object of my faith and I respond to him. But the response is based on the working of the Holy Spirit (1 Cor. 12:3). This response, this decision of faith, is a dual reality (I . . . not I, but the grace of God). This duality reflects the structural duality according to which Christ in me constitutes my life activities.[9]

We find the same kind of relationship in the fourth Gospel, only here it is more clearly present in the relationship between Father and Son. "And thou, Father, art in me and I am in thee" (John 17:21, and passim). But because the relationship between the Father and the Son in the fourth Gospel is analogous to that between Christ and Christians, we can say that the relationship between Christ and his believers reflects the relationship between Father and Son (e.g., John 10:14–15; 15:13; 17:21–23). "Do you not believe that I am in the Father and the Father in me? The words I speak to you I do not speak of myself; but the Father who dwells in me does his works" (John 14:10).

When the Jesus of the fourth Gospel speaks, it is, fundamentally, the Father speaking through him. Once again, therefore, "in me" indicates the ultimate subject of the Son. Yet although the Father and Son are considered to be one, there is also a distinction between them. The Son obeys the Father when Jesus says: "For I have not spoken of myself; but the Father who sent me gave me a commandment, what I should say, and what I should speak" (John 12:49). In John 14:10, Father and Son can be seen as two concentric circles in which the two centers coincide, whereas in John 12:49, Father and Son appear as two centers in an ellipse, the latter obeying the former. It is not likely that one relationship is based on the other, for that would oversimplify the matter. If we think that Christ and God are in all respects two different realities, so that what Christ does coincides with what God does only insofar as Christ obeys God, we lose the essential unity of Father with Son—the unity expressed in the words: "Anyone who has seen me has seen the Father" (John 14:9). Christ is the Son of God insofar as the ultimate subject of the Son is the Father, but also insofar as the Father and Son are distinguished from each other. They are paradoxically one. As verse 10 indicates, those who have encountered Christ and have seen who speaks through him have seen the Father. Because of this unity, the Son reveals the Father. So we cannot categorize one kind of relationship as primary and the other as secondary.

Both types of relationship between Father and Son—concentric and elliptic—remind us of the two kinds of christology in the ancient church: the Antiochean and the Alexandrian. The Antiocheans maintained that there were two centers in the person of Jesus, the divine and the human, and that the human obeyed the divine; the Alexandrians held that both centers coincided. The ancient church, therefore, maintained that both christologies were true when, in the Council of Chalcedon, it declared that the divinity and humanity of Christ were distinguishable but not separable.

Also in Paul's understanding of his relationship with Christ we find the same two concentric and elliptic models. This illustrates how closely christology and anthropology are related. When Paul declares that he is dead and that Christ lives in him, the relationship between them is concentric. On the other hand, he states that it is he who speaks, not Christ. This does not mean that Paul is entirely separated from Christ and much less that he has been cut off from Christ. But it does show how Paul distinguished himself from Christ. We know further that Paul understood himself as the servant of Christ who is the paradoxical identity of the ultimate self and the object of faith. In this servant relationship, the elliptical model is at least implied—that is, the ego of Paul is subordinated to Christ in him, to Christ as the ultimate subject of Paul. So the relationship between the ego of Paul and Christ in him is not only concentric but also elliptic. Indeed, we find this implied in formulas such as "to be led by the Spirit" (Rom. 8:4ff., and passim), by the Spirit—that is, in whom Christ is present (Rom. 8:9f.).

If this understanding of Paul's relationship with Christ is correct, then the christological models—Antiochean/elliptic and Alexandrian/concentric—reflect the structure of the person in which Christ and the believer are neither one nor two[10]—that is, the subjectivity of believers is composed not only of their own ego but also of "Christ in them" as the ultimate subject in them. This is again analogous to Johannine christology in which the Son, who obeys the Father, is at the same time united as one with God, who is present in the Son as the ultimate subject of the Son. In the fourth Gospel, Christ can speak out of and as his ultimate subject when he says "I speak," so that his words are at the same time the words of the Father who speaks through him. And so it can be said that whoever has seen the Son has seen the Father. This is why I said at the beginning of this chapter that it is important to examine closely what "I" means and who, in the last analysis, speaks when one uses the form, "I say to you." As we shall see more closely below, Jesus himself could speak out of and as his ultimate subject when he said "I say to you." The "I" in these words can be the "divine in him," which spoke through the empirical ego of Jesus. This does not contradict the fact that Jesus was just as much a human being as any of us. For all human beings are so constituted, in their very natures, that the divine and the human are at the same time one and two.[11] It is just that most persons have not yet awakened to this reality.

III

We can carry on this same discussion from the perspective of Zen Buddhism. Hisamatsu Shin-ichi (1889–1980), a great Zen Master who was also professor of philosophy of religion at Kyoto University, was a well-known "atheist." This does not mean that he denied the existence of God when affirming the existence of the world and of humanity. Hisamatsu directed his atheism against "theism." For him, God was not something "out there"; he denied God as *das ganz Andere*. In his study entitled "Atheism" (1949),[12] he asserted a paradoxical identity: "the Formless" (ultimate reality) is not something outside, or merely *das ganz Andere*. To those who would insist that the ultimate must in some way be *das ganz Andere*, Hisamatsu responded that at the same time the ultimate is the self insofar as it is the human being's ultimate subject. *Das ganz Andere*, therefore, is also the ultimate self; this means that absolute heteronomy and absolute autonomy are, paradoxically, identical. According to Hisamatsu, "I do" means, at the ground of the human being, "the Formless does." So he could even say, "I do not die."[13]

But is this not the apotheosis of the human being? Some critics made just this accusation against Hisamatsu. To understand what he meant, we have to look beyond the literal sense of his words. When he and I were once having a philosophical discussion, he said to me, "Since I am so old, I may die at any moment. If I die, please carry on a conversation with me who am in you." What he was trying to make clear to me, I think, is just whom I was talking with at that moment.[14] Yet, from what he was saying, it was clear that he was well aware of his own mortality. So for him, "I" had a double structure: it was composed of the ego and the ultimate self (or, the Formless). Both selves for him are essentially concentric. Indeed, from the figure he drew, we see that when the self is awakened, the infinite (Formless) self contains the finite self (ego) within its circle.[15]

The Formless is also at work in the arts where it finds a visible form. (Hisamatsu was a famous calligrapher.) I asked him, "How can one be sure that the Formless expresses itself as a work of art?" He answered, "The Formless itself in the artist sees it." "But how can spectators see it?" I countered. "If spectators are aware of the Formless within themselves, or if the Formless is awakened to itself in the spectators, they can see the expression of the Formless in a work of art." So for Hisamatsu the Formless produces a work of art through the artist and then sees its own expression as and in a spectator, "for it transcends the empirical ego infinitely." This also explains why artists can also fail to express the Formless in themselves.[16]

Although Hisamatsu maintained that the Formless was the self and the self was the Formless, he also held that "to be I" possessed structure and articulation.[17] He could speak directly from the Formless within him. When he said "I do," it meant that the Formless acted *through* his empirical ego, but at the same time *as* his empirical ego, for the Formless expresses itself only through the empirical ego—that is, the ego that is awakened to the Formless. And because the Formless is immortal, he could say "I do not die."

All this became clear to me in a conversation with him. When he said that the Formless was the self and the self was the Formless, I asked him whether there were *bonnos* (the sinful cares of the unenlightened ego when it acts only for itself) in the Formless Self. On the one hand, no human being is free from *bonnos*; on the other, it is impossible for the Formless to produce *bonnos* in the human being. Now if the human self and the Formless are identical, how can there be *bonnos*? He answered me, "I have no *bonnos*." When I pointed out that all human beings have *bonnos*, he answered, "That's true. But suffering is for me the suffering of that which is free from suffering."[18] However one understands what Hisamatsu was trying to say, one does have a sense of what was speaking through him. Hisamatsu was a person who could speak directly from and as the Formless within him. That this is often the case with Zen Buddhists is something we can keep in mind as we turn to our analysis of what Jesus meant when he said "I."

IV

Usually, any attempt to understand the "self-consciousness of Jesus" begins with an examination of what he had to say about "the son of man." As is well known, Jesus in the synoptic gospels speaks about the son of man as an eschatological figure—the son of God (Mark 8:38) who would appear from the heavens at the end of the world and, by destroying the enemies of God, would save God's people. Therefore, it is argued by those involved in "the quest for the messianic consciousness of Jesus," if Jesus called himself the son of man, he was aware of himself as a divine being.

Since the studies of Jackson-Lake,[19] the synoptic passages on the son of man have been classified into three groups: (1) the son of man to come, (2) the son of man who would suffer and be resurrected, and (3) the son of man active on this earth. Rudolf Bultmann, in basic agreement with this classification, argued:

> The third group arose only because of a misunderstanding of the transla-
> tion into Greek. In Aramaic, "the son of man" was not a messianic title
> at all, but signified "man" or "I." The second group comprises *vaticinia
> ex eventu* [prophecies after the fact], which are not found in Q. Only the
> first group contains the oldest tradition. In this group the expression the
> son of man is used in the third person."[20]

It is not necessary to enter into the history of scholarly debate on this issue. After Philipp Vielhauer had negated the authenticity of all the son of man sayings,[21] other New Testament scholars argued for the authenticity of the first groups of sayings.[22] The views of T. W. Manson are especially interesting: he understood the figure of the son of man as a "collective personality."[23]

We have seen that according to Paul, Christ was paradoxically both the ultimate subject and the object of faith. In Hisamatsu, the *das ganz Andere* was paradoxically his ultimate self, so that although he spoke of the Formless in the third person, he could also speak out of and as the Formless within him. Might we not say the same about Jesus? In Mark 8:38 he states, "If anyone is ashamed of me and my words in this wicked and godless age, the son of man will be ashamed of him, when he comes in the glory of his Father and of the holy angels." Although Jesus here refers to the son of man in the third person, he himself is at the same time the representative of the son of man on earth. In this way we can say that Jesus and the son of man are one, despite the qualitative differences between them. We could say that Jesus is here speaking out of and as the son of man. This means that we do not need the theory of a mistake in the Greek translation to interpret the third group of son of man sayings. Rather, we can say that Jesus announced that in his words and actions it was the son of man acting and speaking in and through him, even though from the outside it seemed that his empirical ego was the agent.

For Jesus, therefore, the son of man was both *das ganz Andere* and his own ultimate subject (in a paradoxical unity). Just as only those who are awakened to the Formless in them can see how the Formless expresses itself in a work of art, so only those who are awakened to the reign of God in them can see that the son of man—that is, the son of God—is at work in, through, and as Jesus, in whom the reign of God has been revealed as "the lightning flash that lights up the earth from end to end" (Luke 17:24).[24]

I think we can best understand the unity between the son of man and the reign of God when we assume that the figure of the son of man as used in the words of Jesus is the personification of the reign of God, just as Amida Buddha in Pure Land Buddhism is the personification of the saving activity of the transcendent Amida, who comes from the Formless and reveals it to his believers.[25] This helps us understand the words of Mark 2:27ff.: "The Sabbath was made for the sake of the person and not the person for the sake of the Sabbath: therefore the Son of man is sovereign over the Sabbath." The law is the form that the reign of God (the will of God) assumes on earth in order to show itself, to make itself known to human beings. In this sense, the law is made for the sake of the person. The law itself is not the ultimate, but is a visible form of the invisible reign, will, of God. The law is based on the reign of God, which is personified in the son of man. *Therefore* the son of man is sovereign over the law.[26] This means that a human being through whom the son of man acts—as is the case with Jesus—can break the law if the law is estranged from the reign of God and so binds a person in a heteronomous way. For according to the original nature of every person, the "son of man" (reign of God) is the person's ultimate subject (concentricity), while the empirical ego obeys with inner understanding, so that when one is "enlightened" one understands the law as the expression of ultimate reality. But if the law ceases to be the medium of the reign of God, it can be broken. Therefore Jesus could invalidate the entire ritual system of ancient purification and say: "Nothing that goes into a person from the outside can defile the person. No, it is the things that come out of a person that defile a person" (Mark 7:15).

So the title "son of man" is not a mere self-identification of Jesus. Therefore we can say that the sayings of the third group are for the most part authentic, with the exception of the sayings in which "the son of man" is clearly used only as a way of identifying Jesus or in which the understanding of Jesus in primitive Christianity is clearly reflected (e.g., Mark 8:31; 10:45). With the sayings of the third group, therefore, Jesus declared his work and words to be those of the son of man in him. As we said, the son of man is for Jesus both *das ganz Andere* and his ultimate self. But to those who were not awakened to the reality of the reign of God in them, it seemed that Jesus as an empirical person held himself to be divine and so able to forgive sins (Mark 2:10) and also to break the law (Mark 2:23ff.). So although many of "the Jews" were scandalized at such blasphemy, Jesus' followers went on simply to identify him with the divine, without any distinction between the ultimate subject and the empirical ego of Jesus. But for Jesus himself, it was the son of man who had the right to forgive sins and break the law, not Jesus as an empirical ego. Once again: for him the son of man was both *das ganz Andere* and his ultimate subject. This was Jesus' self-understanding. He did not apotheosize himself, for as an empirical man, he did not hold himself to be divine (Mark 10:18); but he was aware that his actions were those of the son of man in him. Though it was no self-apotheosis, such an awareness could be reached only by someone who "has died" entirely, so that "the son of man" could live in him (cf. Gal. 2:20).

In this context, we can take up the so-called antitheses in the Sermon on the Mount[27] (Matt. 5:21–44) and ask who is actually speaking when we hear "But I say to you":

> You have learned that our forefathers were told, "Do not commit murder; those who commit murder must be brought to judgment." But I say to you: Those who nurse anger against their brother or sister must be brought to judgment (vv. 21f.). . . . You have learned that they were told, "Do not commit adultery." But I say to you: If a man looks on a woman with a lustful eye, he has already committed adultery with her in his heart (vv. 27f.). . . . You have learned that they were told, "Do not break your oath," and "Oaths sworn to the Lord must be kept." But I say to you: you are not to swear at all (vv. 33f.). . . . You have learned that they were told, "An eye for an eye, and a tooth for a tooth." But I say to you; Do not set yourself against the person who wrongs you. If someone slaps you on the right cheek, turn and offer him your left (vv. 38f.). . . . You have learned that they were told, "Love your neighbor, hate your enemy." But I say to you: Love your enemies (vv. 43f.).

With such words, Jesus clearly surpassed the authority of Moses. But whoever is superior to Moses, must be divine. So if Jesus spoke this way, he must have considered himself to be divine. Many did indeed think the same thing about him, and in their confessions, the christology of primitive Christianity can be found.[28] According to this christology, Jesus is a divine being of heavenly origin, the Lord, the son of God who is equal with God. This christology was much discussed in the "quest of the historical Jesus," and many scholars still hold to its views. But such an interpretation does not take into sufficient account that the "I" of Jesus had two centers, the ultimate subject and the empirical ego and that these centers related to each other concentrically as well as elliptically. Still, we have to ask what is the "I" in the antithetical sayings. If it is the empirical ego of Jesus, he is suspect of self-apotheosis. His enemies could accuse him of being a blasphemer of God, whereas his followers thought this empirical man was divine.

I can suggest a different perspective. In the antitheses—really, in the words of Jesus in general—something divine (the reign of God or the son of man as its personification) spoke through the mouth of his empirical person. This was possible because the divine was for him both *das ganz Andere* and his own ultimate subject. To grasp more fully what is really contained in such talk of the divine, one would have to make a further distinction between God, the reign of God (the son of man who is in nature the son of God), and the Spirit of God (cf. Matt. 12:28). At the moment, however, I limit myself to investigating the "I" in Jesus. Jesus was speaking directly from and as the divine when he said, "But I say to you"—that is, he was speaking from his "ultimate subject," which was at one with his humanity (divine-human). The "reign of God" was so clearly revealed in him (to his ego) that he could tell others what it brought forth in the human heart (cf. Phil. 2:13). It called forth love of one's enemy, exemplified in the figure of the good Samaritan; there is an immediacy of love that is so natural and yet so paradoxical that its roots go deeper than the ego, for its roots are the activity of "the reign of God." So Jesus spoke as the divine: the son of God, for the son of God is real in our historical reality only in and through empirical human beings who are aware of the son—just as "Christ" did his work through Paul (Rom. 15:18).

In the depth of the human *self*, the divine and the human are one. We call this reality the incarnate Logos. If my interpretation is correct, Jesus lived *as* the incarnate Logos. An authentic human existence is so structured that the incarnate Logos becomes real in our history in, through, and as the authentic human existence that is aware of its own depths. Yet Jesus also called God *Abba* ("papa"). As an empirical person (the ego), Jesus understood himself to be subordinated to God (cf. Mark 10:18), though, of course, in an intimate union with God.

If this intepretation is correct, we can more clearly understand the antitheses of Jesus; they are by no means only "the highest moral attainment" of humanity. They are not mere morality or ethics, for ethics makes up a moral program valid for the ego. Ethics constitutes social norms for the ego, or the norms for the sociality of the ego. The antitheses in Jesus' sayings are not a matter of the ego; they do not provide social norms for the ego. Rather, they show what is there in the *self* under the reign of God, for they are the words of this reign. Just as the Formless does not produce any *bonno*s in the human heart, so under the reign of God—that is, insofar as it is revealed to the ego and thus works in the human being—there is no anger, nor lustful desire, nor vengence, nor hatred in the human self. When the reign of God in the person is so revealed that it becomes reflected in the ego, then it constitutes the will of the ego (cf. Phil. 2:13); then what is realized is "I will," not "you should."

Of course, to speak as Jesus did is not easy. But it is possible, I think, for all of us insofar as it is based on the activity of God who is at the same time both *das ganz Andere* and the ultimate subject of every human being. If God is merely *das ganz Andere*, the absolutely transcendent that is named only in the third person, then God is something absolutely objective and heteronomous. If this is so, then human beings could know God only through special, supernatural revelation; and such a unique revelation would be the ground for the exclusivity of Christianity. If, on the other hand, God is merely the ultimate subject of the human being, something that speaks and acts only in the first person, then suspicion of the self-apotheosis of the relative is likely. So the understanding of the transcendent as the paradoxical identity of *das ganz Andere* and the ultimate subject of every human being is indispensable not only for our understanding of Jesus but also for our theological thinking today.

V

1. In the first part of this chapter, I mentioned Takizawa's distinction between the primary and the secondary contacts of God with the self. In light of my study of Paul and Jesus, I might interpret that distinction to mean that every human being, a priori, is in the field of God's grace (*in Christo*). The unconditional given of our existence is that God is with each one of us (the primary contact of God with us). This is comparable to the fundamental notion of Mahayana Buddhism that every living thing has a "Buddha-nature." But this reality is found at the depth level of our being (the self as divine-humanity), a level we are generally not aware of; and because we are not aware of it, this reality is not activated in our hearts. And so we do not know God at all.

The primary contact of God with us—the fact that at the ground of our existence we are in the field of God's grace so that our being reflects this field—constitutes and conditions the very existence of each of us. In this sense, the divine and the human are structurally and a priori one. But it is a dialectical oneness. Insofar as the divine does not reveal itself to the ego—that is, insofar as we are not aware of it—this reality is virtually nonexistent and in this sense we are not united with the divine. Or to put it in a Buddhist expression: "There is in the living things no Buddha-nature."[29] But when this reality reveals itself in and to the ego, when the ego becomes aware of it, then the divine begins to act through, in, and as the empirical human being so that the "self" is discovered to be divine-human. The divine realizes itself in our historical reality. This is the second contact of God with the human being according to Takizawa. It is an event. And then we can say that we have become aware of it because it was already there, a priori.

But can we really say that this divine-human oneness is activated or actualized when we become aware of it? And how do we become aware of it? By a decision of faith? Yes. Through enlightenment? That too is possible. In any case, because the reality of the primary contact of God with the human being is virtually nonexistent insofar as the ego is ignorant of it, its "revelation" in the ego is an event that is discontinuous with the ego's past. It has no real grounding in the past. This "revelation" is not a necessary result of the primary contact; it does not have to happen. And so one is justified in speaking of the "Holy Spirit" who gives the gift of faith (1 Cor. 12:3) or brings us to the Truth (John 14:17; 16:13), just as in Jodo-Buddhism the power of Amida Buddha brings forth faith in the person. In such descriptions, the ego is realizing its groundedness in that which transcends it.

If all this is so, we can make a distinction between the self and the ego—that is, between the primary contact at the depths of the self and the secondary contact as an event taking place in the ego. Earlier I distinguished between the self and the ego because of the continuity and the discontinuity between them. Here I am making this distinction for another reason.[30] I am using Takizawa's distinction, but with a necessary adjustment, for it seems to me that Takizawa leaves no room for the role of the Holy Spirit—or, that he does not fully see the meaning of enlightenment.

2. We can extend our analysis to provide an explanation as to how faith in the resurrection of Jesus arose: that which primitive Christianity called the "risen, pneumatic Christ," or "the heavenly Lord," or "the son of God," was none other than that which spoke through the mouth of Jesus of Nazareth when he said "But I say to you. . . . " "The Risen Christ" is what Jesus called "the reign of God" or "the son of man." The disciples of Jesus did not understand Jesus when he was with them. After his death on the cross, "the reign of God" was revealed in them in the same way it was revealed to Paul: "The son of God was revealed to me" (Gal. 1:16). This is the event of religious enlightenment, in which the divine reveals itself in the structure of paradoxical identity between *das ganz Andere* and the person's ultimate subject, and in the oneness of the divine and the human. But the disciples took this experience for the appearance of Jesus who had been resurrected from the dead. For in the activity of that which they had become aware of and that which was realized in and as the depth of themselves, they acknowledged the very same reality that had spoken and acted *as* Jesus when he lived with them.

Furthermore, at that time, "resurrection" would have been the way they interpreted such an event. After the death of John the Baptist, for instance, when Jesus appeared center stage and took the place of his teacher (the Baptist), some said that the Baptist was resurrected and that his power acted in Jesus (Mark 6:14ff.). In the same way, the disciples of Jesus interpreted the event of their enlightenment and believed that Jesus who had been killed on the cross was resurrected and that the power of Jesus was now at work in them, for they had now become "new creatures" (2 Cor. 5:17), agents of Jesus. In other words, the disciples did not distinguish between Jesus' depth and his empirical ego (that is, between the primary and secondary contacts in Jesus, as Takizawa put it), so that they held that Jesus as a historical person was resurrected. In this way, the "event of Jesus" (his death and resurrection) came to be considered the absolute ground of human salvation.

But what they named "the risen Christ" was really what Takizawa would call the primary contact of God with the human being—that is, divine-humanity, Logos incarnate, oneness of the divine and the human at the depth of every human being (self). Therefore Paul could say that "Christ" lived in him when "the son of God" was revealed to him (Gal. 1:16; 2:20). In Takizawa's terms again, primitive Christianity did not distinguish between the primary and secondary contacts of God with the person of Jesus. And so they thought that the primary contact itself—the divine-human oneness—was brought about by Jesus who was resurrected in order to remain with them in the flesh. But the divine-human oneness is not confined to Jesus alone; it is a reality in the depth of every human self, a reality in the church as the Body of Christ in which Christ is truly present (1 Cor. 12), as well as in each believer (Rom. 8:10). In its depth, the divine is one with the human in every human self as well as in humanity as a whole. Here "Christ" remains divinity with flesh, which becomes manifest as well as real in the event of enlightenment, the secondary contact of God with the person. But in its nature, it is prior to enlightenment as the ground common to Buddhism and Christianity.

This is my interpretation and explanation of Takizawa's views, in relation to contemporary New Testament studies. Of course, the results of New Testament studies are not certain; at most, they are probable. Still, it is important that religious pluralism not contradict the results of New Testament studies, just as our investigation of the New Testament is given new stimulus and light from dialogue with other world religions.

NOTES

1. See the discussion of his lectures in "The First Conference of Tōzai Shūkyō Kōryū Gakkai," in *Buddhist-Christian Studies*, 3 (1983) 123–56. In this same volume (pp. 63–97), Tokiyuki Nobuhara compares Takizawa with John Cobb, Jr.: "Principles for Interpreting Christ/Buddha: Katsumi Takizawa and John B. Cobb, Jr."

2. See my own critical comments on his views, *ibid.*, pp. 137–41, 152–53. I should like to add here that even if one accepts Takizawa's distinction, together with his understanding of Jesus, one could in a sense still say with the fourth evangelist that "truth came through Jesus Christ" (John 1:17). Paul is an example; by the grace of God he had been separated from his mother's womb to be a missionary to the gentiles, and yet he was ignorant of all this before the revelation of the son of God in him so that he persecuted Christians (Gal. 1:15–16; cf. 2 Cor. 4:6). But after Christ was revealed in him, he could say "Christ lives in me" (Gal. 1:20), so that from then on, he proclaimed Christ among the Gentiles as Christ worked through him (Rom. 15:18). Therefore, insofar as the self is ignorant of the primary contact of God with the self, this contact is not real; it does not

work in and through the self. It is virtually nonexistent. The fundamental importance, therefore, of "awakening" or "enlightenment" lies in the fact that "Truth" (*dharma*) is activated in the self through enlightenment; it works in the self when the self is awakened to it. In this sense, we can say that "Truth" was virtually nonexistent in history before Jesus (or, in the East, before Buddha) came—or more exactly, before Jesus was awakened to it. It is true that the reason why one can be awakened to the primary contact of God with the self is that it is there prior to the awakening. But it is also true that the primary contact becomes real and is activated in the self only when the self is awakened to it. The same paradox is contained in the well-known statement, "Those who are given to Christ by God believe in him" (John 6:37). And yet, "those who believe in Christ become the children of God" (John 1:12).

3. Takizawa's views contain implications concerning the manner in which the disciples of Jesus came to believe in his resurrection. He holds that after the death of Jesus, the eyes of his disciples were opened to see the primary contact of God with the self—that is, "Christ," "the son of God," which is at the ground of each self. See Takizawa, *Seishono Kiristoto Gendaino Shi'i* ("Biblical Christ and Modern Thinking") (Tokyo: Shinkyō Shuppansha, 1965), pp. 51–53. This viewpoint agrees substantially with my study of biblical faith in the resurrection of Jesus: *Shin'yaku Shisōno Seiritsu* ("Formation of New Testament Thoughts") (Tokyo: Shinkyō Shuppansha, 1963); *Kiristoto Iesu* ("Christ and Jesus") (Tokyo: Kōdansha Gendai Shinsho, 1969). In the context of the "new quest of the historical Jesus," I made a careful comparison of Jesus with Paul, and came to the conclusion that "the reign of God" according to Jesus and "the risen pneumatic Christ" according to primitive Christianity are different names for the same reality. I present this claim in the last section of this chapter, though in a different and abbreviated form. Concerning the thesis that Christianity and Buddhism are based on a common ground, see Seiichi Yagi, *Bukkyōto Kōristokyōno Setten* ("The Point of Contact between Buddhism and Christianity") (Kyoto: Hōzōkan, 1975). My article, "Paul and Shinran: Jesus and Zen," in *Buddhist-Christian Dialogue—Mutual Renewal and Transformation*, Paul O. Ingram and Frederick J. Streng, eds. (Honolulu: University of Hawaii Press, 1986) is a resumé of my book with the same title: *Paulo-Shinran; Iesu-Zen* (Kyoto: Hōzōkan, 1983).

4. Ernst Käsemann, "Das Problem des historischen Jesu," *Exegetische Versuche und Besinnungen*, vol. 1 (Göttingen: Vandenhoeck & Ruprecht, 1960, 1st ed.). Rudolf Bultmann had argued earlier that Jesus' call for a decision on the part of his hearers already implied a christology; see "Die Christologie des Neuen Testaments," in *Glauben und Verstehen,* vol. 1 (Tübingen: J. C. B. Mohr, 4th ed., 1961), p. 266.

5. Ego is the subject of feeling, thinking, and doing—the I, insofar as I am conscious that I feel, think, and do something. When dreaming, I am not conscious that I am producing the dream. The dream is therefore not a product of the ego, but of the unconscious. It is important to bear in mind that "enlightenment" means that the ego becomes aware of the reality of *dharma* which bears the whole existence of the person. If this is so, we have to make a clear distinction between the "ultimate subject" and the "ego." As we shall see below, the ego makes decisions, but it has deeper roots.

6. In affirming this twofold unity of ultimate subject and ego, I think I am in agreement with the views of Donald M. Baillie in *God Was in Christ* (New York: Scribner's, 1948). Baillie finds the mystery of the incarnation reflected in the structure contained in "not I . . . but the grace of God" (1 Cor. 15:10). I agree with this interpretation of the incarnation, but I cannot understand why Baillie, throughout his book, insists on a qualitative difference between Jesus and other believers (for instance,

p. 145). "I do . . . not I, but the transcendent"—these words indicate the very structure of incarnation. Logos incarnate, therefore, is not confined to Jesus; it is a reality in the church as "the body of Christ" (1 Cor. 12) insofar as in this body there is the unity described above. Indeed, Paul can in a sense identify the body of Christ with Christ himself (v. 12). But this unity is not always found in the empirical church or in its members. So we must examine more closely the structure of the person: the relationship between the ultimate self and the ego. Between them, there is both continuity and discontinuity. See below.

7. Akira Satake, *Galatea Sho* ("Galatians") (Tokyo: Shinkyō Shuppansha, 1974), pp. 94–95. I agree with this interpretation as long as "to me" means that the ego becomes aware of the reality of Christ "in me." "Christ was revealed in me" and "Christ was revealed to me" do not really contradict each other, for, as I said above (note 2), "Christ in me" becomes real when "Christ is revealed to me."

8. Hans Conzelmann, *Grundriss der Theologie des Neuen Testaments* (Munich: Kaiser, 1968), pp. 232ff.

9. *The Other Side of God: A Polarity in World Religions*, Peter L. Berger, ed. (New York: Anchor Press, 1981) examines the typology of religious experience proposed by Berger (confrontation and interiority) and finds that many religious personages—Paul, Francis of Assisi, Shinran, for example—evince both a confrontation model and an interiority model in their understanding of the person's relationship with God. According to Figure 1 in my text, the transcendent both "confronts" and "reveals" itself "in" the person. From the standpoint of the religious ego responding to the call of the transcendent, the transcendent is dominantly *das ganz Andere* that confronts it through some medium (e.g., the Bible); but in the experience of inward unity ("Christ in me" constituting my life-activity), the unity of the transcendent and the self is dominant. Here we touch on the roots of mysticism. But I find the *structural* unity in the self, not in the ego.

10. Again, this issue is quite complicated. (1) Christ and the self are one in the depths of the self: "Christ in me" constitutes "my" life-activity. This relationship transcends my consciousness, though it is activated through consciousness. (2) But in the activity of the ego, there is also a twofoldness, insofar as its activity is based on inward unity. There is then a continuity between "Christ in me" and the activity of the ego (concentricity). On the other hand, there is structural discontinuity between the two. In this sense, we can say that the ego obeys Christ, for it responds to the call of Christ in encounter, and it acts through its own decision, though its activity is based on the activity of Christ "in" the person (ellipticity).

11. If "Christ in me" constitutes "my" life-activity, the divine and the human are neither one nor two, or at the same time, one and two. There are many instances in which A constitutes non-A as part or condition of the latter (I call this "front-structure"). So a word from another person, when changed into my own word, constitutes a part of my own thinking. In such mental activity the person and I are at the same time one and two. Or in the case of music, the human heart and physical sounds are neither one nor two. Music is human-physical as the self is divine-human. They are different realities, but insofar as the human heart expresses itself *as* music, they are one. M. Honda sees in the structure "not one, not two" the essence of religious thinking. See his "The Encounter of Christianity with the Buddhist Logic of Soku," in Ingram and Streng, *Buddhist-Christian Dialogue,* pp. 217–30.

12. *Zettai Shutai Dō* ("The Way of the Absolute Subject"), Collected Works of Hisamatsu Shin-ichi, Vol. 2 (Tokyo: Risōsha, 1972), pp. 53–93.

13. *Shinnin Hisamatsu Shin-ichi* ("Hisamatsu Shin-ichi as True Man") (Tokyo: Shunjūsha, 1985), p. 168. Here one of Hisamatsu's leading disciples, Ryūtarō Kitahara, reports what the master said to him: "I do not die though my fleshly body dies. I am always with you."

14. This dialogue between Hisamatsu and Yagi was published as *Kakuno Shūkyo* ("Religion of Awakening") (Tokyo: Shunjūsha, 1980).

15. "Ningenno Bukkyōteki Kōzō" ("The Buddhist Structure of the Human Being"), in *Zettai Shutai Dō*, p. 253.

16. *Kakuno Shūkyo*, pp. 129–31.

17. I understand Hisamatsu in this way: though he maintained the identity of the Formless with the self, he said that the Formless transcends the empirical ego infinitely. So for Hisamatsu, the subject is composed of the self, which is one with the Formless, and of the ego, which is continuous-discontinuous with the self.

18. *Kakuno Shūkyo*, pp. 5–7.

19. *The Beginnings of Christianity*, part 1 (Grand Rapids: Baker Book House, 1979), pp. 368ff. (originally published in 1920).

20. *Theologie des Neuen Testaments* (Tübingen: J. C. B. Mohr, 2nd ed., 1954), p. 31. Translation by Yagi.

21. "Gottesreich und Menschensohn in der Verkündigung Jesu," in *Festschrift für G. Dehn* (Neukirchen: Neukirchener Verlag, 1957), pp. 51ff.

22. Ferdinand Hahn, *Christologische Hoheitstitel* (Göttingen: Vandenhoeck & Ruprecht, 1966), pp. 32ff. Kenzō Tagawa, *Maruko Fukuinsho* ("The Gospel according to Mark") (Tokyo: Shinkyō Shuppansha, 1972), pp. 190–91.

23. For my understanding and criticism of the son of man sayings I am indebted to Norman Perrin, *The Kingdom of God in the Teachings of Jesus* (London: SCM Press, 1963), chap. 7. Shinran, too, affirms the collective figure of Amida Buddha; Amida, the great Light, consists of infinite little lights that are also considered to be Amidas (*Genseiriyaku Wasan 12*, in *Jōdo Wasan*). This reminds us of Christ in Paul: Christ is present in the church as his body (1 Cor. 12) as well as in each member of it (Rom. 8:10).

24. It may not be too bold a conjecture to see in this saying a reflection of the enlightenment of the heart, for cosmological reality is at the same time reality in this world. See Luke 17:21b.

25. "The kingdom of God" and "the Pure Land," or more correctly, "the son of man with the kingdom of God" and "Amida Buddha with his Pure Land" are at least comparable. See Tokuzen Tamaru, "Jōdoto Kamino Kuni" ("The Pure Land and the Kingdom of God"), in *Jōdokōyto Kiristokyō* ("Jodo-Buddhism and Christianity") (Tokyo: Sankibō, 1977). The following parallels are noteworthy: God and Christ in Paul, the relationship between God and "the son of man" (i.e., the son of God, Mark 8:37) in Jesus, and the relationship between the Formless (*Dharma-kāya*) and Amida Buddha (*Sambhoga-kāya*) in Jōdo Buddhism. In other words, "the son of man" in Jesus and "Christ" in Paul correspond to "Amida Buddha" in Shinran. They all come from the ultimate reality (God or *Dharma-kāya*) and represent it, in the role of "savior" (in the case of "the son of man" and Christ, also in the role of judge). It is also noteworthy that both the son of man in our understanding and Amida Buddha are transcendent-incarnate: they are at work in and as human beings. As incarnate divine-human, they are reminiscent of traditional claims of christology. Amida Buddha who is at work in the believer corresponds to "Christ in me" in Paul.

26. In this passage, "the son of man" can also mean true human nature, as Tagawa argues; he also considers this saying to be genuine. See *Maruko Fukeuinsho*, p. 190.

This interpretation does not call into question the point I have been making, for "true human nature" consists in the fact that: I live, not I, but "Christ" in me, or in the case of Jesus, that Jesus lives, not Jesus, but the son of man in him. This is comparable to the "True Person" in Rinzai (Chinese: *Lin-chi I-hsüam*) who is at work in every life activity of the enlightened (*Rinzairoku*, Jōdō, 3: Jishū, 1).

27. Joachim Jeremias, *Die Bergpredigt* (Stuttgart: Calver Verlag, 1959); this little pamphlet offers a fine summary of contemporary understandings of the Sermon on the Mount in Germany. A short history of how the Sermon on the Mount has been understood is given in Ulrich Luz, *Das Evangelium nach Matthäus* (Evangelisch-katholischer Kommentar zum Neuen Testament, vol. 1/1) (Zürich: Benziger Verlag/Neukirchen-Vluyn: Neukirchener Verlag, 1985), pp. 191ff. Here I am not trying to interpret the Sermon on the Mount but only asking "christological" questions.

28. See note 4, above.

29. So Dōgen, *Shōbō-Genzo*, 3 (on the Buddha-nature). Dōgen holds that (1) there is Buddha-nature in every living thing; (2) there is no Buddha-nature in every living thing; (3) Buddha-nature realizes itself when human beings become aware of it (enlightenment).

30. This distinction is perhaps similar to C. G. Jung's distinction between the self and the ego. See *Die Beziehung zwischen dem Ich und dem Unbewussten* (Zürich, 1933). I read this book in translation (translated by Akria Noda, Tokyo: Jinbunshoin, 1982). Jung even refers to Gal. 2:20 (p. 164 of the Japanese translation) and holds the true self to be something divine in us (p. 120 of the translation). Yet Jung's notion of the self is not the same as our "ultimate subject," for in Jung the true self is hidden and does not necessarily show itself in its fulness to those who are aware of it. See his dialogue with S. Hisamatsu in *Tōyōteki Mu* ("Nothingness in the Far East") in the collected works of Hisamatsu Shin-ichi, vol. 1, 1970, p. 389.

PART III

The Ethico-Practical Bridge: Justice

8

Feminism and Jewish-Christian Dialogue

Particularism and Universalism in the Search for Religious Truth

ROSEMARY RADFORD RUETHER

It appears odd to link together questions of feminism and questions of Jewish-Christian dialogue around the common theme of universalism and particularism. On the one hand, one has the dialogue between two patriarchal faiths, both of which are both particularist and universalist, although in different ways. On the other hand, one has the feminist challenge to all patriarchal religions and ideologies. What these two relationships have in common, for the purpose of this discussion, is that both represent challenges to the concept of a single universal biblical faith. I will discuss this question from the Christian side, rather than pretending that I myself can stand outside and discuss this impartially, and from all sides.

JEWISH-CHRISTIAN RELATIONSHIPS, PARTICULARISM AND UNIVERSALISM

Christianity has traditionally regarded Judaism as a religion of obsolete particularism, tied to the idea of God's election of a particular people and land, which has been superceded by the superior revelation of God's redemption of all peoples throughout the earth by the one universal faith. But this view misconstrues the potential of Judaism for its own distinct understanding of universalism, as well as the hidden particularism behind Christian claims to universalism.

Christian claims to universalism were shaped culturally within the Greco-Roman Empire, which believed itself to be a universal empire containing the one true humanistic culture. All persons of other cultures became "human" by assimilating into Greco-Roman culture and accepting its political sway. Those who remained outside this imperial orbit or rejected its culture were seen as "barbarians"—that is, persons of uncivilized status, less than fully human.

In the fourth century, Christianity saw its universalism as an expression of the messianic promises to the Jews that, in the last days, all nations would be gathered to Zion and worship the one God (e.g., Isaiah 26:6–8). This promise, it was claimed, was being fulfilled in Christianity. In Christianity all the nations of the gentiles are to be gathered into Zion in order to worship the true God of biblical faith. Israel itself, unfortunately, failed to recognize and accept its own universal fulfillment.

Christianity synthesized these two kinds of universalism—messianic universalism and Greco-Roman imperialist universalism. Having begun as a Semitic faith in an Aramaic-speaking world, Christianity expanded to the East into the Iranian world toward India, as well as to the West into the Greek- and Latin-speaking worlds. But those forms of Christianity that were not within the Greco-Roman Empire and its culture failed to flourish. Those areas were overrun by the superior ability of Islam to appeal to Middle Eastern peoples as a new universal religion rooted in Semitic and Arabic culture. Modern Christian missions to India, Africa, and Asia have planted churches divided between many denominations, which together comprise only a small percentage of the population, usually among its more westernized groups. Nowhere has Christianity become the predominant form of religion among peoples who are not heirs of Greco-Roman culture. Thus Christian universalism, in practice, has remained mostly limited to areas shaped culturally by Greco-Roman and European civilization.

This cultural limitation of Christian evangelism was recognized by missionaries as early as the Jesuit missions in China in the sixteenth century. Those Jesuits tried to create a distinctively Chinese Christianity that would stand in the same relationship to traditional Confucian culture as Christianity in the West stood in relation to the Hebrew Bible and to Greek civilization. Modern Asian Christians today have taken up this theme in a new way in their discussions of indigenization of Christianity into Asian culture. Asian theologians, such as Kosuke Koyama, in his book *Waterbuffalo Theology* (Orbis, 1974), have recognized that Christianity brings with it Western culture. Asians need to assimilate the distinctive perspectives on historical existence brought by Christianity and Western thought, but they also must integrate these views into Asian spirituality.

This discussion so far has not made it clear whether a Christianity that is truly indigenous to non-Western culture is possible, or whether it would be such a radical translation of Christianity into a different worldview that it would become a new religion. In other words, it is not clear that Christianity actually can be disincarnated from its Greco-Roman flesh and incarnated into a different cultural body. Is there really such a thing as a timeless essence of Christianity that can be separated from its classic theological expressions as a synthesis of Jewish religion and Greco-Roman philosophical culture?

But this question of the relationship between Christianity and culture only raises the deeper question: Is the Christian claim to be the one universal faith by which all persons relate authentically to God still credible? Although the religions of most tribal peoples, such as pre-Christian Europeans and Latin American Indians, faded away under Christian evangelism, Christianity has not succeeded in breaking the power of the great historical religions, such as Buddhism, Judaism, and Islam. These have not been conquered by the great missionary and imperialist expansion of the West in modern times.

In the anticolonialist reaction of Third World peoples, these alternative faiths have experienced vigorous revival. The confident claims of late nineteenth-century Christian missionaries that soon all the world would be Christian, in fulfillment of ancient Christian expectations, is no longer easy to believe. It seems that Christianity will coexist with other faiths for some time to come. Many missionaries have even ceased to define their goal primarily in terms of religious conversion and are instead pursuing goals of social development. Thus Christian faith in its universal mission is in crisis. In recent years, however, discussion of this crisis has been counteracted by resurgent fundamentalisms within Christianity, Judaism, Islam, and even Buddhism, all of which revive their mutually antagonistic claims.

Judaism also had its own version of this dilemma of universalism and particularism, but defined it in a different way. What was clear from the Jewish point of view is that God had elected the Jewish people and given it the Torah as the way of salvation. This was the way that Jews were to walk in order to be faithful to God and fulfill God's command to become a righteous people. Historically, Jews have been surrounded by imperialistic peoples—the Hellenistic, Greco-Roman, Islamic, and Christian empires, each of which have claimed to have the key to the one true humanity and the one authentic relationship to the divine. Jews have preserved their distinctiveness by resisting these universalistic claims, and have been regarded, in turn, as a perverse and misanthropic people because of their failure to assimilate. For Jews, assimilation has posed as great a threat to their status as a distinctive people as has persecution.

Views of other nations, or "gentiles," have varied in Jewish tradition from an ethnocentric hostility that sees the other nations as evil ones that will be defeated and destroyed by God, to a benign liberalism that seeks a modus vivendi among all peoples through common standards of humanitarianism, thus leaving Jews to pursue their own distinctive religious and cultural path. Classic rabbinic Judaism speaks of the Noachite laws, or the laws of general human decency, which God has given to all the nations to bring them up to general human standards, whereas God has given the Torah, as a distinct path of righteousness, to the Jews. Some rabbinic texts even suggested that all peoples could be saved by being faithful to their own paths of righteousness. For Judaism, the key to a final universalism, by which Israel and the nations might worship one God, remains unrevealed. It belongs to the messianic age. The present world remains incomplete.

Judaism, unlike Christianity—which believes that it already has the messianic dispensation—does not have the same impulse toward a universalistic mission to the nations. It has been open to the sincere convert, but it has not sought to evangelize large groups on the assumption that it held in its hands the keys to the final, universal faith for all peoples. The affirmation of Jewish distinctiveness left room for other peoples to affirm their own distinctiveness as well, although it is not clear whether the distinctiveness of the others is really on the same level before God as that of the one "chosen" people.

While Judaism remains unclear about whether its uniqueness really implies a superior status vis-à-vis other nations before God, and Christianity remains unclear about the extent to which its universalism really implies the imperialistic universalizing of one very large, but nevertheless limited, religious-cultural particularism. Theologically, Christianity has never accepted an equal status with other major religions and has shown various ways of relating to other religious traditions. The most negative approach was to view other religions as mere idolatry and demon worship, which must be destroyed, root and branch, in order to be replaced by the one true faith. This view has tended to identify Christianity totally with its cultural expressions and to regard any retention of indigenous culture as a failure of full conversion.

A more benign view has been to see other religions as partial or incomplete expressions of truth, which have glimpses of the true God available through a general or natural revelation but lack the complete or final expression of God's revelation in Christ. This view has characterized the ancient Alexandrian Fathers' view of the relationship of Christianity to Greek wisdom, as well as modern liberal missionaries, and was compatible with an evangelism that sought to express Christianity in the external trappings of a local culture.

Toward Judaism, Christianity has reserved its most intense ambivalence. On the one hand, it acknowledges it as its parental faith and accepted its Bible as its Old Testament in Christian scriptures. But Christianity has regarded its parental religion not only as incomplete, having failed to accept the fulfillment of its own revelation of God in Christ, but also it has seen Judaism and Jews as perverse, deliberately rejecting Christ and seeking to kill him. Thus Jews could be seen as having an especially demonic status as those who should have been able to recognize Christ on the basis of their scriptural predictions of the Messiah, and yet chose to reject and kill him. They are quasi apostates and Christ-killers, not merely ignorant unbelievers. Although these more hostile views have faded away with modern ecumenism and the guilt of Christianity for its contribution to post-Christian anti-Semitism, which culminated in the Nazi Holocaust, Christianity has not succeeded theologically in establishing an alternative to its traditional view that Jews need to convert to Christianity in order to have a final, redeeming relationship to God.

Modern efforts to prescind from the Christian mission to the Jews, without rejecting the finality of Christianity, have varied. Some have suggested that Judaism already contains a sufficient and redeeming relationship to God through its historical revelation in the Torah. Christianity is necessary for non-Jews in order to bring them to a right relationship to God, but not for Jews. This is a Christian variant of the two-covenant thesis. Paul Van Buren has recently sought to reverse the pattern by declaring that it is Christianity that is apostate for having departed from Judaism, as the one true chosen people. Only when Christians accept this unique elect status of the Jews as the basis of their faith can Christ, as the fulfillment of Jewish election, become fully understood by Christians. But this leaves in doubt whether Jews must also recognize Christianity as their mission to the Gentiles in the process.

I believe that we must rethink these views much more radically. The idea that Christianity, or even the biblical faiths, have a monopoly on religious truth is an outrageous and absurd religious chauvinism. It is astonishing that even Christian liberals and radicals fail to seriously question this assumption. My own assumption is that the Divine Being that generates, upholds, and renews the world is truly universal, and is the father and mother of all peoples without discrimination. This means that true revelation and true relationship to the divine is to be found in all religions. God/ess is the ground of all beings, and not just of human beings.

Besides recognizing the less desirable impulses of cruelty, sexism, chauvinism, and violence that have permeated human religiosity, we must also acknowledge that there is no historical basis for assuming that the religiosity of Pueblo Amerindians or ancient Canaanites, who saw the divine power in natural processes of fecundity, as well as in the establishment of human order and harmony, was less moral than Christianity. It is interesting that Judaism and Christianity have traditionally seen ancient Near Eastern religions as the epitome of "immoral religion" because of their possible use of sanctified sexuality, but have not seen their own sanctified warfare as comparatively more problematic. Indeed, it probably would not be difficult to prove that more violence, chauvinism, and hostility between groups have been fomented by Christianity than most other religions, partly because it has had more global power than any other religion. Its commandments of love and universal fellowship between peoples evidently have not served as a check on this internecine warfare. Crusades, witch-hunts, religious wars, and pogroms have all been a part of this violent, chauvinist history of Christianity. Christianity has a tendency to judge other religions in terms of their defects in practice, while speaking of itself only in terms of its ideals. This is unjust. Ideals must be compared with ideals, and practice with practice.

Although there is true relationship to the divine, authentic spirituality, and viable morality in all religious systems, this does not mean that they are all just different words for the same thing. Each religion, like each culture, is a unique configuration of symbolic expressions that has been shaped by the total experience of peoples, their particular histories, and ecological settings. Although there is much overlap among religions, they also represent a broad spectrum of possible ways of experiencing the divine. Some may focus on the historical struggle for justice, some on the renewal of natural processes, and some on mystical ecstasy. Each has incarnated its way of symbolizing life and its relationship to the higher powers in unique ways that make it impossible simply to translate one religion to the other, or to create some abstraction of them all into a universal, ethical faith, as was often imagined among eighteenth-century European rationalists. Even "ethical universalism" is a culturally specific creation of a particular group of West Europeans and Americans who were the heirs of Christianity and Greek philosophy.

We should see ourselves in need of becoming multi-cultural in religious understanding, entering deeply into perhaps two or three cultural configurations of religion and being able to experience our own life renewed through them in different ways. This means that a universal code for all religions eludes us. One can, at most, enter deeply into only two or three such communities of faith, not all of them. But this cultivation of the ability to enter in depth into several symbolic cultures gives us a basic sympathy for the possibilities of truth in all religions.

True universality lies not in trying to make one cultural synthesis that can embrace all possibilities. Such a synthesis will always be limited, and thus become a new cultural imperialism that ignores or denies truth outside its limited construct. True universality lies in accepting one's own finiteness, one's own particularity and, in so doing, not making that particularity the only true faith, but allowing other particularities to stand side by side with yours as having equal integrity. Each is limited and particular, and yet each is, in its own way, an adequate way of experiencing the whole for a particular people at a particular time.

FEMINISM AND UNIVERSALITY

Feminism is a new challenge to Christian claims of universalism that poses different problems from those of interreligious relationships. Interreligious relationships speak of many different ways in which experience of the divine has been localized in human experience and the mutual recognition of these historico-cultural configurations by each other. Feminism speaks of new contexts where the divine needs to be localized. By and large, not only Judaism and Christianity, Islam, and Buddhism, but even ancient tribal religions have not allowed the divine to be experienced in a way defined by women. Feminism looks back at the history of all religions as expressions of male-dominated cultures that have marginalized women to some extent, although women have been more radically and totally marginalized in some religious systems than in others.

Leadership in religious cult, like hunting and war (and in many cultures probably closely related to hunting and war), seems to have been an area where males early took preeminence and put women on the side, giving women some roles as participants and even as leaders, but never allowing them to exercise real command in the shaping of the symbols or in controlling the sacred objects. The *kiva*s or holy underground chambers of the Pueblo Amerindians can be entered only by men. The sacred mysteries of Eleusis, which celebrated the finding again of a daughter goddess by her divine mother, the only mystery religion in antiquity to lift up the mother-daughter relationship, were nevertheless led by male priests.

In Judaism and Christianity this exclusion of women from the shaping of tradition and the handling of sacred objects has been particularly marked. Women, of course, have been worshipers in both religions, but primarily as passive recipients of traditions; they were not allowed to teach or even learn on the scholarly level. Both religions symbolize God as a single male being, although both have vestigal remnants of feminine aspects of God as well. But these have been suppressed and denied. Both look back to key revelatory events where women were shunted to the side.

Interestingly enough, both traditions tell of how women played key roles in the events that led up to the revelatory moment. The sister and mother of Moses and the daughter of the pharaoh conspire together to save the child who will deliver Israel, and Miriam joins with Moses and Aaron in leading Israel out of Egypt. But when the story of the key moment of revelation is told, of the assembly of Israel at Mount Sinai to receive the commandments of God, we are told that God instructed Israel to purify itself for three days by not going near a woman (Exodus 19:15). These are commandments by which Israel is to live, to express its faithfulness to God, and yet women were excluded from Sinai at the giving of the Law. Another story tells of how Miriam was punished and turned into a leper by God for criticizing Moses; thus her equality of leadership in the exodus community was marginalized (Num. 12:1–20).

In Christianity, the women disciples of Jesus, led by Mary Magdalene, are the faithful remnant who stay with him to the bitter end of the crucifixion when all the male leaders have run away and Peter has betrayed his Lord three times. These women are said to have been the first to witness the resurrection. Mary Magdalene is commissioned by the risen Lord to bring the good news back to the male disciples huddled in the upper room. Yet this primacy of women in the apostolic witness is excluded when Paul lists the witnesses of the resurrection who are the sources of apostolic authority (1 Cor. 15:5–8). Mary Magdalene is defined in later Christian tradition as a forgiven prostitute (an idea that does not appear in the New Testament), in order to marginalize her from her position as an apostle and apostolic witness, and to turn her instead into a repentant, sinful woman weeping at Jesus' feet. Thus women, although actually present and perhaps decisive in the actual events that led up to these revelatory moments, are excluded from defining their meaning or being recognized as fonts of authority for the tradition.

Women are excluded from priesthood and from touching the sacred objects of cult in Judaism and Christianity. In Hebrew temple religion this is done by defining women physiologically as unclean. In Christianity it is done by denying their ability to have authority, teach, and preach, although as Christianity becomes more cultic, ideas of women's ritual uncleanliness are also adopted to further exclude women from priesthood. Rabbinic Judaism and historical Christianity have also excluded women from entering the higher schools of theological learning and becoming teachers of the tradition.

This exclusion of women from shaping and teaching the tradition has meant that Judaism and Christianity have been characterized by a pervasive androcentrism. In Christianity, the understanding not only of God, but of Christ, the created nature of "man," sin, and grace, together with the symbolic and structural definition of the church, has been shaped by a male-centered perspective. Women appear around the edges as sinners, as repentant recipients of grace, or as spiritual auxiliaries; but the center of the drama has been the male in relation to the male God.

Today, for the first time in Christian history, substantial numbers of women are being ordained in various Christian churches, and the number of women in theological schools, training for ministry, has increased rapidly over the last decade. Women are also beginning to become professors in the various disciplines of theological education in seminaries as well. For the first time there are now enough women as ministers, teachers, and students of the theological tradition to begin to criticize the androcentrism of the theological tradition itself and to search for alternatives.

This search for alternatives takes several forms. First, there developed a literature that documents the pervasive influence of sexism on theology and religious sciences, and analyzes how it produces a biased interpretation of the tradition. Then there is a search within the tradition for alternatives, both for stories of women's actual participation in religious expression as well as for critical perspectives by which to open up more inclusive ways of developing the tradition itself. A substantial body of mature, scholarly literature has developed since the early 1970s and now provides solid resources in feminist critique of biblical studies, church history, theology, ethics, and pastoral psychology. Although many male professors in religious studies still refuse to learn about this new research or to use it in their classes, it is no longer possible to claim that it does not exist, that it is not sufficiently developed, or that there are no recognized women doing this kind of work.

As women move into ministry, there arises a demand for new models of ministry, new ways of understanding the clergy-lay relationship freed from patriarchalism, new styles of liturgy and prayer. One important expression of this work in the churches, designed for the local worshiping community, is the three volume *Inclusive Language Lectionary* being assembled by a committee of biblical scholars and theologians specially appointed by the U.S. National Council of Churches. In the first volume it provided inclusive forms for all references to God, Christ, and humanity. Jesus' word for God, *Abba,* traditionally translated "Father," was changed to "Father and Mother." The word for Christ's relationship to God was changed from "son" to "child," not to deny his historical masculinity, but to show that the spiritual relationship between humanity and God signified in Christ and shared in by all Christians is not an exclusively masculine one. The expression "Son of Man" became "the Human One," because the term in its original Hebrew form, *ben Adam,* although masculine in form, in fact means simply a human being or, in the ideal sense, the paradigmatic human being. The term "Lord" was changed to "Sovereign" (although in the third volume the word "Lord" was restored, primarily due to protests from black Christians).

These changes evoked an enormous amount of hostility, ranging from sarcasm to outright threats of violence, against members of the committee. This surprised many committee members, especially those white males who believed themselves to be operating out of theological principles rooted in biblical faith and were not prepared for such violence and hostility. Clearly, inclusive language was not just an intellectual issue to be explained by academic exegesis. It struck at persons' emotions. For many it struck at the very basis of the social and cosmic order, for they could not imagine reality as other than male-centered and male-dominated. Male-headship for them was indeed the "order of creation" and, without this symbol-system as descriptive of reality, they could not imagine any order or authority at all.

In the second cycle of readings the inclusive language committee went further and decided that it was not enough simply to change language. They decided that some scriptures were so basically androcentric in structure and so intentional in mandating male-domination that they should be dropped entirely from the readings. One such text is the favorite of conservatives—the text from Ephesians 5: "Wives obey your husbands." Critics accused the committee of editing the Bible, but in fact all lectionary readings, as distinct from Bible translations, have always edited the scriptures. For example, the Levitical codes were put aside by early Christianity as no longer authoritative, and so the teachings of the Levitical codes have never been read in Christian churches. Subsequent lectionaries have picked and chosen among texts to find readings that best appealed to their theological sensibilities and dropped passages that they regarded as distasteful, such as texts encouraging war and hostility to other groups. In the 1930s the precursor to the present American Protestant lectionary dropped the readings from the New Testament that ordered slaves to obey their masters.

There is ample precedent for such editing of biblical readings for lectionary purposes. But this is the first time it has ever been done in behalf of women and to correct the sexist bias of the biblical tradition. Not only did the committee drop certain passages, but it also added biblical texts that had not been used before, especially stories about women, such as the gospel parables of the bent-over woman and the woman with the lost coin. Still, one must wonder whether all these efforts to include women in language and story can really succeed in integrating women into a tradition that has excluded them from its formulation and development for three millennia.

As long as one is limited to the historical Bible as canonized by the rabbis and the church fathers, there are very few stories, even those about women, that are really written from women's perspectives. Much of the awkwardness of translation that offends esthetic sensibilities, even of those who in principle support inclusive language, seems to me to arise not merely from the fact that readers and hearers are more familiar with the old language than they are with the new. Rather, the negativity suggests that, in some more basic sense, the revelations of the biblical tradition were *male* revelations, not female revelations. This does not mean that the divinity to which they point is male, but rather that men received these revelations in the context of male experience and shaped their telling from a male perspective. In the Hebrew scriptures the key locus of revelation is the flight of a people from bondage, surely an event in which women also participated. But male heads of families came to dominate the definition of that people freed by God, and this definition of Israel ultimately determined the description of those who received the revelation at Sinai.

In Christianity we have a first-century rabbi—a member of an office that excluded women—who became a prophet and critic of established religious authorities. Betrayed by powers of religion and state, he was executed by Roman officials as an insurrectionist. This was a tragedy in which women surely participated as his followers, as those who mourned his death and cherished his memory as the Christ. But his prophetic criticism of religion only implicitly, rather than explicitly, included the sexism of religion. It is male suffering at the hands of male religious and political authority, rather than female suffering at the hands of these authorities, that is lifted up as the salvific paradigm, as the place where God is present in suffering unto death and the renewing of life. In Hebrew scripture male suffering and victory in war is a primary focus of revelation. Only once or twice the female agony in childbirth is compared with this male agony on the battlefield. But here also it is a male child that is to be born who serves as the symbol of the renewed Israel. Where, then, is female suffering taken seriously as the locus of revelation of the divine? Is it possible to think of women as battered wives, as victims of child abuse, as victims of rape, as insulted and silenced by patriarchy, as tortured by bound feet, by clitorectomies, and by a thousand other means of sexual objectification and dehumanization, as the place where the divine descends, is present in these agonies as healing power, and brings new life?

I have recently been teaching a course on violence toward women. One of the exercises in this class is a case study in which each student describes and analyzes some crisis in her life or the life of someone she knows. In these case studies, we heard repeated stories of profound suffering of women, sufferings from which each woman managed to emerge a stronger and more autonomous human being. In one such case study a woman described her rape by an unknown man in a ski mask while she was taking trash to a dump near a woods. During the rape she became convinced that she would die and resigned herself to her impending death. But when the rapist left and she found herself still alive, prone on the ground, she experienced all around herself a sudden and compelling vision of Christ as a crucified woman. As she lay transfixed by this vision, an enormous relief swept over her and she realized that she would not have to explain to a male God that she had been raped. God knew what it was like to be a woman who had been raped.

Such an experience of Christ as a crucified woman, making God present in the agony of a woman who had been raped, has not been thinkable in our religious tradition. If any woman had thought it before, she would not have been able to communicate it to the community of faith, or if she spoke of it among believing women, they would not have been able to make it a part of the tradition of authoritative texts from which the church engages in theological reflection, preaching, and teaching.

This is why the feminist challenge to Christianity cannot find sufficient response in the recovery of neglected texts in the Bible or in inclusive translation. Women must be able to speak out of their own experiences of agony and victimization, survival, empowerment, and new life, as places of divine presence and, out of these revelatory experiences, write new stories. Feminists must create a new midrash on scripture or a "Third Testament" that can tell stories of God's presence in experiences where God's presence was never allowed or imagined before in a religious culture controlled by men and defined by male experience. This Third Testament is not simply a religion for women. Just as women have been able to experience themselves in the crucified rabbi from Nazareth, men must be able to experience Christ in the raped woman and thereby come to experience the question mark this directs at a male culture in which the tortured female body is regarded as pornographic, rather than the expression of the sufferings of God.

This new feminist midrash on patriarchal texts and traditions will not only enter into dialogue and controversy with patriarchal religion. It must also open itself to dialogue with feminist exploration of religion in other traditions. There must certainly be a dialogue between Christian and Jewish feminists, and also with Muslim feminists as well. There must also be a dialogue between feminists engaged in the transformation of historical religions and feminists who break with these historical religions and seek to revive, from repressed memories of ancient goddesses and burned witches, visions of new possibilities for women's spirituality today.

This does not mean that such a dialogue between feminists in historical faiths and pagan feminists will be easy. There are many barriers to communication to be cleared away, questions about the historical interpretation of ancient religions and the relationship of female divinity symbols to modern post-Christian patterns of thought. There are also questions about reverse exclusivism and separatism, as well as about exclusivism on the Jewish and Christian side, which is often reinforced today by accusations from male Jewish and Christian theologians who define feminism as "paganism" in order to frighten Jewish and Christian women away from any feminist analysis of patriarchal religion. It may be that feminism done in the context of historical faiths and feminism done in the context of religions of nature-renewal are working with different paradigms of religious experience, so that each side lacks, fundamentally, certain categories that the other sees as essential.

It is not at all certain if such a dialogue between these two types of religious feminism is possible or where it may lead. But what I would like to urge here is that both kinds of feminist religious quest are valid, and each must therefore respect and affirm the basic presence of the divine in and through these several paths. One can dispute about questions of interpretation and their ethical and religious use today. But one cannot dispute that the divine mystery did indeed truly appear in the finding again of Persephone by her Goddess mother, Demeter. It is this new starting point that sets the quest of feminists—whether Christian, Jewish, or pagan—on a new basis.

9

In Search of Justice

Religious Pluralism from a Feminist Perspective

MARJORIE HEWITT SUCHOCKI

Liberation theology has pointed to the invidious effects that follow when one mode of humanity is made normative for others. Such normativeness, combined with power, allows and invites exploitation of all those falling outside the norm. Furthermore, it distorts the perspective of those counted as falling within the norm, leading to problems in adequately knowing either self or others. As liberation theologians—whether feminist, black, or Third World—have dealt with this theme, they have focused on universalized norms in the realm of social, political, and personal structures of existence. The thesis of this essay is that the principle holds for religion as well: universalizing one religion such that it is taken as the norm whereby all other religions are judged and valued leads to oppression, and hence falls short of the norm that liberationists consider ultimate—the normative justice that creates well-being in the world community.

A feminist perspective, therefore, suggests that one must radically affirm religious pluralism, but not without bringing a critical consciousness of well-being in human community to interreligious and intrareligious discussion. Justice is thus to be the fundamental criterion of value and the focus of dialogue and action among religions.

To develop and hold such a position raises interesting problems. First, is it not the case that establishing justice as a norm whereby all religions are judged simply introduces one universal for another, and hence continues the pattern of oppression? Secondly, and closely related to this, who defines "well-being"? Justice is a concept closely aligned to religious convictions, and each concept of justice reflects the religious sensitivities and suppositions of the culture that gave it birth. Thirdly, if the first and second problems cannot be answered adequately, then we must face the situation of religious relativism, which would follow were there no acceptable norms of discernment to be applied to religious positions.

Such relativism involves the supposition that each religion is governed by norms and perceptions uniquely conditioned by the cultural and historical situation of the religion. The only authentic critique of a religion would therefore be an internal critique, developed within the parameters of the normative system or systems within the religion itself. There would be no "meta" view whereby the truth or values of the religion could be judged. An interreligious stance, therefore, would revolve around an open dialogue with no judgments formed as to the truth or value of the religions.

My feminist rejection of absolutizing one religion as the norm for all others accepts the uniqueness and self-naming quality of each religion. I reject, however, the possibility of entering into dialogue with no judgments whatsoever. We are not creatures suspended from some skyhook, impartially surveying the human scene; we are part and parcel of its buzzing confusion, and enter into dialogue value-laden and value-projecting. What is called for is not a nonjudgmental dialogue with other religions in light of the relativism of belief systems, but a shift of judgment from ideological ground to ethical ground, along with an open recognition of the conditioned nature of the norm of justice we bring, and a commitment to critical exploration of the norm in the very dialogue wherein it is brought to bear.

THE CORRELATION BETWEEN RELIGIOUS IMPERIALISM AND SEXISM

Absolutizing one religion, such that it becomes normative for all others, is a dynamic with clear parallels to sexism, whereby one gender is established as the norm for human existence. Therefore the critique of sexism can be extended as a critique of religious imperialism.

The feminist critique of sexism and its effects upon women takes two routes. First, feminists point to the sense in which masculine experience has been universalized in defining all that is fully human. Under such a guise, women's experience is either nonexistent, or subsumed under masculinity. Examples abound, but the most widespread is the "generic" use of the masculine in language. "Son of man," "mankind," "men," and "he," we are told, all refer to women as well as men. Yet the generic language quickly shows its particularist intent when one attempts to apply the language to women. Women may be included within the rubric of "men," until women try to join a "men's club"—whether that club be a social or a professional group. Men's experience is presented as the norm, claiming to incorporate women's experience within it, but when the rule is tested, it becomes apparent that masculinity, rather than humanity per se, shapes the content of the language.

The second route is not to subsume and therefore erase women's experience under the so-called universal norms developed by men, but to assign to women those characteristics that men consider problematic in human existence. Traditionally, these characteristics have been dependence, emotionality, sensuality, and weakness. Given the negative character assigned to these qualities, it follows that for woman's own good she must be under the care of a man who can guide her and control her. When cultural sensitivities shift toward a valuation of the emotive characteristic of human existence, then woman—still the bearer of the quality—is "exalted" by recourse to the "pedestal syndrome." Whereas in the negative valuation she cannot be trusted with independent action, in the positive valuation she is "too good" for the roughness of the everyday world of public life. In both cases she is controlled and excluded from full participation in the human community.

The difference between a sexism that erases woman's experience by subsuming woman under the universality of man (inclusivism) and a sexism that recognizes woman as unique and assigns her certain characteristics (exclusivism) is a difference that finally collapses. The second case is but an instance of the first, for the qualities assigned to women are derived not from women's own testimony but from masculine experience projected upon women. Therefore the apparent recognition of women is as much the erasure of women as is the generic masculine. In both cases women are silenced, save for their ability to echo the dominant voice of man. The consequence of the absolutized masculine norm is oppression of women in all areas of life: public and private, social and spiritual.

Another consequence of the absolutized norm is a distortion of male experience. The particular is made universal, which is itself a distortion of its true nature of particularity. Further, insofar as the norm entails a division of human characteristics, such that men bear some and women others, there is a problem for either sex to own its full humanity. For example, if "tenderness" is a female quality, then must men who are tender describe themselves as feminine? How so, when they are clearly masculine? To call the quality in a man feminine is to distort the fullness of what it is to be masculine. Inasmuch as many men experience no difficulty whatsoever in being tender, the evidence seems to indicate that tenderness is a masculine quality when evidenced by a man. Tenderness in abstraction is neither masculine nor feminine, but simply human. Thus the separation of qualities under a sexist norm leads to a distortion in self-understanding, as well as distortions in other-understanding.

This is a simplified summary of sexism, yet it can serve to show the parallel oppression and distortion that occur when one religion is absolutized, becoming the norm for all others. Just as the universalization of male experience functions either to absorb women within the masculine norm or to ascribe to women those characteristics that men are not willing to name clearly as belonging to themselves, even so the universalization of one religion leads to similar distortions.

I take as an illustration an enormously popular book in Christian theology, Hans Küng's *On Being a Christian*.[1] The book is particularly pertinent: its clear intent, from page 1 through 602, is to demonstrate the superiority of Christianity over against other modes of being human, whether secular or religious. On page 1, Küng acknowledges the challenge of the "great world religions." He asks: "is Christianity something essentially different, really something special?" His answer on page 602 summarizes the argument of the book:

> The Christian element therefore is neither a superstructure nor a substructure of the human. It is an elevation or—better—a transfiguration of the human, at once preserving, canceling, surpassing the human. Being Christian therefore means that the other humanisms are transfigured: they are affirmed to the extent that they affirm the human reality; they are rejected to the extent that they reject the Christian reality, Christ himself; they are surpassed to the extent that being Christian can fully incorporate the human, all-too-human even in all its negativity.

Section A.III of the book, "The Challenge of the World Religions," deals specifically with world religions from the stance of Christian superiority. It begins, however, with a recognition that the 400-year-old Christian mission prior to the second world war was mistakenly aligned with cultural imperialism. The past decades have seen a correction in that now Christians are "striving to discover and evaluate the true inspiration, the great concerns, the wealth of Islam, Buddhism, Hinduism, Confucianism, and Taoism, and make them fruitful for Christian proclamation and theology."[2] Inasmuch as there are elements in these religions that can be used by Christian theology, it is also apparently the case that these religions contain salvific elements: there is salvation outside the church.

Küng follows this suggestion with very brief summaries of what he sees to be the major teachings of Hinduism, Buddhism, Confucianism, Taoism, and Islam. His problem, then, is to ask, given the fact that these religions all contain truth, "Why should Christianity in particular be *the* truth? . . . The fate of Christianity itself is in question."[3]

A curious section follows, beginning on page 100, where Küng warns against belittling other religions in order that Christianity may be seen to be great itself, and then proceeds to do exactly that. Under the guise of not idealizing other religions, he proceeds to point out their negative characteristics. The curiosity is that the characteristics he projects are also Christian characteristics. He speaks of "their actual remoteness from their original positions," but can one argue that Christianity today has no aspects remote from the account in the Gospels? Is "Islam's large-scale veneration of the saints" so different from forms of Catholicism, or has the "use of amulets" no parallels in medals and crosses? "A Chinese anniversary celebration made of archaic Confucian,

Taoist, and Buddhist elements" may not differ all that much from a Western Mardi Gras, and the "fearsome, grimacing gods of Bali" may be no less fearsome than some bloody depictions of a crucified Christ. Küng not only names these as negative features in other religions without noting their parallels in Christianity but, on the contrary, he compares them with elements he considers noble within Christianity. Thus the "grimacing gods" are contrasted with a "wall of icons of Orthodox saints in Zagorsk," and temple prostitution is contrasted with "Christian consecration of virgins."[4] The lingam is contrasted with the cross, and holy wars are contrasted with the love of enemies preached by Christianity.

A "cheap feeling of superiority," is decried, but "the *question of truth* cannot be left out or trivialized."[5] Under this criterion, "encounter with Christianity means for the Asian religions an impetus of unforeseeable extent, to critical introspection, to purification and deepening of the foundations of their own faith, to fertilization with Christian ideas and the development of fruitful possibilities."[6] Presumably, the feeling of superiority—the final result of this encounter for Christians—is precious rather than cheap. Christianity is the norm whereby other religions can continue to improve what is best within themselves. Christians, in turn, can affirm what is positive in other religions, accepting what is of value and discarding the worthless.[7] The criterion of judgment is the essence of Christianity, which is Christ himself—the "ultimately decisive, definitive, archetypal" man.[8]

Parallels with sexism can be drawn in that the norm of Christ is applied to other religions regardless of norms that may be generated from within those religions. Just as the norm of masculinity is applied to women regardless of women's protestations that their own experience of humanity is sufficient to generate their own norms, even so Christian norms are projected uncritically upon non-Christian religions. Such inclusivist stances toward other religions violate their integrity. Also, just as women are measured and judged by masculine experience, even so Küng measures and judges other religions by Christian experience. Further, the form of sexism that separates reprehensible qualities from men and projects them upon women is also operative in Küng's treatment. The qualities which he specifically names as negative in other religions have parallels within Christianity. These parallels are not acknowledged. Rather, they are rendered invisible in Christianity by projecting them as somehow appropriately descriptive of other religions. Here the exclusivist attitude toward women finds its echo in an exclusivist attitude toward other religions.

The consequences of this negation of the value of the other are familiar to women. There is indeed a "superiority-inferiority" syndrome, whether the superiority be deemed cheap or virtuous. This works against the mutuality necessary for full dialogue. There is also exploitation. For women, their labor is devalued and their possibilities are denied. For other religions, their contributions to Christianity are secondary to Christianity's contributions to them. Possibilities for their continuing development are valued not in accordance with their own history, but in accordance with their transformation into closer alignment with Christianity. Measurement against an absolute norm, whether sex or religion, renders invisible or secondary all those in whom the norm is not found.

That the utilization of religious absolutism leads to a failure in self-knowledge is also evident in Küng's account. Just as men, projecting qualities devalued in themselves onto women, fail to have a full understanding of themselves, even so a Christian theologian fails to understand the reality of Christianity when its negative characteristics are projected onto other religions. I have illustrated this dynamic in Küng with regard to his decrying the so-called negative characteristics of the other religions. His projection onto the other inhibits his recognition of the need within Christianity itself to reform in these areas. The presumption of superiority dulls one's self-critical stance.

The same dynamics that promote sexism with repercussions against men as well as women apply with regard to the absolutizing of one religion vis-à-vis all others. Distortions in knowledge and exploitation in relationships follow.

If no religion can set itself up as a norm for all others, do we find ourselves in a situation of unrelieved relativism? Is there no transcendence of our particularity that allows us to determine what is a valid stance toward self and others in the world? I suggest that the norm championed by feminists and other liberation theologians is also a norm for reflection on the world religions. That norm is justice.

JUSTICE: A FEMINIST PERSPECTIVE

The justice applied normatively by liberation theologians centers upon inclusiveness of well-being. The norm is not without problems. Who is to define what constitutes "well-being"? Is not any norm of justice inextricably bound up with the religion that gave it birth? If so, is not a norm of justice simply a "back door" to yet one more invidious form of religious imperialism? These questions will be addressed following exploration of a feminist perspective on justice.

When justice is defined from the perspective of the oppressed, certain consequences follow. First, justice is named as a concrete reality manifested in concrete communities. Laws are to be abstracted from situations that exhibit well-being. Concrete forms of well-being in community provide the norm by which the laws are themselves judged. Consequently, situations reflecting the absence of well-being in community are sufficient reason to call into question the adequacy of the formulated laws governing community life.

Valuation in a concrete mode of justice would begin with fundamental, physical well-being. Food, water, shelter, work, and community are primary, constituting as they do needs fundamental to all human existence. Building upon these values is a second level of justice in terms of human dignity and recognition in the human community. This level involves a self-naming, an appreciation of self and others. A third level of justice is openness to self-development and self-determination within the context of community. The levels are successive, each building upon the other, and each moving toward a multiplicity of forms. The first level, physical well-being, is relatively uniform although, as will be developed subsequently, even here there can be divergent interpretations. The second level of self-naming and dignity in community invites diversity as an essential component of community. The third level carries this openness to diversity further still, indicating not only a diversity of individuals, but of communities. Thus if the forms of justice are actualized in human community, there will be recognition of multiple modes of being human, with this multiplicity valued positively.

A justice that manifests these three levels is one that in principle knows no boundaries, given its tendency toward diversity. For example, self-naming is a function incorporating the unique experience and perspective of individuals and groups within the wider community, but such naming widens the community yet further, and may even create an alternative community. The principle of justice requires the affirmation of alternative communities according to the criterion of well-being.

The ultimate test of justice is precisely the degree to which it knows no boundaries to well-being. A justice that establishes well-being within the context of its own community and ignores the well-being of those outside that community is to that degree unjust. Likewise, a community that establishes its own well-being through exploitation of the well-being of those outside the community is to that degree unjust. A supposition underlying this statement is that the world is a network of interrelationship and interdependence. Thus a value of concrete forms of justice implicitly and explicitly pushes toward an affirmation of pluralism. It provides, however, not only an affirmation of pluralism, but a criterion for judging the forms of pluralism that it engenders.

For example, the justice so described makes room for the development of alternative forms of religion within a major religion. Christianity may well proliferate into many forms; in fact, insofar as it is an embodiment of justice, it should be expected so to proliferate. The norm for judging the value of an alternative form, however, could not simply be doctrinal, but historical and ethical. Historically, the form may be considered authentically Christian if it involves a clear trajectory within the stream of Christian history, and if it names itself Christian. Ethically, the form will be positively valued insofar as it concerns itself with the levels of justice. Does it promote the physical well-being of its adherents? Does it allow the diversity of self-naming and appreciation of self and others within the community? Does it foster the development of each individual within the context of the communal good? Does it define the communal good as extending through and among communities without boundary throughout all existence? Answering the criterion pronounces the new form of Christianity as valuable, despite its divergences from other cultural or doctrinal criteria. Failure of the criterion becomes to that extent a judgment against the value of the form, although it would not necessarily speak to the Christianness of the form. Thus modes of Christianity that systematically engage in destructive action with regard to other groups of persons may in fact be Christian, but they are poor forms of religion in general and of Christianity in particular. Modes that are destructive of justice for their own members are likewise poor forms of religion, regardless of their conformity to intrareligious norms.

To utilize justice as a norm for judging religions is not antithetical to approaches taken by Küng and others insofar as they, too, make use of such a norm. Küng, for example, states on page 106 of *On Being a Christian* that "the manifold failure of Christianity and the world religions in regard to the humanizing of man [*sic*], to involvement in the struggle for justice, peace, and freedom, and their influence—more divisive than unitive—on mankind [*sic*] as a whole form the somber background before which the whole development [of interreligious dialogue] goes on." This statement is meant to stand as a substratum of his whole discussion of the relationship of Christianity to other religions. The problem is that he does not incorporate it into his argument. Indeed, had he done so, his argument would have had to take an entirely different direction. Ideological and esthetic criteria for judging the relative value of religions would have given way to norms of the well-being of the religious community concerned, together with the community's ability to extend its care for well-being to those outside its boundaries. Ideological and esthetic concerns would not be judged by the ideology and esthetics of Christianity; rather, these factors would have been understood according to their function within the religion.

Furthermore, had Küng used a norm of justice rather than the norm of Christianity (more pointedly, the norm of Christ as archetypical and definitive for human existence, which of course is the norm Küng sees as formative for the Christian religion), his understanding of Christianity as well as of the other religions could have developed differently. As it is, his negative judgment of all aspects of the other religions that are unlike Christianity limited his ability to use those ideological/esthetic forms as dialogically instructive for Christianity. This involves the loss of a new basis for self-understanding, self-criticism, and self-development.

JUSTICE AS NORM: PROBLEMS AND POSSIBILITIES

From a feminist perspective, therefore, I argue that religious absolutism is no more valid than is gender absolutism; both serve to devalue all modes of existence falling outside the absolutized religion or gender. But also with a norm of justice, further questions must be raised. These questions deal with the fact that the understanding of justice developed above would by no means command universal assent. The most concrete modes of justice are conditioned by the ideologies that undergird them. The valuation and interpretation of justice reflect the very differences among religions that create the situation of pluralism in the first place. After exploring this relativism of justice, I will suggest that a basis does in fact exist for employing justice as a self-critical norm in interreligious and intrareligious dialogue in a nonimperialistic fashion.

With regard to the relativity of justice, the concrete interpretation of what constitutes well-being is conditioned by one's personal and societal context. The notion of justice can be as culture-bound and imperialistic as any other notion. My attempt to locate justice in specific modes of well-being—physical, societal, and personal—runs into the difficulty that what constitutes these modes of well-being can be differently defined in different societies. The problem for interreligious dialogue is that there are variations of interpretation about what constitutes physical well-being, as well as variations in interpreting societal and personal well-being. Diversity with regard to personal and societal well-being is in fact called for by the norm of justice outlined above, for the norm supports and even expects cultural diversity. Internal rather than external critiques would be most appropriate in these realms. There is a certain intransigence to the norm, however, when it comes to fundamental aspects of human existence, such as peaceful access to food, water, health, shelter, work, and community. To use justice normatively in interreligious dialogue implies, first, a fundamental importance accorded to these values for all peoples, and secondly, a commitment to work cooperatively with any religious group toward the creation of such well-being for the various communities of the world.

Yet it is the case that what constitutes physical ill-being in one culture may be interpreted as well-being in another. I suggest that the reasons for this might possibly be found in historical and economic factors, rather than in any religion's intrinsic valuation of starvation and illness, for example. Religions have in common that they address the problematic in life. Precisely what is deemed problematic varies from culture to culture, and also within cultures. Religion enables the individual or community to deal more successfully with what it judges adverse to its good, and religion is also a tool for formulating a communal vision of present and ultimate good. By no means am I suggesting that this simple description exhausts the nature and function of religion; I am pointing out only that whatever religion is and does, it is at least related to its societal understanding of good and evil in a positive way. When the conditions understood as evil—perhaps hunger, illness, death—are considered overwhelming, or not subject to removal, it is the task of religion to deal with these conditions in a way that makes them bearable. This may be done by positing or discovering within the very experience of the negative that which can lead to the societally defined good. The rational structure that develops around apparently or manifestly irremedial problems may in fact be a functional way of enabling a people to cope with its problems. Paradoxically, this salvific function can also serve to perpetuate the structures that support the problems. The irrational is rendered rational, and the unjust, just, thus incorporating them meaningfully into the social system. Systems that incorporate social ill-being into that which is religiously and societally acceptable do so with a paradoxical understanding of justice. Ill-being becomes well-being within the religiously formulated comprehensive view.

For example, a society may manifest great degrees of poverty, and the religion might explain and eventually justify this poverty as a necessary condition for the attainment of a good not presently seen or experienced. Although poverty and misery may not be deemed good in and of themselves, they are nonetheless judged good as a means to another end. This end may be related to the past or a future: the past, for the poverty could be seen as a way to live out the necessary consequences justly incurred through a previous existence, or the future, for the poverty could be interpreted as a training ground for a higher mode of existence. In either case, the poverty that my own interpretive system would judge "ill-being" could be defined as "well-being" in another interpretive system. Both systems could be grounded in a religious view.

To name ill-being as well-being is certainly not foreign to the Christian tradition. Ideologically, many a theologian has spoken of eternal wretchedness and damnation as an ultimate manifestation of justice. Human sin has been interpreted as meriting infinite punishment, with this punishment balancing out the scales of justice. To those with such views, it is well that the wicked suffer. We need not turn only to ideology to see the paradox; we may look to history as well, as liberation theologians so strongly attest. The ill-being of women, blacks, and others outside the dominant cultural value system has been called well-being within a posited system of order. Irony rather than paradox might be a more appropriate name for such twists, and I, a feminist, cannot in any way consider these views as functions for dealing salvifically with social situations not easily changed. Rather, using justice as an internal basis for criticism, I name such practices evil, and call for their reform.

Yet there are illustrations within Christianity of salvifically naming the negative as good, such as in attitudes toward suffering through persecution. The book of Mark interprets the suffering of early Christians as their identification with Christ; the identification gave hope in that it carried the promise of resurrection as well. To be identified with Christ in suffering was to be identified with Christ in a resurrection to come. This identification gave a salvific interpretation to suffering, allowing it to be borne. Endurance through suffering, in turn, became important to the survival of the infant religion. The sanctioning of suffering became institutionalized through forms such as asceticism, as well as in practices of justifying oppression. Thus my own religion, Christianity, certainly demonstrates that religions can deal with the negative in such a way that the negative is rendered positive within an interpretive grid of meaning. What is considered positive lends itself to forms of institutionalization.

Religions will therefore have different valuations of what constitutes the justice of physical well-being in society, and these valuations may well have their source in the historical development of the religion within its society. Thus agreement concerning physical well-being and even wider understandings of justice should not be sought within the religious interpretations of society. Insofar as they are, then any norm of justice might well be criticized for being as imperialistic as Küng's employment of the norm of Christ, for it takes the notion of physical well-being developed in a culture-specific context and applies it evaluatively to all cultures and religions.

I suggest, however, that there is another base of contact among the religions that allows a nonimperialistic criterion of justice. Oddly enough, the contact puts us back again in the ideological realm we supposedly left behind in calling for justice rather than doctrine as the basis of dialogue. If it is the case that interpretations of well-being are rooted in the salvific interaction of religion with ordinary and extraordinary problems of existence, then it is possible that each religion's deepest valuation of what physical existence should be lies, not in its coping with the exigencies of history, but in its projection of the ideal. By looking at each religion's vision of the ultimately perfect mode of existence for its saints or holy ones, whether that vision be otherworldly or not, we might find some echo of unanimity on the value of freedom from suffering.

My point is that justice is not given a universally acceptable content, not even with regard to physical well-being. Some of the variances in definition may be traceable to the ways in which religions have interpreted and dealt with negative factors in existence. We must be sensitive to these variances, but they do not require a full relativization of justice such that it is rendered useless as a norm to judge that which is of greater or lesser value in and among religions. On the contrary, we must look to the heart of justice in each religion as that which renders life meaningful in light of a vision of what existence should be. Using justice as a norm means that the primary visions within each religion of what societal life should be in a "perfect" world is a source of judgment that can be used internally within each religion to judge its present societal forms of justice. Dialogue among the religions can likewise proceed from the development of mutual concerns for justice that can lead to concerted actions for justice in the world. Justice is a dynamic and transformative notion, capable of being used even to judge itself.

I recognize, of course, that my own determination to ground at least physical well-being as a norm inherently contained within every notion of justice is hardly an impartial or unconditioned determination. My approach is from a feminist perspective, and I have learned the content of justice from experiences of injustice, or that which makes for ill-being. Valuing well-being in the threefold sense outlined earlier means that I look for its traces within that which is given ultimate value in each religion. Nonetheless, I recognize that only the first—physical well-being—can come close to finding common agreement, and even that level has problematic aspects.

What is necessary, then, in looking for a nonimperialistic mode of justice is to look at ultimate rather than penultimate visions of justice. The determinate mode of justice must be drawn from the vision of the termination of adversity, or the ideal form of human existence envisioned in each religion. This vision is far more likely to yield agreement on the value of at least the basic forms of justice dealing with physical existence. If so, then the criterion of justice in that minimal mode can appeal to an internal norm within each religion. This mitigates the charge that the norm of justice as a basis for making value judgments concerning religions is as imperialistic as doctrinal norms.

The situation remains, however, that the second and third levels of justice have an inherent diversity within them such that interreligious dialogues of exploration concerning these diversities can be only that: listening and learning in an openness to the other, which ultimately is self-enriching. Paradoxically, the one employing the norm that affirms diversity must expect to encounter—and affirm—systems that, containing no valuation of diversity, reject or devalue one's norm and the system it reflects. An absolutist, by definition, cannot affirm the pluralist, whereas the pluralist is bound, likewise by definition, to affirm the alternative of absolutism so long as it promotes well-being.

Interreligious dialogue at the societal/personal levels of justice will discover that what constitutes dignity will be defined differently in various cultures. There may be no single standard. The situation may be even more culturally specific at the third level—that is, openness to self-development and self-determination within the context of community. Even to name this as an aspect of justice may be to witness to Western culture, with its emphasis on the individual. However, the phrase "within the context of community" should mitigate even Western individualism, for it indicates that what constitutes self-development is relative to the community in which it takes place. Divergences of communities on these issues are not antithetical to justice, but in fact become the test of justice.

Affirming religious pluralism within the context of justice shifts the focus of dialogue to the concreteness of human well-being. The very exploration of human well-being, however, inevitably directs our attention to questions concerning how we determine what constitutes well-being, or into the heart of the ideological nature of the religions. Interreligious dialogue focused on justice promotes intrareligious dialogue concerning ultimate and penultimate values. The pluralism among religions then finds itself calling attention to the pluralism within each religion; dialogue engenders dialogues. Affirming one another's diversity may grant us the privilege of "listening in" to the internal dialogues, in the hope of understanding and mutual transformations. One vision of justice can temper, criticize, and deepen another, and through dialogue each vision might grow richer in understanding and implementation.

In any case, a norm of justice used in the valuation of religions allows the affirmation of religious pluralism without plunging us into religious relativism, wherein we have no rational ground for distinguishing between a "Jonestown" religion and an Amish village. The norm, however, must be used self-consciously and dialogically in recognition of the fact that the norm is hardly culture-free. In the process of dialogue, justice is not only affirmed, but also created.

NOTES

1. Edward Quinn, tr. (Garden City, N.Y.: Doubleday & Co., 1976).
2. Ibid., p. 91.
3. Ibid., p. 99.

4. Ibid., p. 102.
5. Ibid., pp. 103–4.
6. Ibid., p. 105.
7. Ibid., p. 112.
8. Ibid., p. 123.

10

The Buddha and the Christ:
Mediators of Liberation

ALOYSIUS PIERIS, S.J.

Interreligious dialogue is carried out on three different, but essentially related, levels: the levels of *core-experience, collective memory,* and *interpretation.*

The "core" of any religion is the *liberative* experience that gave birth to that religion and continues to be available to successive generations of humankind. It is this primordial experience that functions as the *core* of a religion, at any time, in any given place, in the sense that it continuously re-creates the *psycho-spiritual mood* proper to that particular religion, imparting at the same time its own peculiar character to the *socio-cultural manifestation* of that religion. It is precisely through recourse to this primordial experience that a religion resolves its recurrent crises and regenerates itself in the face of new challenges. In fact, the vitality of any given religion depends on its capacity to put each successive generation in touch with that core-experience of liberation.

The medium by which the core-experience is made available to successive generations is precisely the "collective memory" of that experience. A religion would die as soon as it is born if it failed to evolve some *means of perpetuating* (the accessibility of) its core-experience. Religious beliefs, practices, traditions, and institutions that grow out of a particular religion go to make up a "communication system" that links its adherents with the originating nucleus—that is, the liberative core of that religion. This is why a religion fades out of history even after centuries of existence when its symbols and institutions lose their capacity to evoke in their followers the distinctive salvific experience that defines the essence of that religion. Did this not happen to the great religions of ancient Egypt, Rome, Greece, and Mesopotamia?

Integral to the functioning of the communication system of the collective memory is "interpretation." In order to be remembered, an experience—in its symbols, beliefs, and rituals—has to be framed in terms of historical and cultural categories. Thus, the core-experience in all religions, insofar as it is remembered, tends also to be interpreted in such diverse ways as to form various philosophical, theological, and exegetical schools.

In Buddhism, the core-experience lends itself to be classed as gnosis or "liberative knowledge"; the corresponding Christian experience falls under the category of agape or "redemptive love." Each is *salvific* in that each is a *self-transcending* event that radically transforms the human person affected by that experience. At the same time, there is an indefinable contrast between them, which largely determines the major differences between the two religions, differences quite obvious even to a casual observer. And yet, it must be recognized that both gnosis and agape are *necessary* precisely because each in itself is *inadequate* as a medium not only for experiencing but also for expressing our intimate moments with the Ultimate Source of liberation. They are, in other words, complementary idioms that need each other to mediate the self-transcending experience called "salvation." Any valid spirituality, Buddhist or Christian, as the history of each religion attests, does retain both poles of religious experience—namely, the gnostic and the agapeic. The movement of the spirit progresses through the dialectical interplay of wisdom and love, or, to put it in Buddhist terms, through the complementarity between *prajñā* and *karunā,* and in the Hindu tradition, the sapiential spirituality known as the *jñāna-mārgā* and the affective-active paths called the *bhakti-* and *karma-mārgā.*

But in order to appreciate and dialogue about both the differences and the complementarity between the core-experiences of Buddhism and Christianity, one must enter into their collective memories. Buddhism and Christianity are both vibrant with vitality today because each has developed its own religious system (of doctrines, rites, and institutions), which can make the original experience available to contemporary society. Hence the conclusion is unavoidable: a Christian who wishes to enter into a core-to-core dialogue with Buddhism must have two qualifications: (1) a preliminary empathic apprehension of the real nature of the other religion's core-experience, and (2) an uninhibited willingness to make use of the religious system that the Buddhist offers to the Christian as the only means of access to that core-experience—in other words, a readiness to enter into a *communicatio in sacris* with Buddhists.

Elsewhere I have gone into greater detail concerning the complementarity between the Buddhist and Christian core-experiences and concerning what a *communicatio in sacris* between the two religions would entail.[1] In this chapter I shall take up the third level of dialogue, that of interpretation (which is ancillary or preparatory to the "real" dialogue that takes place when we so "communicate" that we enter into each others' core-experience). My focus will be on one of the most challenging interpretative difficulties in the Christian-Buddhist encounter, one that motivates the other contributors to this book in their search for a "pluralist theology of religions": the problems that arise when *christology* is confronted with the competing claims of *buddhology*.

As far as Buddhism is concerned, interpretation has reached a high point in the doctrine of the buddhahood—"buddhology," as I shall call it in the following considerations. Similarly, insofar as Christ is the very core of Christianity, christology is both the axis and the acme of all Christian hermeneusis. It should be noted that my emphasis on the essentially hermeneutical character of both buddhology and christology is not intended to deny either the theoretical validity or the historical basis of such interpretations. As already argued, interpretations are a necessary means of communication; and as such they reveal the capacity of a given religion not only to *define* (limit) but also to *redefine* (expand) the boundaries of orthodoxy in the process of allowing its theoretical framework to accommodate the intellectual achievements and historical challenges of a given era.

The focus of Buddhist-Christian dialogue on the level of interpretation is the historical figure of the founders of these two religions, who are believed to play a soteriological role in the lives of their followers. This claim is not made by the adherents of other religions. This is what makes Buddhist-Christian dialogue a dangerous exercise. Far from being a religious conversation about Jesus and Gautama, or a comparative study of their different historical and cultural backgrounds, it can easily explode into a kerygmatic confrontation between Jesus intepreted as *the Christ* and Gautama interpreted as *the Buddha*.

GAUTAMA INTERPRETED AS THE BUDDHA

The Buddhist cultures of Asia project a composite picture of the Buddha. Prof. D. J. Kalupahana, a Buddhist, offers us a slow-motion replay of the process by which the scriptural portrait of the extraordinary human teacher grew, in the minds of his followers, into the Transcendent Being of the Mahayanists.[2] The figure of the human teacher (*satthā*) that Kalupahana draws out of the Pali scriptures was not omniscient; nor was his experience of nirvana thought to be different from that attained by his disciples. Quite unlike Jesus of the New Testament, Gautama of the *Tripitaka* (early Buddhist scriptures) did not seem to have clearly claimed that the Saving Truth or the Liberating Path was identical with his own person. He was only the Path-finder and Truth-discoverer.

But it would be a grave mistake to think of him as a Socrates or a Plato, a mere founder of a school of thought. The kind of Buddhism that Europe imported in the nineteenth century was a "religionless philosophy" and its founder seemed more of a thinker than a holy man.[3] He came to be presented as an areligious person, beloved of rationalists and agnostics, and noted for the "scepticism of his style."[4] This description disregards the fact that the Buddha had listed "logic, inference, and reasoning" among the means that cannot lead to the Truth[5] and put "skepticism" among the five hindrances on the path to nirvana[6] and as one of the three fetters to be freed from.[7]

Much more perceptive in this regard was Clement of Alexandria who was one of the founding fathers of Christian gnosticism; he sensed that the Buddha was more than a mere teacher of a philosophy. According to Clement, those who observed the Buddha's *Regula* (*Monastica*), "regarded him as divine" (*hos theon tetimekasin*) —that is to say, more than human, on account of his superlative sanctity (*di'hyperbolen semnotetos*).[8] It was his sanctity that the medieval Christians celebrated liturgically when they raised St. Joasaph (= *bodhisattva*) to the altars![9]

This is also the image that emerges clearly from the Buddhist cultures in Asia: a saint recognized as such by his followers and therefore revered as the noblest of beings that has ever set foot on earth, higher than the highest of gods, his sanctity alone being the root of his authority over all things in heaven and on earth.

The *locus classicus* that parallels the "Who do people say that I am?" of Matthew 16:13 is found in the *Anguttara Nikāya*.[10] "Could you be a god?" asks a Brahmin, and Buddha's answer is "No." "A *gandhabba* (demigod)?" "No." "A ghost?" "No." "A human being?" "No." The questioner pursues: "What, then, could you be?"[11] The answer begins with a reference to the Buddha's perfect purity: like the lotus that sprouts and grows in water but remains unsullied by that water, so is the Buddha born and nurtured in this world but untouched by it, as one who "has overcome the world" (*lokam abhibhuyya*).[12] Then comes the long-awaited answer: "Remember, Brahmin, that I am Buddha"[13]—for what distinguishes him from all other beings is his spotless purity.

The legend that describes the Buddha's mother, Maya, as a virgin both *ante partum* and *post partum* (before and after giving birth) is a symbolic variant of the simile of the lotus, and is iconographically expressed in the form of a white elephant,[14] just as in Christian art the dove represents the Holy Spirit hovering over Mary to make her the virgin mother of Jesus. In the first centuries of Buddhism, no artist dared to paint or build a human figure of the Buddha; he could not be classed under any category of being, all of which he transcended by his infinite purity. Instead, the early Buddhists resorted to symbols: the riderless horse represented his Great Renunciation (i.e., his leaving home for the forest); a tree with no one seated beneath it represented the enlightenment; the wheel symbolized the first sermon, his death was signified by the *stūpa*, the funeral mound. But when statues did begin to be made in later centuries, they were frequently of gigantic proportions, suggestive of the superhuman stature of his personality. Even today in Theravada countries, to impersonate the Buddha on the stage or in a film is considered blasphemous.

In the medium of the spoken and written word, as in the case of the plastic arts, there was a struggle to formulate this inexpressible dimension of Buddha-hood, a dimension that in no way eclipsed Gautama's humanity but in some way transcended it. Though "docetism" (*lokottaravāda*) was rejected as a heresy especially in southern Buddhism, the Mahayanists equated the Buddha with the *Dharma*, the eternal Truth that preexists Gautama,[15] similar to the way that Jesus of Nazareth was recognized as the preexistent *Logos* in the fourth Gospel.

Hence there has been, from very early times, a desperate effort to create buddhological titles from terms judiciously selected from the religious vocabulary of contemporary cultures. A random survey has come up with forty-six such titles used in the Pali scriptures.[16] Some describe the Buddha's "person" as such (*mahāpurisa* = Supreme Person; *mahāvira* = Great Hero; *purisuttama* and *naruttama* = the Most Exalted of persons; *mahājuti* = the Brilliant, etc.); others indicate his relationship with other humans (*vinayaka* = Leader; *purisa-damma-sārathī* = Trainer of tameable persons; *sārathīnam varuttamo* = the Most Excellent of guides, etc.); still others point to his supremacy over the whole of creation (*lokanātha* = Lord of the Cosmos), and so on.

As one scholar has observed,[17] the long series of epithets cited in the *Upāli Sutta* of the Pali canon[18] recalls the *strotra* (i.e., doxological) literature known as *sata-nāma* ("hundred names") so characteristic of Hindu devotionalism. The first impression one gets is that here affective or devotional spirituality (*bhakti-mārgā*) has replaced the gnostic spirituality (*jñāna-mārgā*) which is proper to Buddhism. The fact, however, is that almost all these epithets refer to the Buddha's gnostic detachment and his internal purity.

Since Buddhahood is conceived as the pleroma of gnosis (*prajñā*) and agape (*karunā*); one can therefore easily understand why Pali commentators linked these two buddhalogical qualities with the two most hallowed buddhological titles—namely, *arahān* (the Worthy One) and *bhagavān* (the Blessed One), respectively. The former implies gnostic disengagement from the world, and the latter connotes his agapeic involvement with the liberation of all beings as well as his sovereignty over the whole of creation.[19] These two epithets occur in the most ancient doxology (used even today at the beginning of any liturgy): "Hail to him, the Blessed One, the Worthy One, the supremely Enlightened One!" The exegetes claim that by gnosis (proper to the *arahān*), Gautama crosses the ocean of *samsāra* and reaches the further shore of nirvana, but by agape (proper to the *bhagavān*) he also gets others across.[20]

The convergence and concentration of *prajñā* and *karunā* in the Buddha (which explains, respectively, his absolute purity and his soteriological impact on the final destiny of others) has also earned for him such titles as *lokavidū* (Knower of the World) and *lokanātha* (Lord of the Cosmos), already in the canonical writings.[21] Also in the subsequent postcanonical literature, his transcendental status and his cosmic lordship began to be indicated through a long string of buddhological epithets such as "King of Kings," "Self-existent," "Self-luminous," "God above (all other) gods (*devātideva*)."[22]

Some eminent Buddhist scholars (e.g., Kalupahana, quoted above) would question the orthodoxy of this development. Perhaps its scriptural roots should be traced back to what we might call the catechetical method or the pedagogy of the Buddha. The scriptures testify that he changed the god-infested cosmos of his contemporaries into an anthropocentric universe wherein humans who fulfill their innate capacity to realize the metacosmic goal of nirvana were held to reach a state far above the level of gods. Thus he divested the gods of all salvific power; even their cosmic influence was restricted to helping or harming humans in their day-to-day temporal needs. The canonical writers make their point when they portray the highest deity of the Brahmanic religion crouching in reverence before the Buddha and his disciples.[23]

This catechetical procedure of the Buddha was continued as a missiological technique in later times in that missionaries did not uproot the cosmic religiosity of the people whom they converted but gave it a metacosmic orientation not only through the doctrine of nirvana but also by installing the Buddha as the sovereign lord immediately *above* and yet wholly *beyond* the local deities of each culture.

This seems to be the origin of what I alluded to as "the composite portrait" of the Buddha emerging from Buddhist cultures. This certainly is what "Gautama the Buddha" means for millions of Asians today. He is as much the Great Being (*mahāsatta*) to be revered and praised, the Lord (*bhagavān*) to be loved and trusted, as he is a human teacher (*satthā*) to be followed and a saint (*arahān*) to be emulated.

This portrait was brought out in clearer focus during a buddhological controversy that erupted some years ago in Sri Lanka. A renowned Buddhist layman and writer, a humanist and socialist, Dr. Martin Wickramasingha produced a Sinhalese novel based on the life of the Buddha, eliminating the mythical and the miraculous elements from the scriptural accounts and focusing on Siddhartha's *human* struggle not only for his own nirvanic freedom but also for *social* transformation. This novel provoked a massive public protest on the part of monks and laity. The great monk-scholar, the Venerable Y Paññārāma, who spearheaded this protest movement, compiled a two-volume refutation of the buddhological and other inaccuracies said to be contained in the novel.[24]

In his critique of the novel, the venerable monk complains that, among other things, in portraying the character of Siddhartha as a human seeker, the novelist had overlooked the quality specific to Siddhartha's Buddhahood.[25] Yet, lest he be accused of docetism (*lokottaravāda*), the monk insists that his criticism should not be construed as a plea for retaining the mythical and the miraculous elements at the expense of Gautama's true humanity. To prove his orthodoxy, he quotes extensively from one of his devotional poems addressed to the Buddha, indeed a credo in the Buddha's historical humanity:

> Had I sensed thee not to be a human
> Never, never indeed would I find in me
> Any love, regard, or fear for thee!
>
> My Lord is indeed a Man!
> Man in body and thought
> In virtue and action!
> Yet, going beyond common humanity
> He bore a Splendour Transcendent![26]

Then, presuming himself to be the Buddha's contemporary, he expresses his longing to nurse his aging Master, to touch and massage his limbs, kiss his feet, and wash his ailing body.

It is very clear that for this defender of orthodoxy, Buddhahood implies a *truly transcendent* dimension of a *truly human* being. Both these aspects are proclaimed with as much firmness as the *verus deus* and the *verus homo* are affirmed of Jesus in traditional christology.

There is also a third aspect implicit in this credo: the soteriological role of the Buddha. In the orthodox Theravada stream, the Buddha is never regarded as a savior. His soteriological role is restricted to his discovering and preaching the *dharma* (the eternal salvific Truth that preexists him) and to the forming of the *sangha* (a community that, like him, realizes this Truth and continues to preach and practice the Path that leads to it). But once the *dharma* was equated with the Buddha, and the *sangha* was devalued (as happened in certain Mahayanist schools, e.g., in Amidism), Buddha became the savior who grants the grace of salvation to those who invoke him in faith. An agapeic religiosity using a personalist idiom has become a characteristic of such schools of Buddhism.

The more intricate element in the Buddha's soteriological influence is his *cosmic lordship,* at least as far as popular religiosity is concerned. However, no recognized anthropologist has really shown so far that the masses ever confuse this lordship with the cosmic function of gods and spirits. Yet, the cult of gods—that is, this cosmic religiosity—includes as one of its manifestations the *socio-political* regulation of human life. This is at the root of the "Divine Right Theory of Kingship," which the Buddha categorically rejected in favor of a social contract theory.[27] Yet the feudal societies that hosted Buddhism in Asia continued to be dominated by the older theory. Hence, the socio-political order, even in Buddhist cultures, continued to be associated with cosmic religiosity to which Buddhism imparted a metacosmic orientation by placing the Buddha, the *dharma,* and the *sangha* above and beyond the socio-political order.[28] The kingdom of Thailand continues this tradition.

Nevertheless, the social dimension of Buddhist ethics is being reclaimed from oblivion and reexpressed as the Buddha's vision of a just political order for today,[29] so that social justice is regarded at least as an inevitable by-product of Buddhist soteriology. An extreme example of such reclaiming can be found in *Dalit Sāhitya* ("Literature of the Oppressed") produced by the schedule castes of Maharashtra in India. Many of them embraced Buddhism as a doorway to social emancipation. The following poem addressed to the Buddha, the liberator of the oppressed, is a sample of *Dalit Sāhitya*:

> Siddhartha
> Never do I see you
> In the Jetavana
> Sitting in the lotus position
> With your eyes closed

Or in the caves of Ajanta and Werule
With your stony lips touching
Sleeping your final sleep.

I see you
Speaking and walking
Amongst the humble and the weak
Soothing away grief
In the life-threatening darkness
With torch in hand
Going from hovel to hovel.

Today you wrote a new page
of the *Tripitaka*.

You have revealed the
New Meaning of suffering
Which like an epidemic
Swallows life's blood.[30]

This indeed is a new interpretation of the Buddha's soteriological role. The belief in his cosmic lordship is hermeneutically extended to the socio-political structures whose radical transformation is believed to be possible under the Buddha's soteriological influence. Undoubtedly, this is "a new page in the *Tripitaka*," as the poet declares.

JESUS THE CHRIST IN THE CONTEXT OF BUDDHOLOGY

The "missionary buddhology" that installed the Buddha as cosmic lord in so many Asian cultures anticipated by centuries the missiology of Paul who did the same with Christ in the Hellenistic cultures that he evangelized. He preached and confessed Jesus to be the Lord of all creation, whom all beings "in heaven, on earth, and in hell" adore in fear and trembling (Phil. 2: 6–11). Far from suppressing the Hellenistic belief in "cosmic elements," Paul acknowledged their existence and their power to enslave human beings (Gal. 4:3) and cause disobedience (Eph. 2:2). Though they appear to be gigantic powers arrayed against humankind (Eph. 6:12), they have all been decisively domesticated by the risen Jesus (Col. 2:15). Thus by liberating us from this "dominion of darkness" (Col. 1:13), Christ has made himself "the head" of all such cosmic forces (Col. 2:10). In other words, he is at once the metacosmic power and the cosmic mediator because in him the whole of existence—in heaven and on earth, visible and invisible—is recapitulated and reconciled (Col. 1:15–16).[31]

Undoubtedly there is a striking parallelism, though not strictly a similarity, between the two confessional formulas, the buddhological and the christological. No wonder that in some Asian countries, the first Christian encounter with Buddhism was to push the Buddha out and install Christ in his place. The Buddhists replied in kind!

In fact, in the polemical mood of the late nineteenth century, when the anticolonial movements had, by historical necessity, to be anti-Christian, the great Buddhist revivalist, Anagarika Dharmapala, took delight in making odious comparisons between the two founders.[32] The "Nazarene carpenter," as he referred to Jesus with disdain, had no sublime teachings to offer, and understandably so, because his parables not only reveal a limited mind, but they also impart immoral lessons and unpractical ethics![33]

> Jesus as a human personality was an utter failure. He made no impression on the public during the three years of his ministry. No thinker or philosopher took the least notice of his philosophy which helped to create imbeciles. The few illiterate fishermen of Galilee followed him as he promised to make them judges to rule over Israel.[34]

In Dharmapala's speeches and essays, Jesus is reduced to the stature of a spiritual dwarf before Buddha's gigantic personality.

But let us humbly acknowledge that this species of Buddhist revivalism owes its anti-Christian thrust to an initial Christian offensive aimed not only against the doctrine but also against the *person* of the Buddha through the written as well as the spoken word.[35]

The peak of this revivalism, as one sociologist sees it,[36] manifested itself in the proliferation of Buddha statues in the major towns of Sri Lanka's western coast; it was an attempt to reaffirm Buddhism, as a socio-political force, against Christianity. May I add my own explanation: Was it not also an attempt to put the Buddha back where he belonged in the urban culture of the westernized Buddhist elite presumably because in that elitist culture the cosmic lordship of the Buddha, taken for granted in the rural areas, was eclipsed by the colonial impact of Western Christianity?

There is also a less aggressive way of affirming the supremacy of the Buddha over Christ and vice versa. The Hindu theology of religions has pioneered this technique. Hinduism neutralizes the challenge of the other religion by absorbing it into its own theological framework. Brought under the Hindu salvific umbrella, Jesus and Gautama become Hindu avatars (incarnations) whom the Christians and Buddhists can hardly recognize as the Christ and the Buddha, respectively.

This ancient theology of religions prevails today on the frontiers of the mainstream churches. The Buddha is accepted as a precursor of Christ, a "holy pagan" preparing the way for Christ the only Savior, as Daniélou, following Guardini, seems to have maintained.[37] Marco Polo's spontaneous observation about the Buddha ("Had he been a Christian, he would have been a great saint of Jesus Christ.") had already anticipated this inclusivist theology of religions. In fact, it was as a saint of Jesus Christ that the medieval church accepted the

Buddha in the Joasaph cult, as mentioned earlier. No Buddhist is going to be flattered by this condescension. Yet this theory has deep roots in the New Testament approach to the patriarchs and prophets of Judaism—the same approach that Islam adopts toward Jesus!

In the same way, many a well-meaning Buddhist condescends to give Jesus a niche in the Buddhist *Weltanschauung*. At best, Jesus receives the welcome given to a *Bodhisattva*, being full of compassion but still on the way to Buddhahood! This is about the maximum that Buddhists can concede to the founder of Christianity. If they concede one bit more to Jesus, they would cease to be Buddhist.

We are, therefore, obliged to conclude that both the exclusivist and the inclusivist theories of religions end up asserting the supremacy of the Buddha over the Christ, and vice versa. There seems to be no way of avoiding the exclusivist model. This is the impasse that any "dialogical" theology of religions, even in its most inclusivist form, runs into. Is there no other way of seeing the problem? Or, another *starting point*?

I believe that the *false start*, which leads theologians into blind alleys, is their obsession with the "uniqueness" of Christ. At the risk of anticipating my conclusions, I would suggest that the real debate is about the "uniqueness" of *Jesus* in terms of the "absoluteness" that Christians indicate with titles like *Christ, Son of God,* and the like—the same absoluteness that Buddhists indicate with similar terms: *dharma, tathāgata,* and the like. To put it more precisely, the crux of the problem is whether it is Jesus or Gautama who is *unique* in the sense of being the *exclusive medium of salvation for all*. That Jesus is unique is obvious even to Buddhists, just as Christians would hardly question the uniqueness of Gautama. Is not each one of us unique? The issue is whether Jesus' uniqueness consists of his absoluteness as conveyed by certain christological titles, and whether the uniqueness of Gautama should be understood in terms of the absoluteness that the word *dharma* or, as in certain schools, *Buddha* seems to convey.

Note that in this context "the Absolute" has a soteriological connotation. Christians know it as the *mysterium salutis* (mystery of salvation) and have learned to distinguish three dimensions in this mystery: (1) *source* of salvation, (2) *medium* of salvation, and (3) *force* of salvation. This is what the "economic Trinity" is all about. In the scriptures these three aspects are distinguished as *theos, logos,* and *pneuma,* respectively; or, more anthropomorphically, as the Father, the Son, and the Consoler/Advocate, who are conceptually clarified in Chalcedonian christology as three distinct *persons* sharing one divine *nature*.

This tridimensionality of the mystery (and process) of salvation is implicitly acknowledged in the soteriology of practically all major religions, as I have suggested elsewhere.[38] In Buddhism, however, the first dimension is not seen as the source of salvation, but seems to be affirmed as the final metacosmic destiny of an individual's cosmic and human history: *nirvana*. Because there is no primordial source of salvation, there is no doctrine of creation (*ex nihilo*), and consequently no doctrine of eschatological consummation, and no theory of grace.

But Christianity sees the source not only as the Alpha, but also as the Omega point of history. Hence, in its agapeic framework, this world and human life itself appears to be *consummated* (fulfilled, perfected) in the *eschaton*. This species of extrapolation characteristic of Christian theology contrasts neatly with the apophatic language of Buddhist gnosticism that sees nirvana as the utter *cessation* rather than the consummation of all that constitutes reality as we now know and experience it. Furthermore, nirvana is the cessation of the human *individual's* history, whereas the *eschaton* is the consummation also of the *collective* history of humankind.

There is, however, a significant point of convergence. Both religions insist: (1) that a positive human endeavor (an ascesis) is a necessary condition for the arrival of final liberation, and yet (2) that this final liberation (the absolute future or the further shore) is never really the result of human effort, for nirvana is beyond the categories of *phala* and *aphala*—that is to say, it defies all human causation, while similarly the *eschaton* is believed to "break in" from the other side of the human horizon.

Though these distinctions and qualifications are necessary when speaking of the source of salvation, there is a greater agreement when we come to the medium of salvation. Salvation implies a paradox: the inaccessible "beyond" (source) becomes one's salvific "within" (force), and the incomprehensible comes within the grasp of human insight. This is possible only because the Absolute contains within its own bosom a mediatory and revelatory self-expression—that is, an accessible dimension: the *Dharma*/the *Logos*. The transhuman horizon stops receding only because there is a path (*mārgā/hodos*) leading toward it. For, in the beginning was the WORD by which Absolute Silence came to be *heard*—and the ICON by which the Invisible was brought within our *sight*!

But how could we humans, who have *dust* as our origin and destiny (Gen. 3:19), ever respond to this medium (*dharma/mārgā/logos/hodos/*word/icon) unless we are equipped with a "response-apparatus" commensurate with that medium? No wonder that all religions seem to postulate a certain *given* capacity within us to seek and find the Liberating Truth, or (as in theistic religions), a certain innate *force* by which the Absolute draws us toward Itself. This "given capacity" appears as the "Spirit" in the Christian's vocabulary.

The Buddhist postulates this capacity in the context of the twofold doctrine: "no soul" and "no God." Because no Primordial Source of liberation is admitted ("no God"), human beings, who are merely a fluctuating series of psycho-physical events without any permanent substratum ("no soul"), have to rely on their own "self" or *citta* for liberation (*atta-sarana*).[39] This *citta* is therefore that which is developed toward the full attainment of Absolute Freedom or nirvana. The idea of a *given* human potentiality for the realization of liberating truth is the most significant presupposition in Buddhist soteriology, though it is never explicitly analyzed.

Having thus clarified the three aspects of salvation in Buddhism and Christianity, I can now proceed, with the aid of a common vocabulary, to juxtapose buddhology and christology, keeping in mind that both are expressions of the *interpretative* level of religious consciousness (as explained at the beginning of this chapter).

Let us note first that there is an "ascending buddhology" and a "descending buddhology," if we may borrow terms from Christain theology. The former defines Buddhahood in terms of a distinctive way of attaining nirvana not attributed to *arahāns*. The term *arahān,* which used to be a buddhological title, is now popularly and frequently used as a synonym for   disciples who attain nirvana in a manner different from the Buddha. The Buddha is therefore a human being who has reached a state that makes him a category of his own, as explained above. This buddhology constitutes the principal orientation in Southeast Asia. But in northern Buddhism the tendency seems to be to equate the Buddha with the eternal preexistent *Dharma.* Gautama, then, would be the human manifestation or incarnation of this revelatory medium of salvation. All buddhological titles are human efforts to express the transhuman dimension of the Buddha in the context of one or the other buddhology. The belief in his cosmic lordship is an interpretive extension of these two basic affirmations.

Christology interprets Jesus as the exclusive medium of salvation for all, the *Logos,* the image, the word, the path, and so on. But as in buddhology, so also in christology, it is not the interpretation that saves! What mediates salvation is the medium itself, in whatever linguistic idiom it may be experienced, recognized, and named. Nor are the titles in themselves salvific. Such titles as "Christ" are only human categorizations limited to a given culture. What mediates liberation is the medium to which one culture as much as another can decide what name to give: Christ, Son of God, and so forth, or *Dharma, Tathāgata,* and so forth—each according to its own religious idiom.

Not even the acclamation "Jesus is Lord" is in itself salvific. For it is not anyone who says "Lord, Lord," but the person who does the will of the Father who is saved (Matt. 7: 21). To say "Jesus is the Word" is not enough; the Word must be heard and executed for one to be saved. To say "Jesus is the path" is not enough; one must walk the path to reach the end. Moreover, not all who obey the Word or walk the path feel obliged to claim its proper name to be Jesus. For what mediates salvation is not the "name" of Jesus in the Hellenistic sense of the term "name," but the name of Jesus and *as* Jesus in the Hebrew sense of "the reality" (or salvific medium) that was seen to be operative in Jesus, independent of the name or designation we may attach to it. In fact, knowledge of the name or title is not expected by the eschatological Judge, but knowledge of the path is (Matt. 25: 37–39 and 44–46).

This holds good for buddhology too. Buddhists must agree with their Christian partners that liberation is possible only through what they both accept to be the "revelatory medium of salvation" and not the titles one gives to it. The major function of christological and buddhological titles is to equate the names of particular historical persons with the salvific medium. The real parting of ways, therefore, begins when either Gautama or Jesus is identified with that medium by means of these titles. It is at this point that dialogue must once more change directions if it will avoid a blind alley, for we are dealing here with kerygmatic affirmations.

A kerygma is always a metalogical proclamation that cannot be demonstrated rationally. The only convincing proof it adduces is *martyrion* (witness), for we are dealing with soteriology, not philosophy or mathematics. That is to say, liberation is the only proof of liberation! To say Jesus is the medium of salvation is to show the fruits of such liberation in the person who says it. A christology that remains a speculative hermeneusis fails to be a soteriological proclamation about Jesus. A christology receives its authenticity from a transforming praxis that proves that in the *story of Jesus that continues in his followers,* the medium of salvation is operative, though it is not the total mystery of salvation (*totus Deus, non totum Dei*—"entirely God but not the entirety of God"). In Christian theological vocabulary, this medium is designated by titles like "Christ," "Son of God," and the like, as applied to Jesus because this liberation is believed to take place through Jesus the man (therefore through every man and woman *in* Jesus).

This is the inchoative christology found in Paul and in need of refinement. But in the process of being refined, this christology splits up into at least two incomplete models. (1) The classic (Chalcedonian) model focused too narrowly on the theandric composition of the incarnate *Logos* (Jesus) and on the philosophical problem of "one and many" with respect to the triune mystery of salvation, thus neglecting the whole process of salvation in its cosmic magnitude and in its eschatological dimension. (2) A popular catechetical model stressed the *divine* lordship of Jesus ("Christ the King" reigning in heaven) over a given, unchangeably created cosmos, without defining this lordship in terms of our co-mediation with him in the task of co-creating—that is, transforming this world psycho-spiritually and socio-politically into his kingdom of peace and justice.

Now this co-redemptive role of the corporate Christ, missing in both these partial christologies, is being supplied by the emergent theologies of liberation, which are essentially kerygmatic and critical of the christology of domination—that is, the theology of the colonial Christ, which could not be "good news" either for Buddhists or for Christians!

A liberation christology sees the medium of salvation in the form of *Jesus on the cross,* the symbol of the twofold ascesis that constitutes the salvific path— the *via crucis*: (1) Jesus' renunciation of biological, emotional, and physical ties that bound him to the "world" (Jesus' *struggle to be poor*), and (2) his open denunciation of mammon, which organizes itself into principalities and powers by dividing humankind into the class of Dives and the class of Lazarus (Jesus' *struggle for the poor*).[40]

The first form of Jesus' ascesis focuses on interior liberation, so well symbolized by the Buddha seated under the tree of gnosis. The second involves a ruthless demand for a structural change in human relationships in view of the new order of love or the kingdom of God, a demand that led Jesus to a type of death reserved for terrorists (zealots) on what has now come to be the tree of agape.

The uniqueness of Jesus (I am not concerned here with the uniqueness of Christ but with the "absoluteness" that titles such as "Christ" were meant to convey) lies in the fact that his claim to be the absolute medium of salvation is demonstrated on the cross by his double ascesis, which, nevertheless, would not be a convincing proof of his claim but an empty boast of his followers unless this double ascesis continues in them as an ongoing salvific process completing in their bodies what is still unfinished in the ascesis of Jesus (Col. 1:24).

This double ascesis is the nucleus around which an Asian theology of liberation evolves into a christology that does not compete with buddhology but complements it by acknowledging the one path of liberation on which Christians join Buddhists in their *gnostic detachment* (or the practice of voluntary poverty) and Buddhists join Christians in their *agapeic involvement* in the struggle against forced poverty.[41] This complementary cooperation is happening today in some basic *human* communities in Asia. Here, co-pilgrims expound their respective scriptures, retelling the story of Jesus and Gautama in a core-to-core dialogue that makes their hearts burn (Luke 24:32). It is only at the end of the path, as at Emmaus, that the path itself will be recognized by name (Luke 24:31).

NOTES

1. In an address given at the "Fünfte religionstheologische Studientagung" on the general theme of "Dialog aus der Mitte christlicher Theologie" ("Dialogue from the Core of Christian Theology"), held at St. Gabriel, Mödling bei Wien, Austria, April 1–4, 1986.

2. *Buddhist Philosophy. A Historical Analysis* (Honolulu: Hawaii University Press, 1976), pp. 112–26.

3. I have briefly described these historical circumstances and given the relevant sources in "Western Christianity and Asian Buddhism: A Theological Reading of Historical Encounters," *Dialogue* (Colombo) n.s. 7 (1980) 66–67. See also my, "Buddhism as a Challenge for Christians," *Concilium*, 183 (1986) 60–65.

4. S. Cromwell Crawford, "American Youth and the Buddha," *World Buddhism* 18/8 (1970) 199.

5. *Anguttara Nikāya* (PTS edition), Vol. I, p. 188, and *passim*. All Pali texts quoted hence forward will be from the PTS Editions (Pali Text Society, London).

6. Ibid., p. 161 and passim.

7. *Majjhima Nikāya*, I:9.

8. *Stromata*, XV:71.6.

9. For references to sources dealing with the Joasaph cult, see my "Western Christianity and Asian Buddhism," pp. 61–62.

10. *Anguttara Nikāya*, II:38–39.

11. In translating this passage, I. B. Horner (*Gradual Sayings*, PTS, 1952, II:46)

insists that the question, as the Pali original has it, is not about what Gautama *is* but what he *will become*, though the final answer is in the present tense—namely, that he *is* (already) the Buddha. For a different view, see Kalupahana, *Buddhist Philosophy*, p. 112. See also note 13, below.

12. Compare John 16: 33.

13. Horner (*Sayings*) translates: "Take it that I am a Buddha." This answer is then summed up in the verse that follows: "Therefore, I *am* Buddha" (*tasmā Buddho'smi*).

14. Maya is believed to have conceived Gautama at the moment when a white elephant appeared to her in a dream.

15. The proof text adduced by the adherents of this theory is *Itivuttaka*, p. 91, where "seeing the Buddha" and "seeing the *Dharma*" are equated. As for the (eternal) preexistence of the *Dharma*, see *Samyutta Nikāya*, II:25.

16. See B.G. Gokhale, "*Bhakti* in Early Buddhism," *Journal of Asian and African Studies*, 15 (1980) 18.

17. Ibid.

18. *Majjhima Nikāya*, I:386.

19. E.g., *Itivuttak'aṭṭhakathā*, I:13, 15–16.

20. Ibid.

21. E.g., *lokavidū* in *Digha Nikāya*, III:76, and *lokanātha* in *Sutta Nipata*, p. 995.

22. See Har Dayal, *The Buddhist Doctrine in Buddhist Sanscrit Literature* (Delhi: Motilal Banarsidas, 1931/1970), p. 24.

23. Cf. *Samyutta Nikāya*, I:235.

24. *Bhavatarana-maga hā Buddha-caritaya*, vol. 1 (1976) and 2 (1978).

25. Ibid., I:20, and passim.

26. Ibid., p. 25.

27. Cf. *Aggañña Sutta,* which is summarized in my "The Political Vision of the Buddhists," *Dialogue*, 11 (1984) 6ff.

28. See the diagram with an explanation of this worldview in my "Toward an Asian Theology of Liberation," *The Month*, May 1979, p. 152.

29. See Piyasena Dissanayake, *The Political Thought of Buddha* (Colombo, 1977).

30. Dayar Powar, "Siddhartha," *Panchasheel*, Oct. 1972, p. 7, translated into English and quoted in J.B. Gokhale-Turner, "*Bhakti* or *Vidroha*: Continuity and Change in *Dalit Sāhitya*," *Journal of African and Asian Studies*, 15 (1980) 38.

31. Cf. Elias Mallon, "The Cosmic Powers and Reconciliation," *Centro Pro Unione* (Rome), 6 (1974) 18–22.

32. See *Return to Righteousness* (Collection of Speeches, Essays, and Letters of Anagarika Dharmapala), Ananda Guruge, ed. (Colombo: Government Press, 1965), pp. 447ff.

33. Ibid., pp. 448–49.

34. Ibid., p. 475.

35. This thesis is documented in Kitsiri Malalgoda, *Buddhism in Sinhalese Society* (Berkeley, 1976), pp. 192–255.

36. G. Obeysekere, "Religious Symbolism and Political Change in Ceylon," *Modern Ceylon Studies* (University of Ceylon), 1 (1970) 43–63.

37. Jean Daniélou, *Holy Pagans of the Old Testament* (London: Longmans, 1957), p. 22.

38. Pieris, "Speaking of the Son of God in Non-Christian Cultures, e.g., in Asia," *Concilium*, 153 (1982) 65–70.

39. For clarification regarding the "self" that is denied in Buddhism and the (empirical) "self" that is identified with *citta*, see my "*Citta, Attā, and Attabhāva* in Pali

Exegetical Writings," *Buddhist Studies in Honor of Walpola Rahula* (London: Gordon Fraser, 1980), pp. 212–22.

40. See the conclusions in "Buddhism as a Challenge for Christians" (note 3, above) and my "To Be Poor as Jesus Was Poor?," *The Way*, July 1984, pp. 186–97.

41. How this theology spells out what is *unique* to biblico-Christian revelation and liberation is discussed in my "Theology of Liberation in Asian Churches?," *Vidyajyoti*, 50/7 (1986) 330–51.

11

Toward a Liberation Theology of Religions

PAUL F. KNITTER

Among the many "signs of the times" that challenge the churches today, there are two that place particularly pressing demands on Christians: the experience of the *many poor* and the experience of the *many religions*. It is not surprising, therefore, that two of the most creative and revitalizing expressions of Christian life and thought today are the theology of religions, responding to the problem of religious pluralism, and the theology of liberation, responding to the greater and more urgent problem of suffering and injustice.

Advocates of these theologies, however, have grown up and continue to live in two neighborhoods of the Christian church. Not that there are any natural barriers between them; it is just that, given their active lives and many concerns, they have not had the time or occasion to get to know each other. In recent years, however, there have been signs that the old neighborhoods are changing—or expanding. Today, members of these two theological camps can and must get to know each other, learn from each other, and work together in their different projects. If they can do this, they will, I believe, be able to contribute all the more creatively and effectively to the life of the church and the world.

In this chapter, I shall try to show why such a dialogue between theologians of liberation and of the religions is necessary and what it promises. Given my own identity as a theologian of religions and, especially, given the theme of this book, my focus will be on what the theology of religions has to learn from the theology of liberation. In particular, I hope to show how principles and guidelines from liberation theology can help us navigate the move toward what in the subtitle of this book is called a "pluralistic theology of religions." As John Hick and I discovered in trying to enlist contributors to the book, there is an imposing phalanx of uncertainties, hesitations, and objections that one must face in endorsing or merely exploring the claim that other religious traditions and religious figures may be as valid as Christ and Christianity. Some of the questions that kept writers from joining our project were: "Is this move really necessary?" "Is it opportune?" "Will it promote or debilitate interreligious dialogue?" And especially, "Can one make this move without abandoning or diluting what is essential to Christian life and witness?"

I should like to suggest how insights and procedures from the theology of liberation can help us grapple with, if not answer, many of those questions. But first, let me offer some background as to why the theological neighborhoods of liberation and of religious pluralism are spilling into each other.

THE NEED FOR DIALOGUE BETWEEN THEOLOGIANS OF LIBERATION AND OF RELIGIONS

1. It is becoming clear how urgently the theology of liberation and the theology of religions need each other. First, from the perspective of those concerned with liberation, the past decade has indicated what an important and powerful role religion can play, for better or for worse, in bringing about socio-political transformation. (Across the spectrum, witness Shī'ah Islam in the Iranian revolution, the Moral Majority in installing and defending the Reagan administration, basic Christian communities in implementing the revolution in Nicaragua and struggling for it in El Salvador.) Some would even endorse the broad philosophico-anthropological claims of historians Arnold Toynbee and Wilfred Cantwell Smith that *only* through the vision, the motivation, the empowerment coming from religious symbols and experience will humankind be able to overcome its innate, warring selfishness; only through the hope and self-sacrificing love born of religious experience will humans be able to "muster the energy, devotion, vision, resolution, capacity to survive disappointment that will be necessary—that *are* necessary—for the challenge" of building a better and more just world.[1]

What this implies, and what especially Latin American liberation theologians need to see more clearly, is that the liberation movement needs not just religion but *religions*! Economic, political, and especially nuclear liberation is too big a job for any one nation, or culture, *or* religion. A crosscultural, interreligious cooperation in liberative praxis and a sharing of liberative theory is called for. This is argued persuasively by Harvey Cox in his book *Religion in the Secular City*; after spending most of his book showing that the highest hopes for the relevance of Christianity in the secular city lie not in fundamentalism but in liberation theology, he urges in a final chapter that liberation theology will be able to do its job only if it "breaks out of . . . [its] regional confines" of Western Christianity and learns to take "more seriously not only the religious experience of its own indigenous populations but also the experience of the world religions."[2]

In fact, if liberation theology is to take root in Asia, and not just in Latin

America, it has no choice but to open itself to dialogue with Eastern religions. As Sri Lankan Aloysius Pieris reminds his Latin colleagues:

> The irruption of the Third World [with its demands for liberation] is also the irruption of the non-Christian world. The vast majority of God's poor perceive their ultimate concern and symbolize their struggle for liberation in the idiom of non-Christian religions and cultures. Therefore, a theology that does not speak to or speak through this non-Christian peoplehood [and its religions] is a luxury of a Christian minority.[3]

A purely Christian theology of liberation, in other words, suffers the dangerous limitation of inbreeding, of drawing on only one vision of the kingdom. An encounter with the liberating potential of Buddhism and Hinduism will reveal to Latin American theologians, for example, that they have perhaps been overinfluenced by the negative views of religion advanced by the two "mighty Karls" of the West—Barth who denied the capacity of religion to channel revelation, and Marx who failed to see how religion can be a vehicle of revolution. Too many Latin American theologians of liberation (e.g., Segundo and Sobrino) are closed to the "liberative and revolutionary potentials of non-Christian religions."[4] A worldwide liberation movement needs a worldwide interreligious dialogue.

2. On the other side, even more clearly and uncomfortably, theologians of religions have in recent years begun to recognize how much they not only can but must learn from the theology of liberation. A growing number of First World theologians, in academe and in the churches, feel themselves shaken and challenged by the liberationist preferential option for the poor and the nonperson. The First World theologians are well aware that their interreligious dialogues have often taken place on mountaintops overlooking favelas and death squads. Thanks to the admonitions and example of liberationist neighbors, theologians engaged in dialogue are realizing that religion that does not address, as a primary concern, the poverty and oppression that infest our world is not authentic religion. Dialogue between inauthentic religions easily becomes a purely mystical pursuit or an interesting pastime affordable only by First World mystics or scholars. Something essential is missing in such otherworldly or ultra-academic dialogue.

Theologians involved in religious dialogue are also recognizing the limits and dangers of an overenthusiastic affirmation of pluralism. Open-minded tolerance of others and eager acceptance of diversity can all too easily lead one to tolerate, perhaps unknowingly, what Langdon Gilkey in his essay has called "the intolerable."[5] Dialogue and pluralism should not be one's first concern; nor should they be ends in themselves. Dorothee Sölle points out the limits of pluralism and tolerance: "The limits of tolerance are manifest by the victims of society. Wherever human beings are crippled, deprived of their dignity, destroyed, raped, that is where tolerance ends."[6] We go out to meet others, liberation theologians would urge, we encounter other religions, not *primarily* to enjoy diversity and dialogue but to eliminate suffering and oppression—not only to practice charity but, first of all, to work for justice. Justice, we are told, takes precedence over pluralism, dialogue, and even charity.

In light of the present state of our world, therefore, both basic humanitarian concerns as well as the soteriologies of most religions would seem to dictate that a *preferential option for the poor and the nonperson* constitutes both the *necessity* and the *primary purpose* of interreligious dialogue.[7] Religions must speak and act together because only so can they make their crucially important contribution to removing the oppression that contaminates our globe. Dialogue, therefore, is not a luxury for the leisure classes of religion; nor is it a "top priority" after we take care of the essentials. Interreligious dialogue is essential to international liberation.

Granting that theologians of liberation and of interreligious dialogue have much to say to each other, I should now like to focus on how liberation theology can help us explore the new terrain of a pluralist theology of religions. More specifically, I shall try to show (1) how the methodology of liberation thought provides a context and starting point for a dialogue that avoids absolutist positions, respects the genuine difference and validity of others, and yet does not fall down the "slippery slopes of relativism," and (2) how ingredients of liberation theology enable us to move "appropriately" toward a pluralist (i.e., beyond both an exclusivist and inclusivist) christology without abandoning the content and power of Christian tradition or witness.

I will be offering the "bare bones" of what a liberation theology of religions might look like. In doing so, I am illustrating, I suppose, what liberation theologians have long been saying: that their method of theology is not meant just for Latin America or the Third World, but that it can and should affect the way theology, in its different disciplines, is practiced in the First World. In its approach and method, liberation theology is for the universal church.

BASIS FOR A PLURALISTIC, NONRELATIVISTIC DIALOGUE

Theologians who argue that Christianity needs a new way of relating to other religions are trying to promote an interreligious dialogue that will be genuinely *pluralistic*—one that will avoid preestablished absolutist or definitive positions in order to allow that all the participants have an equally valid voice and that each participant can really hear, as much as possible, what the other is saying. Yet promoters of such a pluralistic dialogue are well aware of the danger that this kind of conversation can easily boil down to a relativistic pap in which "many" means "any" and no one can make any evaluative judgments. There are three ways in which a liberation theology of religions can help theologians of dialogue maintain the richness of pluralism without allowing it to disintegrate into the pap of relativism.

1. Liberation theologians enter the hermeneutical circle—the process of trying to interpret and listen to the word of God—with a "hermeneutics of suspicion." They suspiciously remind themselves how easily—yes, how unavoidably—intepretations of scripture and formulations of doctrine become *ideology*—a means of promoting one's own interests at the expense of someone else's. All too often the truth that we propose as "God's will" or as divinely revealed is really our own disguised, subconscious will to maintain the status quo or to protect our own control of the situation or our own cultural-economic superiority. Such subtle abuse of the living tradition, liberationists tell us, is always a lurking danger, if not a camouflaged fact, in all doctrine. So their first step, as they take up the task of interpreting God's word, is to be suspicious of and to sniff out, on the basis of their liberative praxis, the ideologies that may be operative in a given Christian context. Ideologized doctrines and practices have first to be detected and revised before God's voice, in both the tradition and in the world, can really be heard.[8]

Theologians of religions have much to gain from adopting such a hermeneutics of suspicion. It would require of them, as the first step in elaborating a Christian theology of other religions or in approaching other believers, to be hermeneutically suspicious of their given Christian positions concerning outsiders. How much has traditional theology of religions, especially its christological basis, served to cloak or condone an unconscious, ideological desire to maintain superiority, or to dominate and control, or to devalue other traditions culturally or religiously. Why, really, have Christians been so insistent on maintaining the doctrine of *extra ecclesiam nulla salus* ("outside the church, no salvation"), or the claim that Christ has to be the final norm for all other religions? Certainly it cannot be denied that in the past such doctrines and such christology have been used to justify the subordination and exploitation of other cultures and religions.

Even if it is not the conscious or subconscious intent of Christians to use particular doctrines to subordinate other cultures or violate their religious sensitivities, still, if such *are* the effects of these teachings, then these doctrines fall under the liberationists' hermeneutical suspicion. "Orthodox" doctrines that bear unethical fruits are, to say the least, highly suspicious. It is, for the most part, only in dialogue, in the voices of other cultures and religions, that Western Christians can begin to feel such suspicions. Third World Asian theologians, for instance, tell us in no uncertain terms that the harvest of missionary expansion in non-European cultures bears an abundance of unethical fruits. They point out how traditional models for a Christian understanding of other religions—even the more inclusivist (Rahner's "anonymous Christianity") and liberal (Küng's "critical catalyst") models[9]—promote a "crypto-colonialist theology of religions," and "cultural imperialism of the West."[10]

Such liberal, inclusivist models for dialogue with other religions are very much like the First World *development* model for promoting the economic welfare of the Third World. As liberation theologians have pointed out, such "development" subtly but effectively leads to further economic dependence and subordination, rather than to true *liberation*. This, indeed, is a form of neocolonialism. And as Tissa Balasuriya puts it bluntly, it causes one to be suspicious: "Can the self-understanding of churches that legitimized sexist, racist, classist, and religious oppression be theologically true?"[11]

It is precisely such "hermeneutical suspicion" about traditional Christian theology of religions, particularly its christological basis, that has impelled many Christian theologians to begin their search for a pluralist theology of religions.

2. If the liberationists' hermeneutics of suspicion can help theologians of the religions clear away ideological obstacles to more effective dialogue, another foundation stone of liberation theology—the preferential option for (or the hermeneutical privilege of) the poor—can help, I suggest, resolve the complex and controversial questions concerning the presuppositions and procedures for interreligious dialogue. Many a scholarly debate has spun its wheels over the "conditions of the possibility" of dialogue—that is, how should we understand religious pluralism and go about conversing so that everyone will have both the full *right to speak* and the genuine *ability to hear*. The traditional view has been that fruitful interreligious dialogue requires the positing, at least hypothetically, of some kind of *common ground* shared by all religions—perhaps a "common essence" within all traditions (à la A. Toynbee) or a "universal faith" (à la W. C. Smith, B. Lonergan) or a common yet undefinable "mystical center" (à la W. Stace, F. Schuon, T. Merton).[12]

Contemporary critics, however, warn against positing a common anything within the religions as a basis for dialogue. Philosophers such as Jeremy Bernstein and Richard Rorty, as well as philosophical theologians such as Francis Fiorenza and George Lindbeck,[13] cast their warnings in terms of the dangers of "foundationalism" or "objectivism." As Bernstein puts it:

> By "objectivism" I mean the basic conviction that there is or must be some permanent ahistorical matrix or framework to which we can ultimately appeal in determining the nature of rationality, knowledge, truth, reality, goodness, or rightness [and religious experience]. . . . Objectivism is closely related to foundationalism and the search for an Archimedean point. The objectivist maintains that unless we can ground philosophy, knowledge, or language [interreligious dialogue] in a rigorous manner, we cannot avoid radical skepticism.[14]

We are urged by the philosophers to resist the siren lure of objectivism and bravely to give up our search for foundations or a "common ground" above or outside the plurality of views. Philosophical maturity demands that we accept that all knowledge is "theory-laden"; different societies have different plausibility structures; each religion is speaking within its own "language game"; the "protocol statements" of the positivists—which claim to report what *anyone* would observe—may not exist. So it seems that there is no common essence or ground, "no way from 'outside' a tradition to assess the meaning and truth of claims made within it. Different religious traditions and schemes of belief and nonbelief reflect frameworks which are ultimately incommensurable."[15]

From a more practical, experiential perspective, theologians such as John Cobb and Raimundo Panikkar echo the philosophers. If we really want to take pluralism seriously, they admonish us, then we must cease our search for a "universal theory" or a "common source" of religion—or even for "one God" within all religions. In his essay in this volume, Panikkar pulls no punches: "Pluralism does not allow for a universal system. A pluralist system would be a contradiction in terms. The incommensurability of ultimate systems is unbridgeable."[16] Cobb chides John Hick, Wilfred Cantwell Smith, and me: "The problem is the quest for what is common. Truly to accept pluralism is to abandon that quest. If our liberal theists really wish to be open, they should simply be open. The openness is inhibited by the need to state in advance what we have in common."[17]

The danger, according to these critics, is that in our desire to establish or distill a common essence or center, we all too easily miss what is genuinely different, and therefore what is genuinely challenging or frightening, in other religions. As Cobb has suggested, maybe there is no one "Ultimate" within or behind all world religions; maybe there are two—and we are afraid to face that fact.[18] Cobb has also leveled some hard-hitting criticisms against John Hick's and my theocentric model for a Christian approach to other faiths showing, quite convincingly I must admit, that by proposing God, instead of the church or Christ, as the common basis for dialogue, we are implicitly, unconsciously, but still imperialistically imposing our notions of Deity or the Ultimate on other believers who, like many Buddhists, may not even wish to speak about God or who experience the Ultimate as *Sunyata*, which has nothing or little to do with what Christians experience and call God.[19]

The critics' point is clear. And yet, when they make this point, when they warn against the pitfalls of foundationalism and common essences, they also warn against the equally menacing pitfall of "radical skepticism" or of a relativism that would so lock religions or cultures in their own language games or plausibility structures as to cut off all communication between them. The philosophers and theologians mentioned above are all, paradoxically, firm believers in the possibility and the value of communication and dialogue between apparently "incommensurable" traditions. They seek a difficult, paradoxical path between foundationalism and relativism; even though there are no preestablished common foundations, we can still talk to and understand each other.

Just how this works is not clear. Cobb and Panikkar (Bernstein as well) seem to take a Habermasian approach; they simply plunge coldly into the dialogue, trusting that, in the very praxis of communication, common ground or shared viewpoints will be discovered or created. Even though this common ground is not at all terra firma, even though it remains "shaky ground,"[20] it can suffice to overcome incommensurability (e.g. between *Sunyata* and God) and can lead to mutual understanding, indeed (as Cobb tells us) to the "mutual transformation" of religions.

Affirming their faith in the value of dialogue, many of the authors who earlier eschewed every trace of "common ground" now try to indicate what makes dialogue possible and valuable and how one should go about communicating. In doing so, they sound, I must say, like they are searching for something "common" within religious history or experience. Disavowing any universal theory for the religions, Panikkar still invokes one aspiration (in the literal sense of one breath) or one inspiration (as one spirit) for all the religions.[21] Bernstein proposes a dialogical model based on reason that can be shared by the plurality of voices.[22] Other philosophers invoke a universal human "bridgehead" of shared perceptions and logical standards that provide a basis for translating between perspectives.[23] Heinrich Ott, though viewing Buddhism and Christianity as two clearly distinct paths, trusts that they are moving through the "same woods" or through a common "neighborhood."[24]

What these authors are sensing is that the different religions cannot, ultimately, be apples and oranges, for if they were, how could they, or why should they, speak and work together? Anyone who affirms the value of interreligious dialogue affirms implicitly that there *is* something that bonds the religions of the world. But the problem is how to indicate it? How to discover it? How to work creatively with it?

This is where a liberation theology of religions may be of great help. If there is no preestablished common ground or common essence that we can invoke before dialogue, perhaps there is a common *approach* or a common *context* with which we can begin dialogue in order to create our shared "shaky ground." For liberation theologians this common context would be the *preferential option for the poor and the nonperson*—that is, the option to work with and for the *victims* of this world. As Harvey Cox puts it with typical clarity: "For liberation theology, the basis for the interreligious dialogue is the struggle of the poor."[25]

The reason why the preferential option for the poor provides such a basis has to do with the epistemological claims of liberation theology—that is, with the hermeneutical privilege of the poor. "Latin American liberation theology, black theology, and feminist theology all claim that the experience of the oppressed is a privileged hermeneutical ground, that identification with the oppressed is the first act in understanding either the Bible or our world today."[26] And we might add: it is "the first act of religious believers toward understanding each other." The liberationists are telling us that without a commitment to and with the oppressed, our knowledge is deficient—our knowledge of self, others, the Ultimate. This is not to imply that we can know the truth *only* in such a commitment but, rather, that without this option for the poor, the truth that we may know is, at best, incomplete, deficient, dangerous.

Because of its hermeneutical priority and potency, therefore, the preferential option for the oppressed (at least in the world as it exists today) serves as an effective condition for the possibility of dialogue—that which makes it possible for different religions to speak to and understand each other. If the religions of the world, in other words, can recognize poverty and oppression as a common problem, if they can share a common commitment (expressed in different forms) to remove such evils, they will have the basis for reaching across their incommensurabilities and differences in order to hear and understand each other and possibly be transformed in the process.

It is important to note the differences between what is being proposed here and "objectivism" or "foundationalism." The fundamental option for the poor and nonpersons serves not as a "foundation" or "Archemedean point" or sure-fire criterion of judgment, but as an approach, a context, a starting point that must itself be clarified as it clarifies and creates new common ground of understanding.

If all this makes some sense, then I think we can go a step further; instead of searching for "one God" or "one Ultimate" or a "common essence" or a "mystical center" within all religions, we can recognize a *shared locus of religious experience* now available to all the religions of the world. Within the struggle for liberation and justice with and for the many different groups of oppressed persons, believers from different traditions can experience together, and yet differently, that which grounds their resolves, inspires their hopes, and guides their actions to overcome injustice and to promote unity. Aloysius Pieris suggests that in our contemporary world, the struggle for liberation and for the transformation of this world provides a cross-cultural, cross-religious basis for defining and sharing religious experience among all religions: "I submit that the religious instinct be defined as a revolutionary urge, a psycho-social impulse, to generate a new humanity. . . . It is this revolutionary impulse that constitutes, and therefore defines, the essence of *homo religiosus.*"[27]

Perhaps better than the monastery or the mystic's mountain, the struggle for justice can become the arena where Hindus and Muslims, Buddhists and Christians and Jews, can sense, and begin to speak about, that which unites them. What makes possible a *communication* in doctrine between believers from different paths is not only what Thomas Merton called a *communion of mystical-contemplative experience*[28] but also and especially a communion of *liberative praxis.* In the words of M. M. Thomas:

> The common response to the problems of humanization of existence in the modern world, rather than any common religiosity, or common sense of the Divine, is the most fruitful point of entry for a meeting of faiths *at the spiritual depth* in our time.[29]

Such a claim corresponds to the insistence of liberation theologians that theory or doctrinal clarity can be acheived only in and through liberative praxis. In order, therefore, to enter into the difficult discussion of whether there is a "common essence" or "ground" within all religions, in order to know whether "God" and "*Sunyata*" might, after all, have something in common, we must not only pray and meditate together, but we must first act together with and for the oppressed. John Cobb, therefore, is right: we cannot know what is "common" between the religions before dialogue—but dialogue now is understood not only as shared conversation or prayer, but as shared praxis. "For the liberationist," Harvey Cox tells us in Western images, "this unseen reality [the hypothetical transcendent unity of religions] lies ahead not beneath or behind. It is eschatological, not primal. It requires faithful love and service, not esoteric insight."[30]

This understanding of the central role of the preferential option for the poor and nonpersons within interreligious dialogue means that the evolution within Christian attitudes toward other faiths that I described in my book *No Other Name?* is incomplete. The evolution, I suggest, is being called to a further stage. If Christian attitudes have evolved from ecclesiocentrism to christocentrism to theocentrism, they must now move on to what in Christian symbols might be called "kingdom-centrism," or more universally, "soteriocentrism." For Christians, that which constitutes the basis and the goal for interreligious dialogue, that which makes mutual understanding and cooperation between the religions possible (the "condition of the possibility"), that which unites the religions in common discourse and praxis, is *not* how they are related to the church (invisibly through "baptism of desire"), or how they are related to Christ (anonymously [Rahner] or normatively [Küng]), nor even how they respond to and conceive of God, but rather, to what extent they are promoting *Soteria* (in Christian images, the *basileia*)—to what extent they are engaged in promoting human welfare and bringing about liberation with and for the poor and nonpersons.

A Christian liberation theology of religions, therefore, will propose as the "common" (though still "shaky") ground or starting point for religious encounter not *Theos*, the ineffable mystery of the divine, but rather, *Soteria*, the "ineffable mystery of salvation."[31] Such a soteriocentric approach, it seems, is less prone to (though never fully immune from) ideological abuse, for it does not impose its own views of God or the Ultimate on other traditions; in this way it responds to Cobb's criticism of theocentrism. A soteriocentric approach to other faiths also seems to be more faithful to the data of comparative religions, for although the religions of the world contain a divergent variety of models for the Ultimate—theistic, metatheistic, polytheistic, and atheistic—"the common thrust, however, remains *soteriological*, the concern of most religions being *liberation* (*vimukti, mokṣa, nirvana*) rather than speculation about a hypothetical [divine] liberator."[32]

John Cobb, however, in his criticism of the first draft of this essay, continued to warn that "posing such a condition [i.e., the preferential option] on dialogue unilaterally from the Christian side is a continuation of the imperialism Knitter opposes . . . he appears to say that he seeks dialogue only with those who share his understanding of salvation." Cobb's admonitions are important. They help clarify that the preferential option for the oppressed is not to be *imposed* as an *absolute condition* for interreligous dialogue; rather, it is offered, or suggested, as an *invitation* to a more authentic and effective dialogue. I am not *demanding* that other religions accept concern for the suffering of oppressed peoples as a starting point for interreligious encounter; but I suspect, and am suggesting, that they can and will want to do so. My suspicions are strengthened by the claim of Pieris that the religions of the world share many more common starting points in their soteriologies than in their theologies. Also, as will be emphasized in the next section, in proposing *Soteria* as a context or starting point for dialogue, I am certainly not implying that there is only one way of understanding "salvation" or that my Christian grasp of it is final or normative. One starts with "shaky" ground that has to be firmed up in the dialogue; the starting point may be clarifed or corrected *after* one starts. But one *does* have a starting point.

3. Harvey Cox summarizes the practical advantages of a soteriocentric approach and signals a further contribution that it can make to a liberation theology of religions:

> In the light of this "Kingdom-centered" view . . . the whole meaning of the discussion among people from different religious traditions shifts. The purpose of the conversation is different. Interfaith dialogue becomes neither an end in itself nor a strictly religious quest, but a step in anticipation of God's justice. It becomes praxis. Similarities and differences which once seemed important fade away as the real differences— between those whose sacred stories are used to perpetuate domination and those whose religion strengthens them for the fight against domination—emerge more clearly.[33]

"Real differences emerge more clearly"—Cox is suggesting how the preferential option for the oppressed might help both academicians and participants in dialogue grapple with another problem within the discussion about religious pluralism: in affirming the independent validity of all traditions and the danger of judging another's truth according to one's own inappropriate criteria, how does one avoid a radical skepticism or a suffocating relativism?' How is one able to resolutely oppose what Langdon Gilkey, in his essay in this volume, terms "intolerable forms of religion and the religious?"[34] So far, I have discussed how the different religions might *understand* each other. Is there any possibility that they might also be able to *judge* each other? In their religious studies and conversations, even academicians are realizing that both the state of our world and the nature of the human spirit (Lonergan tells us that understanding is but a stepping stone to judgment) require us to make judgments, even though tentative, concerning what is true or false, good or bad— or at least, concerning what is preferable. In John Hick's terms, we cannot avoid the need of "grading the religions."[35]

But to call for such evaluative judgments is to rekindle fears of foundationalism, neocolonialism, and ideological abuse. Where are we to find criteria for judging or "grading"—criteria that have some inbuilt protection against being turned into exploitive tools and that can win general consensus in the academy and in the arena of interreligious encounter? Doctrinal criteria—concerning the qualities of the Ultimate, or the activity of a universal Logos, or the presence of an anonymous Christ or Buddha—prove too controversial and prone to ideology. Criteria from mystical experience—Merton's "communion before communication" or Panikkar's "Pneuma before Logos"—are helpful but often, in the end, hard to apply.

Might a soteriocentric basis for dialogue—the preferential option for the poor and nonpersons—provide general criteria that a variety of religions could agree to work with as a basis for grading themselves? Hick himself suggests a criterion of "soteriological effectiveness"—whatever promotes "that limitlessly better quality of human existence which comes about in the transition from self-centeredness to Reality-centeredness."[36] Stanley Samartha holds that the religions of the world can formulate "a global ethic" or a "consensus of conscience" that would not be "a religious fruit salad . . . [but] a set of principles on questions of sharing power and resources both within the national community and between nations in the global community."[37] Hans Küng has proposed that the first ingredient in an "ecumenical criteriology" for determining "true religion" is the *humanum*—those "fundamental values and fundamental demands" essential to being human. "Should it not be possible to formulate a general ethical fundamental criterion with an appeal to the common humanity of all which rests upon the *Humanum*, the truly human, concretely on human dignity and the fundamental values accorded to it?"[38]

A liberation theology of religions would affirm such suggestions but would warn against their dangerous lack of specificity. *Whose humanum* are we talking about? Or, as liberationists persistently ask: Who is the interlocutor for these theologians? "Soteriological effectiveness," "a global ethic," the *humanum* need to be preferentially focused on the oppressed, the marginated, the powerless of our world, which means that these criteria have to be formulated and concretized in the actual praxis of liberation for the oppressed. Otherwise, such criteria run the risk of sinking into ineffectual theory or First World ideology. Can the religions of the world agree on the necessity and value of such liberative criteria? The declaration of the World Conference on Religion and Peace in Kyoto (1970) is a hopeful indication; among the convictions that the religions "possessed . . . in common" was "a feeling of obligation to stand on the side of the poor and oppressed against the rich and the oppressor."[39]

Such soteriocentric criteria, although focused on the poor and nonpersons, need not lead to a new form of foundationalism or an ethical Archimedean point outside the praxis of liberation and dialogue. As already stressed, we are not starting with preestablished absolutes. In her contribution to this volume, Marjorie Suchocki illuminatingly points out the complexity and persistent pluriformity in coming to a common understanding of "justice."[40] Soteriocentric criteria, therefore, serve as a *heuristic device* rather than as a defined basis.

The criteria—what elements contribute to authentic, full liberation—can be known only in the actual praxis of struggling to overcome suffering and oppression, and only in the praxis of dialogue. What are the causes of suffering, of oppression? How best eliminate them? What kind of socio-cultural analysis is needed? What kind of personal transformation or alteration of consciousness is required? The preferential option for the poor does not provide prefabricated answers to such questions. And yet the starting point for struggling, together, toward answers is given in the fundamental option for and commitment to the oppressed.[41]

Furthermore, as Hick has indicated, in applying the liberation theology soteriocentric criteria in interreligious conversation, one should not expect to be able to give one grade *in globo* for an entire religion or to rank religions in a kind of ethical hierarchy.[42] As W. C. Smith has made clear, the reality of religion transcends our rational, Western constructs about "religion."[43] Still, by applying the criteria of liberative praxis, by asking, for example, how a particular Hindu belief or Christian ritual or Buddhist practice promotes human welfare and leads to the removal of poverty and to the promotion of liberation, we might be able to arrive at communal judgments concerning what is true or false, or what is preferable, among different religious claims or practices.

In holding up *Soteria* as the source of ethical criteria for interreligious dialogue, one need not be ideologically naive. Even though there may be general agreement about promoting justice and removing oppression, each religion or tradition will have its own understanding of what *Soteria* and liberation entail. Here, as Gavin D'Costa has pointed out in his criticism of my book, every theocentric or soteriocentric approach remains, in a sense, inherently Christocentric (or Buddhacentric, Krishnacentric, Quranocentric).[44] We all have our particular viewpoints, our perspectives, or different mediators. The criteria by which we understand what liberation means or what makes for authentic or deceptive salvation are provided by our particular mediators. The Universal, therefore, whether it be *theos* or *Soteria,* is always experienced, understood, and responded to via a particular symbol or mediator. In no way is Christ left behind; he remains the Christian's way, truth, and life.

But what makes the soteriocentric approach different from christocentrism or theocentrism is its explicit recognition that before the mystery of *Soteria,* no mediator or symbol system is absolute. The perspective on *Soteria* given by any one mediator is always open to clarification, completion, perhaps correction by the viewpoints of other mediators. So again, the absolute, that which all else must serve and clarify, is not the church or Christ or even God—but rather, the kingdom and its justice. And although Christians understand and serve that kingdom *through* Christ, it is in seeking first the kingdom and its justice that all else will be added to them, including a clearer, perhaps corrected, understanding of that kingdom *and* of Christ. This brings us to a consideration of how the method of liberation theology might clarify the christological component of a theology of religions.

LIBERATION THEOLOGY OF RELIGIONS AND THE UNIQUENESS OF CHRIST

Besides clarifying the context and starting point for a genuinely pluralistic interreligious dialogue—beyond both exclusivism and inclusivism—the method of liberation theology can also help resolve the even more knotty problem of the uniqueness of Christ. In order to avoid preestablished absolutist positions that prevent a genuinely pluralistic dialogue, Christians must, it seems, revamp or even reject their traditional understanding of Jesus Christ as God's final, definitive, normative voice. Can they do this and still call themselves Christians? To show how a liberation theology of religions can help answer such christological quandaries, I offer the following four considerations.

1. As already mentioned, liberation theology insists that *praxis* is both the *origin* and the *confirmation* of theory or *doctrine*. All Christian beliefs and truth claims must grow out of and then be reconfirmed in the praxis or lived experience of these truths. According to liberation theology, one does not first know the truth and then apply it in praxis; it is in action, in doing, that truth is really known and validated. What this means for christology has been made clear by theologians such as Jon Sobrino and Leonardo Boff: we cannot begin to know who Jesus of Nazareth is unless we are following him, putting his message into the practice of our lives.[45] This was the process by which the New Testament titles for Jesus came to be formulated; they were the fruit, the joyful kerygma, derived from the experience of following him. And because this experience varied according to the various communities and contexts of the early churches, the titles for Jesus proliferated.

Praxis, therefore, was the starting point of all christology. And it remains the criterion of all christology, for everything we know or say about Jesus must be continually confirmed, clarified, and perhaps corrected in the praxis of living his vision within the changing contexts of history. In this sense, therefore, as Boff tells us, nothing we say about Jesus is final; "no title conferred on Christ can be absolutized."[46]

What this primacy of praxis means for a christology of interreligious dialogue is implied in a remark made by Sobrino:

> [Jesus'] universality cannot be demonstrated or proved on the basis of formulas or symbols that are universal in themselves: e.g., dogmatic formulas, the kerygma as event, the resurrection as universal symbol of hope, and so forth. The real universality of Jesus shows up *only in its concrete embodiment.*[47]

In other words, the Christian conviction and proclamation that Jesus is God's final and normative word for all religions cannot rest only on traditional doctrine *or* on personal, individual experience. We cannot know that Jesus is

God's last or normative statement only on the basis of being told so or on the basis of having experienced him to be such in our own lives. Rather, the uniqueness of Jesus can be known and then affirmed only "in its concrete embodiment," only in the praxis of historical, social involvement. This means, concretely, that unless we are engaged in the *praxis of Christian dialogue* with other religions—following Christ, applying his message, within the dialogue with other believers—we cannot experience and confirm what the uniqueness and normativity of Christ mean.

But has such praxis taken place? Have Christians actively learned from and worked with other religions to such a degree that they have experienced the uniqueness and normativity of Jesus over all others? Has their praxis of dialogue with other believers been extensive enough to make the universal claim that Jesus surpasses and is therefore normative for these other faiths? I think not.

Although it is true that the church for centuries has been "going forth to all nations" and religions, it is only in this century that the Catholic Church, in Vatican II, and the Protestant churches, through the World Council of Churches, have taken up a conscious, extensive dialogue with other religious traditions. From the perspective of a liberation christology of religions, there- fore, Christians will have to admit that at least at the moment it is *impossible* to make claims of finality and normativity for Christ or Christianity. This means that we have "permission"—maybe even an obligation—to enter into a dia- logue with other believers without making our traditional claims of "no other name" or "one mediator." In making this step we are strengthened and consoled by Boff's reminder that no christological title is absolute; even those titles claiming finality or normativity for Jesus may, as a result of our praxis of religious dialogue, have to be revised.

2. Another related ingredient in the theology of liberation—the *primacy of orthopraxis over orthodoxy*—assures Christians that if claims about the final- ity of Christ/Christianity are not presently possible, neither are they *necessary*. The primary concern of a soteriocentric liberation theology of religions is not "right belief" about the uniqueness of Christ, but the "right practice," with other religions, of furthering the kingdom and its *Soteria*. Clarity about whether and how Christ is one lord and savior, as well as clarity about any other doctrine, may be important, but it is subordinate to carrying out the preferen- tial option for the poor and nonpersons. Orthodoxy becomes a press- ing concern only when it is necessary for orthopraxis—for carrying out the preferential option and promoting the kingdom. If orthodox clarity is not required for such purposes, it can wait.

I think it can wait. Christians do not *need* orthodox clarity and certainty concerning Jesus as the "only" or the "final" or the "universal" savior in order to experience and fully commit themselves to the liberating truth of his mes- sage. What Christians *do* know, on the basis of their praxis of following Jesus, is that his message *is* a sure means for bringing about liberation from injustice and oppression, that it *is* an effective, hope-filled, universally meaningful way of realizing *Soteria* and promoting God's kingdom. Not knowing whether Jesus is unique, whether he is the final or normative word of God for all times, does not interfere with commitment to the praxis of following him and working, with other religions, in building the kingdom. Such questions need not be answered now. In fact, as we just saw, they cannot be answered now. In the meantime, there is much work to be done. Not those who proclaim "only Lord, only Lord," but those who *do* the will of the Father will enter the kingdom (Matt. 7:21–23).

These christological conclusions drawn from the liberationists' insistence on the primacy of orthopraxis over orthodoxy end up sounding very similar to H. Richard Niebuhr's recommendation, way back in 1941, that Christians adopt a *confessional approach* to peoples of other faiths. He urged his fellow believers in Christ to relate to other believers "by stating in simple, confessional form what has happened to us in our community, how we came to believe, how we reason about things and what we see from our point of view." And today he could have added: "and by putting into praxis what we have come to believe." Niebuhr urged that such a confession, in word and deed, need not, should not, be accompanied by any attempt to "justify it [Christianity] as superior to all other faiths." Such "orthodox" claims about the superiority or normativity of Christ over all religions were not only not necessary for the living out of the Christian confession; they were, in Niebuhr's prophetic words, "more destructive of religion, Christianity, and the soul than any foe's attack can possibly be."[48]

3. The possibilities, described earlier, of using the preferential option for the poor as a working criterion for "grading the religions" contain further christological implications. If liberating praxis with and for the poor and nonpersons is an indicator and measure of authentic revelation and religious experience, then Christians, whether they like it or not, have the means to discern not only whether but *how much* other religious beliefs and practices may be genuine "ways of salvation"—and further, whether and *how much* other religious figures may be genuine liberators and "saviors." In other words, the soteriocentric criteria for religious dialogue contained in the preferential option for the oppressed offer Christians the tools to critically examine and possibly revise the traditional understanding of the uniqueness of Christ.

Simply stated, from their ethical, soteriological fruits we shall know them— we shall be able to judge whether and how much other religious paths *and* their mediators are salvific. Judgments can go in different directions. In their academic and personal encounter with other believers and other paths, by applying the criteria of liberative praxis, Christian theologians may find that although there are other "saviors" in other traditions, still, Jesus the Nazarean appears to them—and perhaps to other believers too—as the unique and somehow special liberator—as he who unifies and fulfills all other efforts toward *Soteria. Or*, Christians may discover that other religions and religious figures offer a means and vision of liberation equal to that of Jesus, that it is impossible to "grade" saviors or enlightened beings in the sense of ranking them. For instance, they may conclude that the liberative, transformative power of the Buddhist notions of enlightenment, dependent co-origination, and compassion, as they are being practiced in the "family gatherings" of the Sarvodaya Movement in Sri Lanka, are just as salvific as are the symbols of the kingdom of God and redemption and grace as they are being lived out in the *comunidades de base* in Nicaragua. Jesus would then be unique—together with other unique liberators. He would be universal savior—with other universal saviors. His universality and uniqueness would be not exclusive, nor inclusive, but complementary.

And yet, according to a soteriocentric liberation theology of religions, whether such discernments about uniqueness and finality are eventually made or not is, in the final analysis, not that important—as long as we, with all peoples and religions, are seeking first the kingdom and its justice (Matt. 6:33).

4. A liberation theology of religions offers help in dealing with another obstacle facing those who are exploring possibilities of a nonabsolutist or nondefinitive understanding of Christ. The final touchstone, it can be said, for the validity and appropriateness of a new understanding of Christ as "one among many," in a relationship of "complementary uniqueness" with others, is whether such a view will, eventually, be *received* by the faithful. Reception by the faithful was the final criterion for the validity of the early ecumenical councils, and it remains such a criterion today for popes, councils, and theologians.[49] Christian theologians, in other words, cannot ply their trade in well-padded ivory towers; belonging as they do to the "public of the academy," they must also be able to communicate and find a home in the "public of the church."[50]

But this is precisely the reason why a number of very open-minded theologians feel they cannot endorse a pluralist theology of religions and move to a view of Jesus that would diminish his "once and for all" (*epaphax*, Heb. 9:12) uniqueness. Such a view could never be received by the "sense of the faithful." Monika Hellwig and Frans Josef van Beeck insist, sensitively yet firmly, that "to claim only that Jesus offers a way of salvation to us which is one among many is to fall short of fidelity to the classic statements about Jesus in the bible and the tradition."[51] Avery Dulles argues that any diminishing of the *lex credendi* (the law of believing) concerning the "utter uniqueness and transcendence of what happened in the career of Jesus Christ" will weaken the *lex orandi* (the law of praying) of the community. "If this [Christ's utter uniqueness] is obscured, the Christ event will not elicit the kind of worship and thanksgiving needed to sustain the Christian community in its vibrant relationship to God."[52] And Hans Küng has told me personally, and has said publicly, that although to move in the direction of a nonabsolutist christology might make logical sense, he himself could not make this move, mainly for two reasons: it would alienate him from his faith community and it would tend to diminish the depth and firmness of Christians' personal commitment to Jesus Christ.[53]

All these reservations, which come not from the Falwells and Ratzingers but from some of the more liberal thinkers in our communities, are based on the perceived clash between the new nonabsolute views of Christ and the *sensus fidelium*. So, if these new christologies have any future within Christian theology, they need a better *ecclesial mediation* in order that they might be "received" by the faithful.

Liberation theology can lend a helping hand in working out such ecclesial mediation. First of all, although liberation theologians are extremely sensitive about operating with and from the "sense of the faithful"—liberation theology was born from the womb of the basic Christian communities—they would not be so worried about stirring up and challenging the faithful. What happens in the basic Christian communities is not simply a reflecting upon Christian beliefs but a sharpening, indeed a transformation, of the sense of the faithful. Liberation theologians consider themselves not only teachers and learners but also, where need be, *prophets*. (Gustavo Gutiérrez has said, "In the United States I am called theologian. In Peru I am an activist.")[54] Liberation theologians might suggest to Hellwig and Küng that they must be ready to push and prod the faithful instead of only reflecting on their experience. (As if Küng needs any encouragement to push and prod!) As the American bishops themselves have recently discovered with their pastoral letters on nuclear war and on the economy, theologians must sometimes rush in where the ordinary faithful fear to tread. Especially in this question of the uniqueness of Christ, I have found that congregational fears and hesitations can be overcome—indeed, that many of the faithful are happy someone is finally pushing and challenging them.[55]

But liberation theology can offer more than exhortation in solving this problem of ecclesial mediation. The basic liberationist maxim that orthopraxis holds a primacy over orthodoxy is not only a challenging epistemological insight; it is also a workable pastoral tool for mediating the new nonabsolutist christologies to the *ecclesia*. By understanding and affirming the primacy of orthopraxis, the faithful can, I suggest, be helped to see that in "receiving" these new views of Jesus, they are not only remaining faithful to the witness of the New Testament and tradition, but are also being challenged to an even deeper commitment to Christ and his gospel.

I suspect, for instance, that the "sense" of most Christian faithful—insofar as they are brought into touch with their own experience through a liberative praxis of their faith—will resonate with the claim made above that the right practice of following Jesus and working for his kingdom is more important for Christian identity than is the right knowledge concerning the nature of God or of Jesus himself. Those Christians who are challenged and enabled to make the link between their own experience, the gospel, and liberative praxis will agree, I am quite certain, that the essence of being a Christian is *doing* the will of the Father rather than knowing or insisting that Jesus is the one and only or the best of the bunch. In fact, the psychology of love and commitment would seem to suggest that the deeper and more secure one's commitment to a particular path or person is, the more one is open to the beauty or truth of other paths and persons. Christians can be led to see that neither their commitment to Jesus nor their ability to worship him (the *lex orandi*) need be jeopardized just because there may be others like him. Why, really, must something be "one and only" in order to merit our devotion and commitment? The Christian faithful will also grasp how much sound evangelical sense such an nonabsolutist approach to Christ makes: others will be much more readily convinced by Christians who give simple witness to how much their savior has actually done for them than by Christians who insist that "our savior is bigger than yours."

Recognition of the primacy of orthopraxis over orthodoxy can also be used pastorally to enable Christian believers to understand the nature of New Testament language and what it means to be faithful to this language. On the basis of their own experience of pondering and praying over the scriptures, the faithful can readily grasp that the power and purpose of biblical language is first of all to call forth a way of life rather than a body of belief. More precisely, the christological language and titles of the New Testament had as their primary purpose not to offer definitive, ontological statements about the person or work of Jesus, but to enable men and women to feel the power and attraction of Jesus' vision and then to "go and do likewise." This is not to deny that the New Testament communities were trying to say something real about Jesus; they were making cognitive claims about him. But these claims were not the primary intent; they were, in a sense, means to an end—or better, calls to discipleship.

In my book, I called New Testament talk about Jesus "survival" and "love" language in order to distinguish it from philosophical language.[56] It would be more accurate and pastorally effective, I think, to call the New Testament claims about Jesus "action language." He was called "one and only" or "only begotten" not *primarily* to give us definitive theologico-philosophical statements, and not *primarily* to exclude others, but rather to urge the action or practice of total commitment to his vision and way. In order to urge that action, the New Testament authors used their "one and only" language. Now, *if* Christians today can continue with that same action, if they can continue to follow Christ and work for the kingdom *without* the traditional "one and only" language, then they are still holding to the core content of the original message. If recognizing the possibility of other saviors or mediators does not impede this praxis, then it is compatible with Christian identity and tradition.

In fact, it might be argued that today such a recognition of others is necessary for remaining faithful to the original witness about Jesus. Theologians who are exploring a pluralist theology of religions and a nonabsolutist christology are doing so not merely for the sake of novelty or for the sake of joining the excitement of a truly pluralist interreligious dialogue; rather, they do so because "the love of Christ urges them" (2 Cor. 5:14). They want to be faithful to the original message of the Nazarean—that to which Jesus always subordinated himself: the kingdom of love, unity, and justice.

In order to serve and promote that kingdom, we want to dialogue and work with others and be open to the possibility that there are other teachers and liberators and saviors who can help us understand and work for that kingdom in ways as yet beyond our hearing or imagination. "Anyone who is *not against us* is *with* us" (Mark 9:40). This present volume was assembled with the suspicion and trust that there are others, perhaps many others, *with* Jesus— and many other religious paths, *with* Christianity. Each very different, each unique—but *with* each other.

NOTES

1. Wilfred Cantwell Smith, *The Faith of Other Men* (New York: Harper & Row, 1962), p. 127.

2. Harvey Cox, *Religion in the Secular City: Toward a Postmodern Theology* (New York: Simon & Schuster, 1984), pp. 223, 233.

3. "The Place of Non-Christian Religions and Cultures in the Evolution of Third World Theology," in *Irruption of the Third World: Challenge to Theology*, Virginia Fabella and Sergio Torres, eds. (Maryknoll, N.Y.: Orbis Books, 1983), pp. 113–14.

4. Ibid., p. 122, also pp. 117–20.

5. Gilkey, p. 44, above.

6. *Strength of the Weak: Toward a Christian Feminist Identity* (Philadelphia: Westminster, 1984), p. 66.

7. Below I will urge that shared liberative praxis, flowing from the shared preferential option for nonpersons, constitutes not only the *primary purpose* but a *condition of the possibility* and the essential *first step* in interreligious dialogue. Liberative praxis, in a sense, is the substance of dialogue among world religions—that from which shared prayer/meditation and shared reflection/doctrine can flow.

8. Juan Luis Segundo, *The Liberation of Theology* (Maryknoll, N.Y.: Orbis Books, 1976), pp. 7–9. In another sense, ideologies cannot and should not be avoided; they are not necessarily opposed to God's word. Liberationists claim that a divine ideology runs through the Bible—God has taken the side of the poor. See *ibid.*, pp. 97–124; idem, *Faith and Ideologies* (Maryknoll, N.Y.: Orbis Books, 1984), pp. 87–129.

9. Karl Rahner, "Anonymous Christianity and the Missionary Task of the Church," in *Theological Investigations*, vol. 12 (New York: Seabury, 1974), pp. 161–78; idem, "Observations on the Problem of the 'Anonymous Christian,' " in *Theological Investigations*, vol. 14 (New York: Seabury, 1976), pp. 280–94; Hans Küng, *On Being a Christian* (Garden City, N.Y.: Doubleday, 1976), pp. 110–12.

10. Pieris, "The Place," p. 114; idem, "Speaking of the Son of God in Non-Christian Cultures, e.g., in Asia," in *Jesus Son of God?*, Edward Schillebeeckx and J. B. Metz, eds. (*Concilium*, 153) (New York: Seabury, 1982), p. 67; Ignace Puthiadam, "Christian Faith and Life in a World of Religious Pluralism," in *True and False Universality of Christianity*, Claude Geffre and Jean-Pierre Jossua, eds. (*Concilium*, 135) (New York: Seabury, 1980), pp. 103–5.

11. "A Third World Perspective," in *Doing Theology in a Divided World*, Virginia Fabella and Sergio Torres, eds. (Maryknoll, N.Y.: Orbis Books, 1985), p. 202.

12. Arnold Toynbee, "The Task of Disengaging the Essence from the Non-essentials in Mankind's Religious Heritage," in *An Historian's Approach to Religion* (New York:

Oxford University Press, 1956), pp. 261–83; Wilfred Cantwell Smith, *The Meaning and End of Religion* (New York: New American Library, 1964), chaps. 6 and 7; Bernard J. F. Lonergan, *Method in Theology* (New York: Herder and Herder, 1972), pp. 101–24. Walter T. Stace, *Mysticism and Philosophy* (Philadelphia: Lippincott, 1960); Frithjof Schuon, *The Transcendent Unity of Religions* (New York: Harper & Row, 1975); Thomas Merton, *The Asian Journal of Thomas Merton*, Naomi Burton et al., eds. (New York: New Directions, 1975), pp. 309–17.

13. Jeremy Bernstein, *Beyond Objectivism and Relativism: Science, Hermeneutics, and Praxis* (Philadelphia: University of Pennsylvania Press, 1983); Richard Rorty, *Philosophy and the Mirror of Nature* (Princeton University Press, 1979); Francis Schüssler Fiorenza, *Foundational Theology: Jesus and the Church* (New York: Crossroad: 1984), pp. 285–311. George A. Lindbeck, *The Nature of Doctrine: Religion and Theology in a Postliberal Age* (Philadelphia: Westminster, 1985).

14. Bernstein, *Beyond Objectivism*, p. 8.

15. Thomas B. Ommen, "Relativism, Objectivism and Theology," *Horizons*, 13 (1986) 299.

16. Panikkar, p. 110, above. See also idem, "A Universal Theory of Religion or a Cosmic Confidence in Reality?" in *Toward a World Theology of Religions*, Leonard Swidler, ed. (Maryknoll, N.Y.: Orbis Books, 1987).

17. "The Meaning of Pluralism for Christian Self-Understanding," in *Religious Pluralism*, Leroy S. Rouner, ed. (University of Notre Dame Press, 1984), p. 172.

18. *Beyond Dialogue: Toward a Mutual Transformation of Christianity and Buddhism* (Philadelphia: Fortress Press, 1982), pp. 86–90, 110–14; idem, "Buddhist Emptiness and the Christian God," *Journal of the American Academy of Religion*, 45 (1979) 11–25.

19. *Beyond Dialogue*, pp. 41–44.

20. Mark Kline Taylor, "In Praise of Shaky Ground: The Liminal Christ and Cultural Pluralism," *Theology Today*, 43 (1986) 36–51.

21. Panikkar, "A Universal Theory of Religion."

22. Bernstein, *Beyond Objectivism*, p. 172.

23. Martin Hollis, "The Social Destruction of Reality," in *Rationality and Relativism*, M. Hollis and S. Lukes, eds. (Cambridge: MIT Press, 1984), pp. 67–86; Steven Lukes, "Relativism in Its Place," ibid., pp. 261–305.

24. "The Beginning Dialogue between Christianity and Buddhism, the Concept of a 'Dialogical Theology' and the Possible Contribution of Heideggerian Thought,' in *Japanese Religions*, Sept. 1980, pp. 87–91, 96.

25. Cox, *Religion in the Secular City*, p. 230.

26. Lee Cormie, "The Hermeneutical Privilege of the Oppressed," *Catholic Theological Society of America Proceedings*, 33 (1978) 78.

27. "The Place," p. 134.

28. Merton, *Asian Journal*, pp. 309–17.

29. *Man and the Universe of Faiths*, as quoted in Richard Henry Drummond, *Toward a New Age in Christian Theology* (Maryknoll, N.Y.: Orbis Books, 1985), p. 129, emphasis added.

30. *Religion in the Secular City*, p. 238.

31. Pieris, "Speaking of the Son of God," p. 67.

32. Pieris, "The Place," p. 133.

33. *Religion in the Secular City*, p. 238.

34. Gilkey, p. 44, above.

35. "On Grading Religions," *Religious Studies*, 17 (1981) 451–67.

36. Ibid, p. 467, see also pp. 461–64. See also Hick's essay in this volume.

37. *Courage for Dialogue* (Maryknoll, N.Y.: Orbis Books, 1982), pp. 126–67.

38. "What Is the True Religion? Toward a Three-dimensional Ecumenical Criteriology," in *Toward a World Theology of Religions*.

39. Ibid.

40. Suchocki, pp. 156–60, above.

41. I believe that this responds to the concern of John Cobb in his commentary on the first draft of this chapter: "When they [Hindus and Buddhists] think of liberation, they have something other than social change in mind, and they would like to share this other concern with us. They believe it to be of the utmost importance for everyone regardless of its effects on outward social conditions. Should we refuse to listen because it is our judgment that the plight of the poor is now more important than the liberation of the religious?" Certainly not! With some reservations about Cobb's exclusion of social change from all Hindu or Buddhist understanding of liberation, I would recognize that Christians concerned with social liberation must listen to the Eastern insistence that such liberation is impossible or emphemeral without enlightenment or religious liberation—that one must therefore also make a certain "preferential option" for personal enlightenment. At the same time, I am hopeful that Buddhists and Hindus will (as many do) recognize that although enlightenment is valid without effecting social conditions, enlightenment can and, in the world of today, must bring about such effects, especially for those who are among those suffering most in this world.

Yet what about religions that deny any relationship between the transformation of this world and personal salvation or enlightenment, that call upon their followers to abandon all concern for this world and concentrate only on the next? In view of his contribution to this book, Gilkey would perhaps see this as an example of what is *intolerable* in religion. If, as we said above, there are limits to tolerance, then there are also limits to dialogue. At the most, one can say that given the pressing needs of our present world, we "choose" not to dialogue with such other-worldly religions. When, or if, there is time, such a dialogue can be taken up in the future.

42. "On Grading Religions," pp. 465–67.

43. *The Meaning and End of Religion*, pp. 109–38.

44. Review of *No Other Name?* in *Modern Theology*, 2 (1985) 83–88; see also Gavin D'Costa, "An Examination of the Pluralist Paradigm in the Christian Theology of Religions," *Scottish Journal of Theology*, 39 (1986) 211–24.

45. Jon Sobrino, *Christology at the Crossroads* (Maryknoll, N.Y.: Orbis Books, 1978), pp. 346–95; Leonardo Boff, *Jesus Christ Liberator* (Maryknoll, N.Y.: Orbis Books, 1978), pp. 32–48, 264–95.

46. *Jesus Christ Liberator*, pp. 229–31.

47. *Christology at the Crossroads*, pp. 9–10.

48. *The Meaning of Revelation* (New York: Macmillan, 1962), pp. 39, 41.

49. Avery Dulles, "The Magisterium in History: A Theological Reflection," *Chicago Studies*, 17 (1978) 269.

50. David Tracy, *The Analogical Imagination: Christian Theology and the Culture of Pluralism* (New York: Crossroad, 1981), pp. 3–33.

51. Monika Hellwig, *Jesus the Compassion of God* (Wilmington: M. Glazier, 1983), p. 133; Frans Josef van Beeck, "Professing the Uniqueness of Christ," *Chicago Studies*, 24 (1985) 17–35.

52. *The Resilient Church: The Necessity and Limits of Adaptation* (Garden City,

N.Y.: Doubleday, 1977), p. 78; see also idem, *Models of Revelation* (Garden City, N.Y.: Doubleday, 1983), pp. 189–92. Van Beeck expresses the same reservations in *Christ Proclaimed: Christology as Rhetoric* (New York: Paulist, 1979), pp. 385–95.

53. At conferences in Philadelphia, Temple University, Oct. 1984, and in Toronto, Toronto University, Nov. 1985.

54. Quoted in Robert McAffee Brown, *Makers of Contemporary Theology: Gustavo Gutiérrez* (Atlanta: John Knox Press, 1980), p. 20.

55. Paul Knitter, "The Impact of World Religions on Academic and Ecclesial Theology," *Catholic Theological Society of America Proceedings*, 1985, pp. 160–65.

56. *No Other Name? A Critical Survey of Christian Attitudes toward the World Religions* (Maryknoll, N.Y.: Orbis Books, 1985), pp. 182–86.

Postscript

12

The Case for Pluralism

TOM F. DRIVER

I

In human systems, as in physical, a principle of inertia induces a body to remain in its present state, whether of motion or of rest, as long as possible. If this principle gives stability to our worlds and continuity to our histories, resisting anarchy and confusion, it also makes the envisionment and realization of new possibilities extremely difficult.

The contributors to the present volume, attempting to envision a new state of affairs and wanting Christianity to move in a certain direction with respect to other religions in the world, have encountered no small measure of inertial resistance, some of it external and some resident within ourselves. What is more, and this is by no means unusual in human projects, the external and internal obstacles are closely related.

At the meeting in Claremont, California (March 1986), where the authors of this book, together with appointed critics, assembled to discuss their first drafts, the critics, by design of the book's editors, represented the external inertia. Most of them took the so-called inclusivist position, according to which, although salvation can indeed be found outside the Christian fold, this is so by virtue of the fact that non-Christians are somehow included in the saving grace that comes from God through Christ, however hidden, anonymous, or mysterious the presence of such grace may remain. In short, the inclusivists maintained, in line with tradition, that Christ is the way, the truth, and the life. That is, in the last analysis Christ is the *only* way unto salvation: no one comes to God except through Christ, even if non-Christians do not know this or call upon Christ by name.

Judgments concerning inertia, like all other judgments, are relative. It has taken no little overcoming of inertia in Christian history to envision and articulate the inclusivist position itself, for it has been a bold step beyond that time-honored Christian exclusivism that held, and in many quarters still holds, that persons (some conservative voices say nations) that do not confess Christ are for that reason condemned and lost to all eternity.[1]

In the eyes of the writers of this present volume, however, Christian inclusivism, however more charitable than the conviction that all who do not confess faith in Christ are damned, still represents an unwarranted attachment to a traditional kind of christology that is no longer in the best interests of the world or the church. A strategy of embracing all members of the human race, of whatever religious tradition, in the Christian dispensation seems to us an inertial turning back to familiar modes of thought, however sincerely or brilliantly defended, at a time when these modes of thought have become not only insufficient but in many ways deleterious to a more constructive Christian presence in the world.

Meanwhile, we who would make a new departure have a certain momentum of our own. Having moved a certain distance along a trajectory defined by incorporating into Christian theology our best judgments concerning the course of world history in the twentieth century, we do not wish to be turned back toward worldviews, cosmologies, or modes of theologizing that seem insensitive to the ethical and spiritual demands of the present *kairos*.

At the same time, it would be false to imply that we crossers of the river, or strikers out for new territory, or whatever metaphor be used to describe us, have none of the inclusivist's inertia within ourselves. We too are concerned about continuity with Christian tradition, about bearing a true witness to Christ, and about Christianity's claim to universality. Hence, the siren call, as I shall uncharitably dub it, of the christocentric inclusivists at the Claremont meeting held a certain fascination, with the result that we spent most of the time at the meeting discussing *whether* the move we propose to make beyond inclusivism can be justified, instead of analyzing carefully *what* the move really is and what issues arise once the proposed move is assumed.

Our work raises two different sets of questions. One has to do with whether it is possible or advisable for Christians to move beyond inclusivism to something else, usually called pluralism. The other has to do with the character of pluralism itself: What is meant by the term? Is it intelligible? How is it to be understood in conjunction with the mission of Christianity, on the one hand, and the world situation on the other? And so on.

This set of questions, although by no means forgotten during our preparatory discussions for this book, did not become their focus. Hence, it is pluralism itself that I wish to discuss in this chapter. That is not because the topic has not been set before the reader in the foregoing chapters, where indeed it has received much skilled attention, but because I hope that a certain focus on it may be appropriate for this concluding essay, the only one in the book that has been written with the Claremont discussions in hindsight.[2]

II

One of the critics of the manuscripts discussed at the Claremont meeting, Prof. Kenneth Surin of the College of St. Paul and St. Mary in Chettenham,

England, refused to enter into the terms of the debate. Declining to identify himself with inclusivism, with pluralism, or with the dispute between them, he seemed to call a plague upon both houses. It is perhaps well to begin with some of his observations, which I shall take principally from what he has chosen to call "A Naive Letter" to all the authors and critics of this book, written after his return home.

"The cries of those who hunger," he wrote, "point to the lie in even the most profound theological teleologies or universal histories." It seemed to Surin that the whole question of inclusivism vs. pluralism was parochial. Our words concerning a new global situation and a turning point in history seemed to him little more than ideology of a Western, liberal sort. Inasmuch as the theological issues being debated did nothing, as he thought, to address the situation of those who are starving, they functioned as ideological cover for a status quo that is hostile to the kingdom of God.

Hunger, destitution, and oppression, especially on the massive scale evident in the world today, stand as a rebuke to all who envision a conjunctive or harmonious universe. A happy ending to the world's misery envisioned under the banner of an all-inclusive Christ working hiddenly to redeem all peoples is as unwarranted an expectation as one conceived through the imagery of a pluralistic world in which diversity is embraced wholeheartedly.

Surin pointed us to the fissures that separate the world from the kingdom of God, the wealthy from the starving, ideals from their realization, human pretension from human actuality. What he heard in "pluralism" was perhaps, to use the poet Adrienne Rich's phrase, "the dream of a common language," a dream Surin regarded as no less ill-fated than the tower of Babel. He was therefore put in mind of Louis Althusser, Roland Barthes, and other commentators upon language who have pointed to the ruptures that exist within the apparently smooth fabrics of human discourse:

> Why did the grid of intelligibility [of our discussion of pluralism] generate a plethora of mutualities, commonalities, unities, conjunctions, consonances, etc., when the material position of the faith-traditions in the hegemonic culture of late capitalist society requires us to valorize something radically different—viz., disjunctions, disunities, (countervailing) distances, dissonances, etc.?

He was accusing us of crying "Peace! Peace!" when there is none.

Surin was also reminded of Max Weber's analysis of modernity as a process of rationalization whereby each realm of discourse (Weber had in mind each scholarly, professional, or technological discipline), arriving at an autonomy free of outside influence, proceeds by its own "inner logic." From this perspective, pluralism, with its view that every religion has its own particular integrity, is a product of modern, Western rationalization. Pluralists are modernists who think that autonomy is the highest good. Pluralism's pretended globalism is no less particular than is the universality claimed for Christ in traditional dogmatics. In Surin's words: "Without the intellectual legacy of modernity . . . the notion of 'religious pluralism' would lack historical grounding in any kind of socially supported code or public discourse."

These critiques bear pointedly upon the dilemmas of liberal Christianity at the present time, especially in two respects: the liberal tendency to view the whole world as like unto itself, and its distance, even if it be a sympathetic distance, from the wretched of the earth.

It will be the better part of wisdom to acknowledge, even to stress, that the whole discussion about "religious pluralism," as it is represented in this book, belongs to Western liberal religious thought at the present time. One of the characteristics of any pluralism I myself would want to espouse is that it not only permits but positively requires that persons know and make known the life-situation from within which they speak. Ours is not a "universal" point of view but one conditioned by a First World liberal Christianity trying to make theological sense of the fact that the First World, with which the fortunes of Christianity have long been identified, is not the whole of the world nor the norm of its potentialities. It is true that four contributors to this volume (Raimundo Panikkar and Stanley Samartha of India, Seiichi Yagi of Japan, and Aloysius Pieris of Sri Lanka) write from an Asian perspective. When Panikkar or Samartha spoke at the Claremont meeting (Pieris could not attend) they brought to the room resonances very unlike those of the other participants. Indeed, their eloquence, combined with the points of view they expressed, often produced a response of silence, as if for the moment they had brought us Western theologians to the edge of our awareness. From there we would scramble back to the words we know, and know how to manipulate. The agenda of this book, however, is certainly Western, and there is no reason to deny that it is couched in Western terms, addressed to Western audiences, and aimed at the Western conscience.

It is fashionable to say that the world has become one, that our problems are global, and that we are going to survive or perish together. These ideas have much truth in them, but they are not the whole truth. It is less fashionable (especially in North America), though equally true, to say that the world is broken into many pieces, subject to unfathomable misunderstandings, engaged in unending warfare between nations, social classes, racial groups, and genders. The world may be one, but there are sides to be taken. Langdon Gilkey's sage chapter, wisest of all in its confession of ignorance concerning where the path of pluralism will lead, summons the courage to say that even from within a pluralistic point of view some things are "intolerable." He is not ready in the name of pluralism to compromise with Nazism, or with reactionary fundamentalism. Nor should he.

And yet. . . . (Here the fissures so keenly noticed by Surin start madly and subtly to become irony. The opposites will not stay opposite. They love to reverse themselves. This is not only a linguistic but also a political truth.) And yet. Raimundo Panikkar turned to Langdon Gilkey and said, "Intolerable? Did you say intolerable? But you do tolerate them—for they exist." He smiled. "Oh yes, my friend, you tolerate them."

III

That we exist in a world torn apart by injustice, severed by incompatible systems of meaning, and subject always to ironic juxtapositions should remind us that pluralism is not the resolution of anything and should not be entertained as an "end." This is something it pains me to say, for I love variety, and the thought of a peaceful coexistence of all manner of creatures warms me to the core. I make my home in New York City because the infinite variety of its megalopolitan life never stales. Variation turns me on, and I could write a hymn to it now. Yet I know full well that one person's pluralism can be another's disaster. Love of variety contains no insurance against dilletantism, no protection against trifling with love, no guarantee that the suffering of political prisoners in torture chambers will not be countenanced as part of life's "infinite variety."

No, pluralism is not an ultimate concern. It is something more serious. It is an immediate concern. Espousing pluralism, I take a stand not as proposing something "universal," or as having discovered a new norm of truth for all the world to follow, but rather as proposing a step that is ethically, and therefore theologically, necessary for Western Christianity now to take.[3] At stake is Christianity's self-understanding, its view of its own place in history, and its understanding of God. Pluralism is a demand laid now upon us Christians, brought upon us by our own history, which has largely been one of "universal colonialism."

Born within an empire, in one of Rome's minor but troublesome colonies, Christianity soon proved upwardly mobile and found itself, in about three centuries, established as the official religion of the colonizing state. "Christendom," the "rule of Christ," came to be. From that time, most of Christianity's expansion in the world has accompanied and often rationalized the colonizing adventures of nations. Moreover, its attitude to other religions has been shaped by the colonial mentality: The "other" religions that Christianity encountered in its expansions were to be subdued and brought into conformity with Christian ideas and practice, the pattern most evident in the christianizing of Europe. Local divinities frequently became Christian saints. Local feasts found their way into the Christian calendar. Syncretism was strongly opposed only when it threatened the hegemony of the Christian church, just as colonialist nations tolerated local customs as long as it remained clear who was in charge. When local religions could not be brought under the Christian banner, and if there was sufficient power, these religions were eradicated, not infrequently by the burning of books, destruction of symbols, and the torture and slaughter of "infidels." Practices contrary to the mores of the missionaries' home country were usually discouraged or forbidden, with little or no attempt to understand their meaning locally.

In all this, there was precious little attempt to listen or to learn. Even when Christian mission has been informed by sophisticated political and anthropological thought, this knowledge has mostly been used in the service of communicating *to* others, not to learn *from* non-Christians, particularly not in the weighty matters of theology, ethics, and spiritual life.

Near Cap Haitien, I visited a medical missionary from the United States who had worked in Haiti some twenty-five years. He had built a hospital and was providing some of the best medical services in the whole country. He talked to me a solid hour without cease, telling me what he had learned about "the Haitian mind." Well read in recent linguistic theory, he used its jargon in a fascinating way to explain to me why there would never be any meeting between "the Haitian mind" and "the European mind." He then explained why the future, in God's providence, belonged to the European way of thinking and not the Haitian. It was a rather dazzling performance, and I did not begin to tire of it until it was well over half finished. When at last he stopped, I said, "I see that you have in your years here learned a very great deal *about* the Haitians. I envy you this knowledge. Now, please tell me: What have you learned *from* the Haitians?" The question threw him. It seemed never to have crossed his mind that in some respects the Haitians might be wiser than he.

The history of Christianity is, by and large, one of not listening to followers of other spiritual roads. On the contrary it has largely been a history of combating, to the death if necessary, those who worship "other gods." To do so is enjoined in Christian scriptures, a duty as convenient now as it was in Old Testament times for those who would employ religious prejudice in the conquest of territory. America, which many of the early European settlers saw as a new land of Canaan, was particularly guilty in this respect, in that the christianizing of America decimated Amerindian religion and civilization, and attempted to stamp out all traces of African religion in slaves.

The crusading mentality among Western Christians is far from dead, although perhaps today it is not much found among liberals. It seems at present to be focused mostly on "godless communism." The temptation for liberals is not crusading but complacency. It is to assume that by taking a positive rather than a negative attitude toward other religions, these can somehow be politely affirmed in their existence without the need for Christianity to undergo any significant change in itself.

IV

Two strategies of such liberal complacency in the affirmation of other religions may be noted. The one is the inclusivist position I have already mentioned. Because the inclusivist already "knows" that the source and means of salvation for every person in the world is Christ Jesus (something that the non-Christian does not yet know), there is no need to listen to the non-Christian at any fundamental level. To be sure, inclusivists might see that other religions contained some practices and insights that might "enrich" their understanding of Christ, but there would be no reason to listen at the level at which their own form of faith, their commitment to Christ, might be called radically into question. In short, the other religion would not be taken as seriously, in its own right, as is Christianity.

Rosemary Ruether's essay in this volume is of great importance because it shows the parallel between Christianity's condescension to other religions and its condescension to certain categories of persons within its own ranks, notably women. In matters concerning other religions, the Christian inclusivist either is or is like a "benign" Christian patriarchalist, one who agrees that women are indeed fully human and full members of the church but fondly supposes that they have no need of independence, autonomy, and elevation in the hierarchy because they are "included" in the representation of all humanity that is made by the male priesthood. Or such a patriarchal inclusivist may even countenance the ordination of women and their elevation to higher sacerdotal orders, provided only that they do not rock the boat by bringing to their office any ethical, spiritual, or theological insights that challenge those of their male predecessors. In other words, the inclusivist supposes that the *defining terms* of the enterprise, usually codified as scripture, tradition, and creed, are not to be tampered with. They are often very happy to include all manner of outsider as long as inclusivists set the terms of inclusion.

This is why it is wrong for persons deeply concerned about justice, liberation, and the kingdom of God to suggest that the question of Christianity's attitude to other religions is irrelevant. Ruether demonstrates the connection between Christianity's attitudes to "others" who are outsiders and "others" who are within. There is every reason to suppose that the question of "the other" is a fundamental ethical and political question, just as it is a question crucial for theology. Or, to say this more pointedly, it is a crucial theological question *because* it is ethical and political.

A second strategy or type of liberal complacency that may be adopted while encouraging Christianity to take an affirmative stand toward other religions is to decide that all religions are basically the same. I suppose that the most sophisticated modern argument for the similarity, even the identity, of all "major" religions is that of Fritjof Schuon in *The Transcendent Unity of Religions*.[4] In his interpretation, all the major religions contain an esoteric core that affords mystical participation in the form of transcendence usually called the divine. At this core, religions are the same, even though they differ markedly in their exoteric shells. Many followers of a religion never penetrate to the core, but those who do arrive at something known also to the spiritual elite of other religions.

My point in mentioning Schuon is not to argue with a book I regard with high ambivalence as both profound and misguided. I cite it only as an illustration, perhaps familiar to many readers, of an approach to the multiplicity of religions that is *not,* in terms of the case I am making here, pluralistic. My logic brings me to the same judgment concerning all attempts to define an essence of religion such that it can be shown to form the basis or core of every particular religion. Studies in the philosophy of religion are prone to this kind of analysis, and it is sometimes to be found in studies in the history of religions as well. Let no one say that such exercises have no value. However, they bypass the issue of pluralism in their preoccupation with what the various religions have in common. They are but casually, not deeply, concerned with difference, something that the Western philosophical tradition has tended to consign to the realm of the accidental.

"Contact," said the Gestalt psychologist Fritz Perls, "begins in the appreciation of difference." Where differences are ignored, or perhaps discounted, entities tend to merge, distinctions blur. Psychologists speak then of confluence, which is the lack of awareness of the dividing line between self and other.

In the political and economic sphere, confluence is disastrous: it invariably leads to the domination of the weaker by the stronger. And here we may see a bitterly ironic convergence of opposite attitudes hovering over an exaggerated preoccupation with identity. The oppression of women by men, for instance, is maintained by two principal arguments logically incompatible: first, that there is no difference between women and men, because all are children of God and members of the same species; second, that the two genders are categorically different, each having its own proper sphere. The first argument tries to blind one to any problems of inequity that may exist. The second serves to keep women "in their place." Together, the two arguments maintain a situation of confluence or symbiosis, which accounts for the fact that the oppression of women has for the most part been ignored in history, although it is probably the oldest form of the subjugation of one group by another.

Movements for liberation are separatist. Their first task is to make groups conscious of their own identity, which means they must not only come to see but also to affirm their differences from others, especially from their oppressors. The main difference between men and women is not their anatomy, for this difference, important as it may be, does not prevent their being capable of most of the same activities, thoughts, and feelings. The main difference is their histories.

V

As for religions, the main differences between them are not rites and symbols, striking as such differences appear. Nor are the differences principally doctrinal or philosophical, although differences of that order are real and important. The main differences among religions are historical. A religion, like a person or a nation, is what it has become in history and carries that history within itself, even if many of its devotees know little about the past.

That religions are historical is a point of central concern in Gordon D. Kaufman's chapter in this volume. I would say that socio-economic factors are more important in the history of a religion than Kaufman's treatment suggests, with its emphasis on "human imaginative creativity in face of the great mystery."[5] Raimundo Panikkar writes that "geography as much as history is a religious as well as a human category."[6] And, we may remind ourselves, so are wealth, poverty, means of production, and class conflict, all of which belong, as does religion, to history.

Kaufman's emphasis upon the historicality of religions properly leads him to stress that theology is a human construction:

> Religious frames of orientation, then, and religious reflections, are just as important today as ever—but (in the light of modern historical understanding) they should be conceived now much more explicitly in terms of human imaginative creativity.[7]

So they are, but let us be clear that this does not preclude any part that God may have had in bringing them to be. As Schubert Ogden pointed out in his critique of Kaufman's manuscript at Claremont, "our theological statements and claims are not *simply* ours." They are ours, I would say, quite as much as any human creation can be, and it is necessary from an epistemological as well as an ethical point of view that we human beings should acknowledge responsibility for what we have produced. Even scripture, I have argued elsewhere, is the creation of us human beings, and when we do not acknowledge this, we start a process by which scripture ceases to be a medium of revelation and instead becomes an idol.[8] But human beings do not create alone. It is as false to say that they do as it was of some neoorthodox theologians to maintain that human beings do not create at all, because, as these theologians fancied, only God is creator.

Pluralism discerns that creation comes about by collaboration, encounter, exchange. Creation is the product not of one alone but of at least two in interaction. Pluralism is attuned to the *mix* that makes life. Hence, the pluralist is out to remind Christian theology how important it is not to regard God as basically remote from humanity, lest when theology comes to emphasize, as now it must, the historicality of the human condition, it would sound as if it had ceased to speak about God. On the contrary, one should recognize that within the purview of a Christian incarnational theology the more radically one addresses the human condition, the more one speaks of God.

This way of thinking, however, requires a theological move enabling one to affirm not only that human beings have histories but that God does also. Just as, from a historicistic point of view, having a history and existing in history are constitutive of human beings, so also does history belong to the being and the becoming of God. It is something that process theology, in its own way, has taught. And Panikkar, although not of that school, writes, "Neither dogma, nor Christian self-understanding are ahistorical and ageographical facts."[9] It follows, if we take theological language as seriously as we should, that neither is God unhistorical and nongeographical. The transcendence and holiness of God should not be construed as separating God from incarnation in time, place, and human struggle.

Christianity, Judaism, and Islam have almost always taught that God is active in history, but they have tended to combine this teaching with an unfortunate concept of divine transcendence that suggests (and sometimes insists) that God's essence is outside time and space. When applied to Jesus as the Christ, such ideas have long been regarded as docetic, as if the essence of Christ were beyond history, and its instantiation in Jesus of Nazareth was more apparent than real. Today I think we are being led to see that there may be a docetism in doctrines of God as well as in christology, and that this will occur whenever divine transcendence is permitted to diminish the divine immanence, as if the essence of God were "elsewhere," and the presence of God as active agent in human affairs is only apparent or, as is usually said, "symbolic."

To combat this docetic tendency in theology, I have proposed that transcendence be understood as radical immanence.[10] God surpasses human beings by becoming *more*, not less, involved in creation. God is God by virtue of being more, not less, historical than we. (That is, God does not avoid or seek to escape history, as humans frequently do.) We Christians need to turn away from a passive notion of God, according to which God dwells high above in great Mystery, whereas human beings struggle in history to understand and to approximate an unchanging divine will. However eloquent their expression, the root of such notions is absentee landlordism. Patterns of landownership probably have much more to do with theology than is commonly taught in school.

To a historicistic understanding of both God and humanity, the pluralist adds a perhaps startling thought: God may have more than one history. God is participant not only in Jewish and Christian history but also in Hindu. I stress "participant" because I do not think it is adequate simply to affirm God's providential surveillance of all world history. It is a matter of God's active involvement in peoples' histories, and it is a matter of these being multiple and different. If there is a "salvation history" delineated and forecast in Christian scripture, there are other "salvation histories" outside it; and in them God has different names, different identities, and moves in different ways. Inasmuch as God has different histories, then God has different "natures." In pluralist perspective, it is not simply that God has one nature variously and inadequately expressed by different religious traditions. It is that there are real and genuine differences within the Godhead itself, owing to the manifold involvements that God has undertaken with the great variety of human communities.

VI

It is not easy to know in what sense either God or the world is "one." God is one; the word itself is singular. But God is many, inasmuch as the ways and histories of God are more than can be named. The world is one: the word itself is singular, and events seem to ramify throughout the globe. But the world is also a yard full of old junk, amid the clutter of which are objects of great worth and beauty that cannot all be classified in the same system.

Shall we vote for the unity or the plurality? The pluralist is a funny bird who says, "Let's have it both ways." As I view the matter, the present condition of life is multiplicity, and the paramount ethical dilemma with which humanity has to wrestle is how to "order" the diversities in such way that the integrity and destiny of each is preserved. We start in otherness, we aspire to unity. If we sacrifice (kill, bind, or lame) otherness to find a shortcut to unity, we attempt to trump history, and we fall into sin. Christianity has done this in its triumphalism, the vestiges of which remain in latter-day inclusivism. The pluralist says to Christianity and to other religions, "Put to sea in little boats. Cast your self, your faith, and your tradition upon the waters. See what happens."

For Christians at the present time, the imperative is to ponder the integrity and destiny of religions not our own. We have too long supposed that their destiny was to give way to the rule of Christ.

Neither individuals, religious traditions, nor theological images can jump out of their historical skins. Pluralism is the recognition of this as real, more or less necessary, and good. That is to say, although human history is pervaded with evil and injustice, there would be more if this history had been unitary rather than multiple. In diversity there is truth. Nothing but the truth? Certainly not. But truth there is nonetheless, and of a sort as important to affirm for ethical as for esthetic reasons. Variety is not only the "spice" of life: without it, evil is the more likely to go unchecked, potential for good more apt to perish unrealized.

One might be able to adduce some physical and metaphysical arguments in favor of the pluralist point of view I am expressing, but I shall not do that here.[11] However interesting, such arguments are not conclusive. Panikkar is well advised to observe, in his chapter above, that "pluralism belongs also to the order of myth." "Pluralism is not," he writes, "a mere symbol. It expresses an attitude of cosmic confidence (in the Spirit, which is not subordinate to the logos), which allows for a polar and tensile coexistence between *ultimate* human attitudes, cosmologies, and religions."[12]

But what shall we say of such "confidence in the Spirit" when we are in the presence of those fissures, those cries of the hungering, of which Kenneth Surin reminded us? This question leads to consideration of some linkages between pluralism and liberation, but before coming to those I want to comment on one of the most important theological issues raised during our discussions at Claremont and in the foregoing pages of this book: idolatry.

Panikkar says, as we have just seen, that pluralism allows for a "tensile coexistence between *ultimate* human attitudes." How could something that is ultimate be considered as coexisting, even tensely, with *other* ultimates?

At the end of our authors' meeting at Claremont, during a forum open to the public, two memorable images were described. Marjorie Suchocki, from the platform, told the audience that during our discussions the following image had presented itself to her. Some pilgrims were ascending the mountain of religion. They could not see its summit because they were making their way up through clouds, but after a long time they climbed to heights above the clouds and stood on the upper reaches of their mountain under a clear sky. Then they could see, to their surprise, that there were other mountains. And on their peaks, beyond the valleys that lay concealed beneath the clouds, were other pilgrims. So the pilgrims cry out over the distance, "Halloo! Halloo!" And that is all that they communicate.

Suchocki's image paid tribute to the difficulty, perhaps in some respects the impossibility, of interreligious dialogue. It immediately evoked from a member of the audience a contrasting image. Prof. Dianna Eck of Harvard University, who had been present throughout our discussions, informed us that certain Hindus speak of a mountain that is upside down. Like an inverted pyramid, it is narrow at the bottom, wide and broad at the top. A persistent religious seeker, climbing this mountain with great difficulty, finds at the end of the climb a broad summit where dwell every variety of creature and all manner of Gods.

If the one image stresses the separateness and disjunctiveness between religious traditions, and the other celebrates "coexistence," both are mini-dramas containing a recognition scene in which adherents of a religion discover after a lifetime, or even ages, of devotion that their known path is not the only way.

VII

The knowledge that there are other spiritual ways has, from Old Testament times onward if not before, generated the concept of idolatry. The habit (unless we should honor it by calling it the tradition) in Christianity has been to speak of the religions of others as idolatries, a usage in line with the Old Testament, where "idol" is a word to name the icons employed by persons who worship gods other than the God of Israel. Such figures are considered to be no gods at all, false gods, or perhaps demons, and their icons no more than wood and stone, presumably in high contrast to Yahweh, the one true God, of whom no image can be made. But of course images of Yahweh *are* made, if not "graven" in stone then "writ" in concepts and metaphors that become sacrosanct—for example, the surety on the part of many Christians that it is proper to call God Father but improper to say Mother.

Iconoclastic movements in Christian history have often inveighed against idolatry. The word took on a somewhat different meaning in the twentieth century when it was used by neoorthodox theology to characterize German Nazism, which came to vaunt itself as absolute and to require a kind of devotion suitable only to deity. The usage was then extended to refer to all instances of treating as absolute anything other than God, and this usage is rather frequent in theology today.

The chapter in this volume by Wilfred Cantwell Smith takes a very important next step. It proposes that there is an idolatrous way of interpreting the most sacred images and doctrines of one's own religion, even (perhaps especially) if one is a Christian. "For Christians to think that Christianity [itself] is true, or final, or salvific, is a form of idolatry. . . . Christianity has been our idol."[13] This raises the question "Has the figure of Christ served as . . . an idol through the centuries for Christians?"[14] Smith is not entirely clear about his answer, but I think it necessary to say that the idolization of Christ—let us call it "christodolatry"—is not only possible but in fact frequent. Indeed, I would go further and say that there is even such a thing as an idolatrous devotion to God.

Readers familiar with the work of Paul Tillich will recognize here a point of view akin to what that theologian called "the protestant principle." This perhaps unfortunately chosen phrase was not meant to refer to Protestantism as such, for it is a principle, said Tillich, that is to be found also in Catholicism and in other religions, too, and Protestantism itself dishonors the principle as often as not. "The protestant principle" refers to a critique of every finite form, particularly every form of *religious* expression, in the name of the infinite. It is protest against any finite form claiming ultimacy for itself or having that claim made for it by overly zealous devotees. In the name of the protestant principle Tillich coined the phrase, "the God beyond God," signaling the fact that what we name and worship as God ordinarily is a finite form and, as such, open to idolization.

This Tillichian point takes on new coloration, however, when Smith proposes it in the context of interreligious coexistence and dialogue, for this context forces one to recognize that one's religion in its entirety is, within the comparative or pluralistic frame of reference, not ultimate. At the top of the mountain, one sees other mountains.

In the light of Smith's chapter it seems to me that Paul Tillich's own christology would come under judgment, for Tillich, in line with Christian tradition generally, regarded Christ as the "final revelation." Tillich had a paradoxical way of linking this ultimacy with Christ's total self-emptying, so that in the end what is "final" about Christ is devoid of any particular content. Tillich's christology is rather mystical in that way. Nevertheless, Tillich maintained that such self-emptying ultimacy was to be found uniquely in the crucified Christ and that therefore the event of Jesus as the Christ constituted a "center" for all human history. However, it is precisely this determination of a single, concrete center for the whole of human history that is incompatible with pluralism and lays Christianity open to the charge of serving an idolatrous christology.

Being in fundamental agreement with Smith's words about idolatry, the only thing I want to emphasize is that there are reasons for opposing "christodolatry" that arise within a Christian framework itself, more or less apart from the matter of religious pluralism. This is important to see, for it indicates that one of the benefits of pluralism is its inducement to get one's own theological house in order. As I have attempted to say all along in this essay, the concern of this book is the ethical and theological challenge that pluralism presents to Western Christianity.

It was for reasons internal to Christianity that I included in a book on christology several years ago a critique of Christ as center, model, and norm, a critique of Christ as once for all, and a critique of biblicism. The only interreligious concern prominent in the book is the relationship of Christianity to Jews and Judaism, a long and shameful aspect of our history. The book was primarily motivated by two other concerns: the pluralism that exists *within* Christianity and the pluralistic consequences of modern historical thinking. The latter is the subject of Gordon D. Kaufman's chapter, as I have already mentioned.[15] The former has reference mainly to racism and sexism.

Rosemary Ruether's essay above, as I have already noted, astutely points out the parallel between Christianity's regard of the "others" outside its fold and the "others" within. The divinity and centrality of a male Christ have been used by the church throughout most of its history to rationalize the otherness of women and to remove them frc n recognition as fully human. In service of racism, Christ Jesus has been imaged as white, implying that nonwhites are contrary to the Christic norm. Mostly, however, racist christology works by identifying Christ with centers of power, which has the effect of distancing him from slaves, servants, women, the poor, and all the others who are excluded from the corridors of power. Most of all, both sexism and racism are supported by the doctrine of a single, unique, unsurpassable Christ who has appeared "once and for all" in the past. This produces what I call a "fixation," upon a single channel of grace, the net effect of which is to discourage all variety that may exist in humanity and in the life of the divine. In point of fact, Christians worship a great many different Christs, and have done so from the earliest decades after Jesus' death and resurrection. Denial of this diversity leads to the fabrication of a single Christ whose worship is based on denial and is therefore idolatrous.

We can, on the basis of this insight, enunciate a principle: denial of diversity, refusal to entertain alternatives, avoidance of disjunctions and ruptures in the human fabric, and insistence upon oneness result in idolatry.[16] Idolatry is the insistence that there is only one way, one norm, one truth. It is the refusal to be corrected or informed by the "other."

VIII

In conclusion, I return to the cries of the hungering, with which, thanks to Kenneth Surin, I began. The cries have not gone away as I have been writing. Nor will reading this quiet them. Nevertheless, as is today rather obvious even to the secular press, theology is not irrelevant to the socio-economic and political structures that enforce so much oppression in the world.

Several essays in this book are specifically concerned with liberation praxis in the context of religious pluralism, notably those by Paul Knitter, Aloysius Pieris, Rosemary Ruether, and Marjorie Suchocki. All of them see, as do I, a positive correlation between concern for pluralism and concern for justice. We might even say that pluralism is itself a justice issue, and I for one would say that if it is not, then theology should waste no time on it.

The task of Christian theology, formally speaking, is to help churches and individual Christians to determine what views they ought to be propagating and what actions they ought to be taking in the world. In the light of the judgment under which every Christian stands because of Jesus' proclamation of the realm of God, everything that Christians do and say should be governed by concern for justice, freedom, and grace, and never any one of these without the others.

"Were it not for the fact of the political decolonization of the world," writes Panikkar, "we would not be speaking the way we are today.[17] Over the whole discussion of pluralism there hangs the specter of colonialism, neo-colonialism, imperialism, exploitation of the weak, and warfare. It is this history that makes the topic urgent. We have learned that, unfortunately, technology alone does not diminish injustices or of itself bridge differences. These require a liberative praxis.

It is only such praxis, where undertaken with the requisite degree of commitment to eradicate structural injustices, that can save pluralism from degenerating into mere tolerance. In the absence of strong ethical commitments directed toward the doing of God's will on earth as in heaven, Christianity's opening itself to other religions cannot be deep but will tend toward complacent compromise with the status quo, which the New Testament calls "the world." It is only a passion for *doing* the truth that turns pluralism from a mere contemplation of variety into a serious theological matter.

Liberation theology speaks of a "commitment to the poor." Pluralism must learn to speak of a "commitment to the other." Moreover, we must never forget that most of the "others" are poor. Concentration upon the world's "great" or "major" religions—usually considered to be Christianity, Judaism, Islam, Buddhism, and Hinduism—in interreligious dialogue usually obscures the differences between elitist and popular forms of these religions. Moreover, it ignores the many other religions, followed by countless millions, which the rational scholarly community has refused to denominate as "great."

In order to protect itself against elitism and complacency, the pluralist cause must come to see that particular religions are delivered from idolatry not only by reflection upon "otherness" and diversity but also by commitment and action in behalf of the poor. Transcendence is not just a matter of thought or prayer. In the first instance, and also in the last, it is action in service of that for which it is imperative to give one's life. Transcendence is radical immanence. The way to the universal is through particular pathways of liberative praxis. There we can find, perhaps to our surprise, but certainly as Marjorie Suchocki has invited us to see, that pilgrims discover each other best not at the tops of mountains but along the trails that have to be bushwhacked from where the world is now to where, thanks to God, it is called to be.

NOTES

1. For a survey of Christian attitudes toward religious pluralism, see Paul F. Knitter, *No Other Name? A Critical Survey of Christian Attitudes toward the World Religions* (Maryknoll, N.Y.: Orbis Books, 1985).
2. In what follows I shall make no attempt to survey or summarize all that went on at

the meeting, or to assess the contributions of the various participants. However, I shall refer to some of them in order to highlight the issues connected with pluralism that I discuss.

3. In this connection, one might ask whether Christianity in toto should be regarded as a Western religion. If continuity with the past be decisive, then the answer is yes. At the present time, however, many Christians in Africa and Asia are attempting to realize an indigenous form of Christianity. This points to a pluralism *within* Christianity that is no less significant than a pluralism *embracing* Christianity.

4. Wheaton, Ill: Quest Books, 1984.

5. Kaufman, p. 8, above.

6. Panikkar, p. 98, above.

7. Kaufman, p. 9, above .

8. See *Christ in a Changing World* (New York: Crossroad, 1981), chap. 5, "Critique of Biblicism."

9. Panikkar, p. 99, above.

10. Tom F. Driver, *Patterns of Grace: Human Experience as Word of God* (San Francisco: Harper & Row, 1977); and *Christ in a Changing World*.

11. It would be harder to come up with specifically theological arguments drawn from Western Christian traditions, because Christianity's "radical monotheism," as H. R. Niebuhr called it, has tended in almost all connections to say that unity is a higher value than diversity, just as it has tended to hold that infinity is of greater value than finitude, transcendence than immanence, eternity than time, and for that matter, the male more normative than the female, the West than the East, white than black. Such dualisms are happily being questioned today, most vigorously perhaps by feminist theology. My own extended critique of dualism is to be found in *Christ in a Changing World*, especially chap. 6.

12. Panikkar, p. 110, above.

13. Smith, p. 59, above.

14. Ibid., p. 62, above.

15. There are also other grounds within Christian tradition for objecting to the idolization of Christ—for example arguments based on the rational criticism of myth, such as those to be found in *The Myth of God Incarnate*, John Hick, ed. (London: SCM Press, 1977) , or those based on strict interpretations of monotheism, such as were made by H. Richard Niebuhr in *Radical Monotheism and Western Culture* (London: Faber and Faber, 1943).

16. "Can it be," Stanley J. Samartha writes in his essay here, "that plurality belongs to the very structure of reality? Or can it be that it is the will of God that many religions should continue in the world?" Discussing the Hindu concept of *Satyasya Satyam* (the Truth of the Truth), he aptly points out that "according to one particular Hindu view [it] cannot even be described as 'one.' It is 'not-two' (*advaita*), indicating thereby that diversity is within the heart of Being itself and therefore may be intrinsic to human nature as well" (p. 75, above).

17. Panikkar, p. 96, above.

Contributors

Tom F. Driver is the Paul J. Tillich Professor of Theology and Culture at Union Theological Seminary, New York. Among his books are *Romantic Quest and Modern Query: A History of the Modern Theater*, *Patterns of Grace: Human Experience as Word of God*, and *Christ in a Changing World: Toward an Ethical Christology*. He is currently working on a book about rituals in crosscultural, interreligious, and ethical perspectives.

Langdon Gilkey is Shailer Mathews Professor of Theology at the Divinity School of the University of Chicago. His interest in both the possibilities and the problems raised by the plurality of religions stems from an early sojourn in China (1940-45), a visiting professorship at Kyoto University (1975), close relations for over a decade with the Western Sikh Shalsa, of which his wife, Ram Rattan, is a member, and participation in groups devoted to Buddhist-Christian and Confucian-Christian dialogue. Notable among his many books are *Reaping the Whirlwind*, *Message and Existence*, and *Society and the Sacred*.

John Hick is Danforth Professor of the Philosophy of Religion, Chair of the Department of Religion, and Director of the Blaisdell Programs in World Religions and Cultures at the Claremont Graduate School, California. He is the author of *Faith and Knowledge*, *Philosophy of Religion*, *Evil and the God of Love*, *Arguments for the Existence of God*, *God and the Universe of Faiths*, *The Second Christianity*, *Death and Eternal Life*, *Problems of Religious Pluralism*, and editor of *Faith and the Philosophers*, *The Existence of God*, *The Myth of God Incarnate*, *The Experience of Religious Diversity*, *Christianity and Other Religions*. His Gifford Lectures on *An Interpretation of Religions* will be published soon.

Gordon D. Kaufman is Edward Mallinckrodt, Jr. Professor of Divinity at Harvard Divinity School. He is also an ordained minister of the Mennonite Church. His interest in religious pluralism stems from teaching fellowships in India and Japan and from his involvement in Buddhist-Christian and Jewish-Christian dialogue. Among his recent books are *The Theological Imagination: Constructing the Concept of God* and *Theology for a Nuclear Age*.

Paul F. Knitter first became interested in crosscultural, interreligious dialogue as a member of the Society of Divine Word Missionaries. He is presently Professor of Theology at Xavier University, Cincinnati, where he teaches courses in world religions and theology of religions. Besides numerous articles on religious pluralism, he has published *Toward a Protestant Theology of Religions* and *No Other Name? A Critical Survey of Christian Attitudes toward World Religions*. He is also serving as General Editor of Orbis Books' new series "Faith Meets Faith."

Raimundo Panikkar was born into and has lived within two cultures: Hindu and Christian, Eastern and Western. After completing doctoral studies in chemical sciences, he went on to earn doctorates in philosophy and in theology. He has studied and lived in Spain, Germany, Italy, India, and the United States and has served as professor at the universities of Madrid, Rome, Harvard, and California. His thirty books have appeared in several languages and his over three-hundred articles deal with philosophy of science, metaphysics, comparative religions, theology, and indology. Recently become Professor Emeritus of the University of California, he now divides his time between India and Spain. His book, *The Silence of God: The Answer of Buddha,* will soon be published by Orbis Books.

Aloysius Pieris, Sri Lankan by birth, entered the Society of Jesus in 1953 and went on to study philosophy in India and theology and music in Italy; he graduated in Pali and Sanskrit studies from the University of London and in 1972 became the first Christian to earn a doctorate in Buddhist philosophy from the University of Sri Lanka. He is presently Director of the Tulana Research Center in Kelaniya (north of Colombo) which promotes Buddhist-Christian encounter on the threefold basis of philosophical-textual study, experience of popular religion, and theological-pastoral reflection in the context of social transformation. Author of *Theologie der Befreiung* (Herder, 1982) and of about sixty articles, he has lectured at several universities including the Gregorian University in Rome, the Graduate Theological Union in Berkeley, University of Cambridge in England (Teape Wescott Lecturer 1982), and is Professor of Asian Religions and Philosophies at the East Asian Pastoral Institute in Manila. His book *An Asian Theology of Liberation* will soon be published by Orbis Books.

Rosemary Radford Ruether received her M.A. and Ph.D. in religious studies from the Claremont Graduate School in Claremont, Ca. She is author of twenty-one books and numberous articles on feminist and liberation theology. Among her more recent works are *Sexism and God-Talk: Toward a Feminist Tehology* and *Woman-Church: Theology and Practice of Feminist Liturgical Communities.* Over the past years she has contibuted and expanded her feminist-liberation concerns in an ongoing dialogue among Buddhist-Christian scholars. Presently professor at Garrett-Evangelical Theological Seminary, she was recently scholar in residence at the Ecumenical Institute for Theological Research in Tantur, Jerusalem.

Stanley J. Samantha is Visiting Prosessor at the United Theological College and a consultant to the Christian Instutute for the Study of Religion and Society, both in Bangalore, India. For ten years he served as the first Director of the Dialogue Program of the World Council of Churches in Geneva, Switzerland. Besides numerous edited works during his tenure at the WCC, he has written *The Hindu Response to the Unbound Christ* and *Courage for Dialogue: Ecumenical Issued in Inter-religious Relationships.*

Wilfred Cantwell Smith is Professor Emeritus of the Comparative History of Religion, Harvard University. He taught for some years at the University of the Panjab in India (now Pakistan); founded and directed the Institute of Islamic Studies at McGill University, Montreal; was director of the Center for the Study of World

Religions at Harvard; and was for a time at Dalhousie University, Halifax. He is the author of numerous articles and books, most recently *On Understanding Islam* and *Toward a World Theology*, the latter completing a trilogy along with his *Belief and History* and *Faith and Belief*. He is currently at work on a comparative study of the idea of scripture and the role of scriptures in world history.

Majorie Hewitt Suchocki is presently Academic Dean at Wesley Theological Seminary, Washington, D.C. She had previously taught and directed the Doctor of Ministry Program at Pittsburgh Theological Seminary. In her teaching and publications she combines her central concerns for process theology and feminism with interest in and dialogue with world religions. She has written *The End of Evil: Process Eschatology in Historical Context* (forthcoming), *God-Christ-Church: A Practical Guide to Process Theology*, and numerous articles.

Seiichi Yagi completed his graduate work in Western classics at Tokyo University before continuing his study of the New Testament at the University of Göttingen in Germany. Presently Professor at the Tokyo Institute of Technology, he has also taught at Tokyo University, the International Christian University in Tokyo, the Hanazono Zen University in Kyoto and Berne University, Switzerland. He is considered one of the leading figures in the Buddhist-Christian dialogue in Japan; his books, such as *Christ and Jesus*; *Contact Points between Buddhism and Christianity*; and *Paul/Shinran—Jesus/Zen* (translations of Japanese titles) have sold widely throughout Japan. He is currently working on a study of the transformation of Christianity through dialogue with Buddhism, to be published by Orbis Books.

Index

Compiled by William E. Jerman